The Beauty and Glory of the Reformation

The Beauty and Glory of the Reformation

Edited by
Joel R. Beeke

Reformation Heritage Books
Grand Rapids, Michigan

The Beauty and Glory of the Reformation
Copyright © 2018 Puritan Reformed Theological Seminary

Published by
Reformation Heritage Books
2965 Leonard St. NE
Grand Rapids, MI 49525
616-977-0889
e-mail: orders@heritagebooks.org
website: www.heritagebooks.org

Printed in the United States of America
17 18 19 20 21 22/10 9 8 7 6 5 4 3 2 1

ISBN: 978-1-60178-621-0 (hardback)
ISBN: 978-1-60178-622-7 (e-pub)

For additional Reformed literature, request a free book list from Reformation Heritage Books at the above address.

With heartfelt appreciation for

Randall Kirkland

a faithful Barnabas (encourager),
a kind friend and "fellow soldier" (Philemon 2)
in Christ, and
a loyal attendee and supporter
of PRTS's annual conferences.

—JRB

Contents

Preface

This past year marked the five-hundredth anniversary of Martin Luther's affixing his Ninety-Five Theses of protest against the Roman Catholic Church to the church door in Wittenberg, Germany. Through Luther's bold words, the Holy Spirit blew into flame the smoldering coals of other movements across Europe, and the land which lay in darkness for so long began to grow bright under the uncovered beauty of God's Word.

The reforming work begun by John Wycliffe, Jan Hus, and others was now vigorously promoted and furthered by scores of Reformers who fully embraced Luther's breakthrough doctrine of justification by faith alone. The hearts of many were turned to the Lord. The enabling Spirit promised to the church by Jesus Christ in John 14 made the Reformers effective witnesses of Jesus Christ to the nations.

The Reformation possessed as its heartbeat a devotion to the pure truth of the Holy Scriptures, especially manifest in the passionate exposition of the biblical doctrines of salvation by grace, true worship, and the pursuit of holiness. The Word of God preached was properly held to be the central engine for the breaking down of Satan's realm and the upbuilding of God's kingdom.

Some five hundred of us gathered this past August in Grand Rapids to drink in teaching flowing from this wonderful reformation. The stated purpose of the conference was to teach how to grow as faithful sons and daughters of the Reformation.

The conference highlighted several important Reformers. Michael Haykin painted the beautiful picture of William Tyndale's irrepressible desire that the Word of God would reach the common people, and then spoke also of the Reformation's emphasis on the primacy of preaching through the history of Hugh Latimer. "Take away preaching," Latimer had said, "and take away salvation." Elias Medeiros laid before us John Calvin's intensely practical concern for missionary work and the spread of the gospel through all the nations. William VanDoodewaard described for us the "company of pastors" in Geneva, emphasizing God's use of the epigones of the Reformation to carefully build up His church.

Two talks from Ian Hamilton drew us into the experiential heartbeat of the Reformation. The first brought to our attention the deep and abiding importance of proper worship of our glorious and triune God. The second stirred us to a deeper admiration and love for Christ by proving from Scripture that only the eternal Son of God is the way, the truth, and the life.

Multiple sessions also brought to our attention practical lessons from the Reformation's people, teaching, and work. In two addresses Carl Trueman highlighted Augustine's remarkable insights into human nature and Luther's biblical theology of preaching. Joel Beeke provided contemporary applications from the life and work of William Perkins, warming our hearts to this man who in forty-four short years accomplished an incredible amount of God-honoring work as so-called "father of the Puritans." Rebecca VanDoodewaard presented the moving stories of five noteworthy women of the Reformation, giving stimulating insights into how women build up the kingdom of God. Stephen Myers clearly expounded to us the Christology of the Reformation, lifting up before us a sin-atoning, righteousness-imputing Christ who is wondrously both fully God and fully man. The practical talks of the conference concluded with Elias Medeiros's colorful and inspiring contemporary applications from the Reformation's work in world missions.

Those of us who attended last year's Puritan Reformed Theological Seminary conference were grateful for the God-honoring, passionate, and clear teaching of the speakers under whom we sat. We hope also that you will consider joining us for this coming conference in August 2018—not only for the excellent teaching on "The Beauty and Glory of the Last Things," but also for the warm fellowship (www.puritanseminary.org). Please also pray for the work of the seminary, that God's Spirit would fill the faculty, staff, and students with love, faithfulness to the Scriptures, holiness of life, and Spirit-worked power for ministry.

Many thanks go to Rod MacQuarrie for his assistance in editing this manuscript, Gary den Hollander for proofing it, Lois Haley for transcribing a few of these addresses, Linda den Hollander for typesetting, and Amy Zevenbergen for the cover design.

We pray that the Lord will use this book to move us to a deeper appreciation for the rich Reformation heritage that has been entrusted to us, so that we will praise Him from whom all blessings flow.

BRIGHT LIGHTS IN THE HISTORY OF THE REFORMATION

CHAPTER 1

William Tyndale and
Sola Scriptura

Michael Haykin

In 1994 the British Library paid the equivalent of well over two million dollars for a book which Dr. Brian Lang, the chief executive of the Library at the time, described as "certainly the most important acquisition in our 240-year history." The book? A copy of the New Testament. Of course, it was not just any copy. In fact, at the time there was only one other known New Testament like this one in existence, and that one, which is in the library of St. Paul's Cathedral, London, is lacking seventy-one of its pages. The New Testament that the British Museum purchased was lodged for many years in the library of the oldest Baptist seminary in the world, Bristol Baptist College, Bristol, England. It had been bequeathed to the College by Andrew Gifford (1700–1784), a London Baptist minister. It was printed in the German town of Worms (pronounced "warms") on the press of Peter Schöffer the younger in 1526 and is known as the Tyndale New Testament. The first printed New Testament to be translated into English out of the original Greek, it is indeed an invaluable book. Its translator, after whom it is named, was William Tyndale.

Of his overall significance in the history of the Church, the article on him in the famous eleventh edition of the *Encyclopædia Britannica* rightly states that he was "one of the greatest forces of the English Reformation," a man whose writings "helped to shape the thought of the Puritan party in England."[1] There is a portrait of Tyndale that hangs in the dining-hall of Hertford College, Oxford. His right hand in the painting is pointing to what appears to be a Bible, under which there is a Latin couplet, of which the translation runs thus:

---

1. *The Encyclopædia Britannica*, 11th ed. (New York: Encyclopædia Britannica, 1911), 27:499.

To scatter Roman darkness by this light
The loss of land and life I'll reckon slight.[2]

This painting accurately captures Tyndale's view of God's Word. As he wrote in 1530 in his "Prologue" to his translation of Genesis:

> The Scripture is a light, and sheweth us the true way, both what to do and what to hope for; and a defence from all error, and a comfort in adversity that we despair not, and feareth us in prosperity that we sin not.

And if need be, Tyndale was willing to give his life so that his countrymen might have this treasure.

The Years of Preparation

Though we know the general area in which Tyndale was born—the county of Gloucestershire next to Wales—we have no idea of the exact town or village in which he first saw the light of day. David Daniell, his most recent biographer, suggests that the "most likely region of his origin is within a few miles of Dursley, between Bristol and Gloucester."[3] Nor do we know the exact date of his birth—the usually cited date of 1494 is most probable, though not altogether certain. Nor is the identity of his parents known, although it is evident that he came from a family that "included reasonably wealthy merchants and landowners."[4] Indeed, the details of his early life are also shrouded in obscurity. Our first solid evidence of him is in the first decade of the sixteenth century when he was a student at Oxford University—he obtained his B.A. there in 1512—and then later studying at Cambridge.[5]

It was at Cambridge that he would have definitely encountered the works of Erasmus (1466–1536), the foremost scholar of his day in western Europe and a satirical critic of the morals and lifestyle of the clergy and leadership of the Roman Catholic Church. Early 16th-century Europe was undergoing a series of massive transformations during the life-time of Tyndale—social, political, religious, and intellectual—and Erasmus proved to be a prime catalyst in the

---

2. See David Daniell, *William Tyndale. A Biography* (New Haven, CT/London: Yale University Press, 1994), photograph 4, between pages 214 and 215.
3. Daniell, *William Tyndale*, 9.
4. Daniell, *William Tyndale*, 10–11.
5. Daniell, *William Tyndale*, 9.

process of change. In the hope of recovering the life and experience of the Early Church, Erasmus had printed, for the first time ever, a copy of the New Testament in Greek in 1516. Prior to this point in time, the New Testament was only generally available in western Europe in a Latin translation dating from the end of the fourth century, a translation that by the late Middle Ages definitely obscured a number of key areas of Christian doctrine. Erasmus openly expressed the desire that his Greek New Testament would be read by many of the working-class in Europe and that it would reveal the vast difference between the simplicity of New Testament Christianity and the degenerate state in which the Roman Church found itself at the beginning of the sixteenth century.

Erasmus, it should be noted, was content to critique the morals of the Roman Church. Its doctrine, in many areas just as aberrant as its morals, he did not really view as a problem. But those who read his Greek New Testament, men like Martin Luther (1483–1546) as well as Tyndale himself, came to the realization that nothing was going to change with regard to the morals of Rome until there was a return to New Testament doctrine. This is one of the most decisive differences between the Reformers and various critics of the morality of the Roman church like Erasmus. The former found the ground of the Roman Church's corruption in her doctrinal errors, while the latter were content to criticize the moral failings of the Roman Church and recommended a return to the simplicity of life in the New Testament church. For critics like Erasmus, doctrine was not an issue. J. I. Packer and O. R. Johnston, in their introduction to their translation of Luther's *The Bondage of the Will*, compare Erasmus's program of church renewal to a person going on a diet: the problem was simply the removal of some surplus pounds or excess fat. To the Reformers, including Tyndale, however, doctrine was foundational to restoring biblical Christianity, because true religion is first and foremost a matter of faith, and faith is inextricable from truth and doctrine.

It was probably during his time at Cambridge, around 1520, that Tyndale came to evangelical convictions. In 1521 he left Cambridge University to become chaplain and private tutor in the home of Sir John Walsh at Little Sodbury Manor, a Cotswold house twelve or so miles south of Stinchcombe, just off the M5. It was while in Walsh's employ that Tyndale came to another firm conviction. He came to see that the printing of the New Testament in Greek was merely the first step in reforming the church. Since it was in Greek it still remained a closed book to all who were not scholars and who could not read that language. Tyndale therefore determined to translate God's Word into English.

Nothing better reveals Tyndale's determination to translate God's Word than the story of what took place one evening during his time in Sir John Walsh's household. Walsh was an extremely hospitable man, and it often transpired that there were guests for dinner. On this occasion, according to Richard Webb of Chipping Sodbury, who was a servant of Hugh Latimer (c. 1490–1555), a high-ranking cleric was present and Tyndale was outlining the problems of the Church of Rome in the light of God's Word. The cleric responded by saying that he would rather have the Pope's laws than those of the Word of God. His response and general tone of his conversation revealed a profound ignorance of God's Word and its preciousness. Tyndale, amazed by the man's words and his disdain for the Scriptures, replied, "I defy the Pope and all his laws,… if God spare my life, ere many years I will cause a boy that driveth the plough shall know more of the scripture than thou dost."[6]

In England, however, it was illegal to translate the Scriptures into English, let alone for a ploughboy to read them in his own native tongue. A law actually forbidding such a translation had been passed in 1408 after John Wycliffe (c. 1330–1384), the so-called "morning star of the Reformation," had translated the Old and New Testaments from Latin into Middle English in the hope of bringing about a reform of the Church. To stifle the aims of Wycliffe and his followers, known as the Lollards, it had been made illegal to put the Scriptures into English, to have such a translation in one's possession, or even to read such a translation without express permission of a bishop. But Tyndale was not to be deterred from the pursuit of what he was coming to regard as God's calling for his life.

Initially he sought for a wealthy and powerful patron who would support him in his translation work. He approached the Bishop of London, Cuthbert Tunstall (1474–1559), reputedly a friend of Erasmus, for such patronage, but to no avail. Soon Tyndale came to the conviction that he would have to go abroad to the Continent to

---

6. Daniell, *William Tyndale*, 79.

undertake such a translation. So, in the spring of 1524, he sailed from England for the port of Hamburg, Germany, little knowing that he would never see his native land again.

Translating the New Testament
He spent a year or so in Wittenberg, where he met the great German Reformer Martin Luther. He could have stayed in Wittenberg, and translated the Scriptures in relative security and with all of the scholarly aids that he needed. Instead he chose to go to Cologne, one of the three great trading ports of northeast Europe. The major reason for the move undoubtedly has to do with the fact that Cologne was on the Rhine River that flowed out into the North Sea and boats would come there on trading trips from England. And Tyndale wanted his translated Scriptures to be taken to England where they could be read. An English translation would do very little good in the heart of Germany.

In Cologne he finished his translation of the New Testament from the Greek. Accompanying it were marginal notes, many of which he took from Martin Luther's translation of the Scriptures into German—an indication of his use of Luther's German New Testament, which had appeared in 1522.[7] All that has survived, however, is a manuscript down to Matthew 22, since, just as he was about to print it, he was betrayed to Roman Catholic authorities. Tyndale managed to escape with his translation and made his way up the Rhine to Worms.

In Worms, on the printing press of Peter Schöffer the younger (his father, Peter Schöffer the elder [c. 1425–c. 1503], had been an apprentice of Johann Gutenberg), three or six thousand copies[8] of the first printed New Testament to be translated into English out of the original Greek were run off. It was a small octavo, that is, it was made by folding each sheet three times to form a quire of eight leaves. Unlike the Cologne translation, there were no marginal notes, though there would be such notes in his definitive 1534 edition. Nor

---

7. Heinz Bluhm, "Martin Luther and the English Bible: Tyndale and Coverdale" in Gerhard Dünnhaupt, ed., *The Martin Luther Quincentennial* (Detroit: Wayne State University Press, 1984), 112–25.
8. It is not clear how large the print run exactly was. See Daniell, *William Tyndale*, 134.

was there a prologue. The title-page, which is missing from two of the copies that have survived (a more recently discovered copy in 1996 by Eberhard Zwink[9] does have the title page), did not contain Tyndale's name. It reads thus:

> The new Testament as it was written and caused to be written by them which heard it. To whom also our Saviour Christ Jesus commanded that they should preach it unto all creatures.

There were no verse divisions, which did not come into vogue until the 1550s, only simple chapter breaks. Also, it is noteworthy that in the 1526 edition, Tyndale followed Luther's arrangement of the New Testament in his 1523 translation, in which Hebrews, James, and Jude as well as Revelation were placed at the end of the Bible.

The Tyndale New Testaments were then smuggled back into England on boats, hidden in bales of cloth and other innocent looking containers, and Tyndale's dream of giving the common person the Word of God started to become a reality. By early 1526 they were being sold openly in England. Price: a week's wages for a laborer like a mason.

Response from church authorities, however, was not slow in coming. When word of Tyndale's translation reached the ears of Cuthbert Tunstall, the Bishop of London began to scour the boats coming into English harbours and ports for the precious books. Many of the New Testaments were seized or even bought, and Tunstall had them publicly burned in the heart of London in 1530. He described the Tyndale New Testament as a "pestiferous and pernicious poison." Ironically, the money that was paid for the copies eventually found its way back to Tyndale, who simply used it to finance another edition!

A Literary Master

There is little doubt that Tyndale had a solid handle on the Greek language, its idioms, shades of meaning, and idiosyncrasies. It is now recognized that Tyndale was a brilliant Greek scholar. In fact, he had remarkable linguistic skills, being the master of at least eight languages, including Greek.

---

9. See Eberhard Zwink, "Confusion about Tyndale: The Stuttgart Copy of the 1526 New Testament in English" (http://www.wlb-stuttgart.de/fileadmin/user _upload/sammlungen/bibeln/Tyndale_1526_NT_English.pdf; accessed February 1, 2017).

Equally important was his impressive grasp of the words and rhythms of the spoken English of his day. He knew how to render the Scriptures into the English vernacular so that they spoke with force and power. In fact, as Daniell notes, "what still strikes a late-twentieth-century reader is how modern" Tyndale's translation actually is.[10] The reasons for this are twofold. First, in translating the New Testament, Tyndale aimed to reproduce "clear, everyday, spoken English." Second, Tyndale aimed to impact the heart of his readers.

In fact, many of his words and phrases became part of everyday English—words and phrases such as "under the sun," "signs of the times," "let there be light," "my brother's keeper," "lick the dust," "fall flat on his face," "the land of the living," "pour out one's heart," "the apple of his eye," "go the extra mile," "the parting of the ways," "peacemaker," "longsuffering," the "salt of the earth," "fight the good fight," "God forbid," "the spirit is willing," "there were shepherds abiding in the fields," and "this thy brother was dead, and is alive again: and was lost, and is found."[11]

So good in fact was Tyndale's translation of the New Testament that, when the King James Version (KJV) translators came to fashion a new translation at the start of the seventeenth century, they went back to Tyndale's work and used no less than ninety per cent of it,[12] which also speaks volumes for his grasp of Greek.

Translating the Old Testament

After completing the translation of the New Testament, Tyndale turned his attention to the Old Testament. His translation of Genesis, which appeared in 1530, was the first English translation ever made from a Hebrew text. Only a tiny handful of Oxford and Cambridge scholars, if any at all, knew this language. In fact, most of the ordinary population would have been astonished to discover that Hebrew had anything to do with the Bible. For them, all of their religion was wrapped up in Latin.[13] Translations of a number of other books of the Old Testament followed: including the rest of the Pentateuch in 1530 and Jonah in 1531.

---

10. Daniell, *William Tyndale*, 135.
11. Melvyn Bragg, *William Tyndale. A very brief history* (London: SPCK, 2017), 87.
12. Daniell, *William Tyndale*, 1.
13. Daniell, *William Tyndale*, 287.

Where Tyndale learned Hebrew we have no idea. It is quite unlikely he learned it in England, since so little Hebrew was known there in the 1520s. Hebrew studies only began to take root in England during the reigns of Elizabeth I and James I. He had to have learned it, therefore, on the Continent, probably in Germany—David Daniell suggests that Tyndale may have studied Hebrew at Wittenberg when he was there in the mid-1520s.[14] As with the Greek New Testament, Tyndale displays a wonderful facility for rendering the Hebrew Scriptures—a linguistic world utterly unlike any other in Europe at that time—into English. And coinages that he made, like "Jehovah," "Passover," "scapegoat," "shewbread," and "mercy seat" have become a part of standard English.

Jonah incidentally was an important book for the Reformers. Luther, for instance, translated it separately in 1526. At its heart is the account of the preaching of repentance to a terribly sinful nation—the powerful message of repentance despite the weakness of the preacher. Just as God's Word had been preached to the Ninevites with the threat of judgment if repentance was not forthcoming, so God's Word had to be preached to the English. Thus, Tyndale can say in his introduction to this translation of Jonah:

> The Pope sanctifieth us with holy oil, holy bread, holy salt, holy candles, holy dumb ceremonies and holy dumb blessings, and with whatsoever holiness thou wilt—save with the holiness of God's word which only speaketh unto the heart and sheweth the soul her filthiness and uncleanness of sin, and leadeth her by the way of repentance unto the fountain of Christ's blood to wash it away through faith...[and] if thou confess with a repenting heart and acknowledge and surely believe that Jesus is Lord over all sin, thou art safe. Beware of the leaven that saith we have power in our freewill before the preaching of the Gospel— to deserve grace, to keep the law....
>
> Neither can actual sin be washed away with our works— but with Christ's blood: neither can there be any other sacrifice or satisfaction to Godward for them—save Christ's blood. For as much as we can do no works unto God—but receive only of his mercy with our repenting faith—through Jesus Christ our Lord and only Savior: unto whom and unto God our Father through

---

14. Daniell, *William Tyndale*, 291, 299.

him, and unto his Holy Spirit—that only purgeth, sanctifieth & washeth us in the innocent blood of our redemption—be praise for ever.[15]

"Lord! open the King of England's eyes"

By the early 1530s Tyndale was living in Antwerp, from whence the smuggling of the Scriptures across to England could be easily carried out. In 1535, he was hard at work on translating the books of Joshua to 2 Chronicles, as well as making some minor revisions to his 1534 New Testament. The translation had not yet progressed beyond the manuscript stage when he was arrested on May 21 of that year. Tyndale was betrayed into the hands of Roman Catholic authorities by a certain Henry Phillips, an appalling and perfidious individual who was probably acting under orders from John Stokesley, the Bishop of London at the time.[16] He was imprisoned in the infamous prison of Vilvoorde, six miles north of Brussels. There he was put on trial for heresy—specifically for being a Lutheran—found guilty and condemned to be burned to death. Two word-pictures from the last year of his life reveal the character of the man.

The first comes from a letter that he wrote in the Vilvorde prison in the autumn of 1535. It was found during the last century and is the only surviving example of his handwriting. Writing to the governor of the prison, the Marquis of Bergen, Tyndale requested

> a lamp in the evening; it is indeed wearisome sitting alone in the dark. But most of all I beg and beseech your clemency to… permit me to have the Hebrew Bible, Hebrew grammar, and Hebrew dictionary, that I may pass the time in that study.[17]

To the end Tyndale was intent on the study and translation of God's Word—that precious book that Tyndale knew God the Holy Spirit would use to shed the light of God's salvation throughout benighted Europe. It is unlikely his petition was granted.

The other word-picture comes from the day of his death, traditionally October 6, 1536. The executioner, in an act of mercy to Tyndale, strangled him before he lit the wood piled around him. According to

---

15. William Tyndale, "Unto the Christian Reader" to his trans., *The Prophete Jonas* (Antwerp: M. de Keyser, 1531).

16. Daniell, *William Tyndale*, 367–68.

17. Daniell, *William Tyndale*, 379.

the martyrologist John Foxe, the last words that Tyndale was heard to utter were, "Lord! open the King of England's eyes."

Up until this point the king, Henry VIII, had been firmly opposed to the free circulation of Tyndale's translation, despite his break with Rome over his desire to get a divorce from his first wife, Katherine of Aragon.[18] Yet, within a year of Tyndale's death his New Testament was being openly published in England, though not under his name. That Tyndale was not recognized as the translator would not have bothered him at all.

"I did my duty"

A few years before his martyrdom Tyndale had written the following in the preface to his book *The Parable of the Wicked Mammon* (1528) regarding his translation of the New Testament:

> Some man will ask, peradventure, Why I take the labour to make this work, inasmuch as they will burn it, seeing they burnt the gospel? I answer, In burning the New Testament they did none other thing than what I looked for: no more shall they do, if they burn me also, if it be God's will it shall so be.
>
> Nevertheless, in translating the New Testament I did my duty.

What a glorious duty that was! Enshrined in the King James Version, his New Testament lived on for centuries after his death. As David Daniell has recently noted in what is the definitive biography of Tyndale, it was Tyndale that made the English people a "people of the Book."[19]

Conclusion

Nearly thirty years after the appearance of the first edition of his New Testament, an English Protestant named John Rogers (d. 1555) was on trial for his Christian faith. Rogers, who had been converted through Tyndale's witness, was told by Stephen Gardiner, the Lord Chancellor of Mary I and the man who was judging his case, that

---

18. On the influence of Anne Boleyn for good, see "The Royal Household of Henry VIII. Part One: A Changed Ann Boleyn," *The Sword and the Trowel* (1997, no. 2): 12–14.

19. Daniell, *William Tyndale*, 3; Iain Murray, "William Tyndale" (address at the Free Reformed Church of Dundas, Dundas, Ontario, October 24, 1994).

"thou canst prove nothing by the Scripture, the Scripture is dead: it must have a lively [i.e. living] expositor."

"No," Rogers replied, "the Scriptures are alive." Rogers's conviction in this regard was in part shaped by the achievement of Tyndale, whom God had used to make the Scriptures live forever in the hearts and minds of a multitude of English men and women.

CHAPTER 2

"Meat, not Strawberries": Hugh Latimer and Biblical Preaching in the English Reformation

Michael Haykin

In the early days of the Reformation in Germany, Martin Luther (1483–1546) reflected on why the Reformation truths that he and his colleagues were preaching and publishing were making such a deep impact on various parts of German-speaking Europe. To the biblicistic Luther, the answer was patent:

> I simply taught, preached, and wrote God's Word; otherwise I did nothing. And while I slept or drank Wittenberg beer with my friends…, the Word so greatly weakened the papacy that no prince or emperor ever inflicted such losses upon it. I did nothing; the Word did everything.[1]

In emphasizing that the "Word did everything," Luther is not simply giving his own personal opinion, but making plain a vital theme in the history of the Christian faith. In times of spiritual advance, the church is borne along by the Word of God as that Word, applied by the Holy Spirit, lays bare the secrets of human hearts and brings sinners to repentance and conversion.[2] Speaking of this pattern in the history of the church, Iain Murray put it this way: "The advance of the church is ever preceded by a recovery of preaching [the Word]."[3] The Reformation, a time of great spiritual advance, was no exception.

Further evidence of the importance of preaching during the Reformation is found in the fact that the leading term used by the Reformers

---

1. Martin Luther, *The Second Invocavit Sermon*, in Ronald J. Sider, ed., *Karlstadt's Battle with Luther: Documents in a Liberal-Radical Debate* (Philadelphia, Pa.: Fortress Press, 1978), 24.
2. See Heb. 4:12–13; James 1:18.
3. "Lloyd-Jones: Messenger of Grace," *The Banner of Truth*, no. 536 (May 2008): 32.

to describe leadership in the local church was not the word "priest," which had been the case in medieval Christendom, nor "pastor," which only came into regular employ in the eighteenth century, but "preacher."[4] The main reason for this was the conviction held by all of the Reformers that utterly central to ecclesial leadership was the preaching of the Word of God. When Luther singled out the main problem with the medieval church, for instance, he cited the fact that

> God's Word is not proclaimed; there is only reading and sing-ing in the churches. Second, because God's Word has been suppressed, many unchristian inventions and lies have sneaked into the service of reading, singing, and preaching, and they are horrible to see.[5]

In this analysis, the ultimate failure of the mediæval church lay in its refusal to preach the Word of God. And this entailed nothing less than profound religious error and the loss of the gospel. The English Reformer, Hugh Latimer (*c.* 1485–1555), had a similar critique:

> Preaching is necessary; for take away preaching, and take away salvation. I told you of *Scala coeli* [the ladder of heaven], and I made it a preaching matter, not a massing matter. Christ is the preacher of all preachers, the pattern and the exemplar that all preachers ought to follow. For it was he by whom the Father of heaven said, *Hic est Filius meus dilectus, ipsum audite,* "This is my well-beloved Son, hear him."[6]

For Reformers like Luther and Latimer, there is little doubt that preaching was the central means of grace in God's great work of ecclesial renewal and revival. For these men, along with the other Reformers, hearing was *the* key sense of the Christian man and woman. As the French Reformer John Calvin (1509–1564) stressed:

---

4. Wilhelm Pauck, "The Ministry in the Time of the Continental Reformation," in H. Richard Niebuhr and Daniel D. Williams, eds., *The Ministry in Historical Perspectives* (New York: Harper & Brothers, 1956), 116.

5. Cited in Pauck, "The Ministry in the Time of the Continental Reformation," 111.

6. Hugh Latimer, *The Fourth Sermon preached before King Edward, March 29, 1549,* in *The Works of Hugh Latimer,* ed. George Elwes Corrie (Cambridge: Cambridge University Press, 1844), 1:155. See also Hugh Latimer, *The Fifth Sermon preached before King Edward, April 5, [1549],* in *Works,* 1:178: "*Scala coeli* is a preaching matter, I tell you, and not a massing matter. God's instrument of salvation is preaching."

genuine "faith cannot flow from a naked experience of things, but must have its origin in the Word of God."[7] Mediæval Roman Catholicism had majored on symbols and images as the central means of teaching. The Reformation, coming as it did hard on the heels of the invention of the printing press in the fifteenth century, turned back to the biblical emphasis on "words," both spoken and written, as the primary vehicle for cultivating faith and spirituality. As Calvin aptly put it, "The Word is the instrument by which the Lord dispenses the illumination of his Spirit to believers."[8] In the minds of the Reformers, there could be neither true Reformation nor genuine spirituality apart from the Scriptures.[9]

Moreover, for the Reformers, the preaching of the Scriptures was a key mark of a true church. Luther put it thus in 1523: "The certain mark of the Christian congregation is the preaching of the gospel in its purity."[10] Sixteen years later he made the same point when he maintained: "Whenever you hear or see this Word preached, believed, confessed, and acted on, there do not doubt that there must be a true holy catholic church, a Christian, holy people."[11] Similarly, Calvin stated: "Whenever we see the Word of God purely preached and heard, and the sacraments administered according to Christ's institution, it is not to be doubted, a church of God exists."[12]

In what follows, the spotlight is placed on one of the remarkable cadre of preachers raised up during the Reformation, the English preacher cited above, Hugh Latimer, whom the twentieth-century historian Patrick Collinson once described as one of the greatest English-speaking preachers of the sixteenth century.[13] In fact,

---

7. Cited in Nigel Westhead, "Calvin and Experimental Knowledge of God," in *Adorning the Doctrine* (London: The Westminster Conference, 1995), 18.

8. John Calvin, *Institutes* 1.9.3, trans. Ford Lewis Battles, ed. John T. McNeill, *Calvin: Institutes of the Christian Religion* (The Library of Christian Classics, vol. 20; Philadelphia: Westminster Press, 1960), 1:96.

9. Otto Gründler, "John Calvin: Ingrafting in Christ" in E. Rozanne Elder, ed., *The Spirituality of Western Christendom* (Kalamazoo, Mich.: Cistercian Publications, 1976), 175.

10. Cited in Sam Chan, *Preaching as the Word of God: Answering an Old Question with Speech-Act Theory* (Eugene, Ore.: Pickwick Publications, 2016), 62. I am indebted to Dr. Chan for drawing my attention to his work and then making it available to me.

11. Cited Chan, *Preaching as the Word of God*, 63.

12. Cited Chan, *Preaching as the Word of God*, 71.

13. Patrick Collinson, *Archbishop Grindal 1519–1583: The Struggle for A Reformed Church* (London: Jonathan Cape, 1979), 48.

in many ways Latimer was "the Preacher of England" during the Reformation era.[14] J. C. Ryle gave some reasons why: "If a combination of sound Gospel doctrine, plain Saxon language, boldness, liveliness, directness, and simplicity, can make a preacher, few...have ever equalled...Latimer."[15] Nor is this a recent perspective on Latimer. In the 1560s, it was apparently a common saying in the university town of Cambridge that when "Master [Hugh] Latimer preached, then was Cambridge blessed."[16] And according to Augustine Bernher (fl. 1550s–1570s), a Francophone pastor who was mentored by Latimer and later pastored during the reign of Elizabeth I (1533–1603), "if England ever had a prophet, he was one."[17]

"The child of everlasting joy"[18]

Hugh Latimer's father, also called Hugh Latimer, was a yeoman-farmer in Thurcaston, a small village in Leicestershire. According to his son's witness in a sermon he preached before Edward VI, his father was a "yeoman, who had not lands of his own; only he had a farm of three or four pounds by year at the uttermost."[19] The younger Latimer was the only son among seven siblings, and having profited from his early education, he entered Clare Hall (now Clare College) at

---

14. *Clare College 1326–1926* (Cambridge: Cambridge University Press, 1928), 1:135.

15. J. C. Ryle, *Five English Reformers* (1890 ed.; repr. London: The Banner of Truth Trust, 1960), 110.

16. From Thomas Becon, cited in Marcus L. Loane, *Masters of the English Reformation* (London: Church Book Room Press, 1954), 97.

17. Cited in John T. McNeill, "Book Reviews: *Hugh Latimer, Apostle to the English*. By Allan G. Chester," *Church History*, 24 (1955): 78. The statement is taken from Augustine Bernher, "To the Right Honourable, the Lady Katherine the Duchess of Suffolk," in *The Works of Hugh Latimer*, ed. George Elwes Corrie (Cambridge: Cambridge University Press, 1844), 1:320–21.

18. For studies of Latimer's life and thought, see Robert Demaus, *Hugh Latimer: A Biography* (London: Religious Tract Society, 1904); Harold S. Darby, *Hugh Latimer* (London: Epworth Press, 1953); Allan Griffith Chester, *Hugh Latimer, Apostle to the English* (Philadelphia: University of Pennsylvania Press, 1954); Alister McGrath, *Passion for the Gospel: Hugh Latimer (1485–1555) Then and Now* (London: The Latimer Trust, 2005); Michael Pasquarello III, *God's Ploughman. Hugh Latimer: "A Preaching Life" (1485–1555)*, Studies in Christian History and Thought (Eugene, Ore.: Wipf and Stock, 2014).

19. Cited in *Clare College 1326–1926*, 1:132. See Hugh Latimer, *The First Sermon Preached Before King Edward, March 8, 1549*, in *Works*, 1:101.

the University of Cambridge when he was 14—so around 1507.[20] He was at Clare for the next 23 years or so, till 1530. He received his BA in 1510 and his MA four years later, in 1514.[21] Around the time that he received his MA, he was ordained a priest at Lincoln.[22] In 1524 he obtained his BD, which proved to be a key turning-point in his life.

Up until this time he had been a staunch Roman Catholic. As he stated later, "I was as obstinate a Papist as any was in England."[23] While gifted in Latin, he was typical of many scholars in the Roman Church who were neither deeply conversant with Greek nor the Scriptures. Before his conversion, he considered the study of Greek, which at that time was an innovation in the university, with deep suspicion. In fact, on one occasion he urged his hearers to "study the school divines, and not meddle with the Scripture itself."[24]

On receiving the BD, though, Latimer was expected to deliver a public speech. He used the occasion to deliver a bitter attack on the teaching of Philip Melanchthon (1497–1560), the German Reformer and co-worker with Martin Luther. Now, among those listening to Latimer was Thomas Bilney (c. 1495–1531), who was at Trinity College and the earliest of the Cambridge Reformers. Bilney was concerned by what he heard and after the lecture, he went to speak with Latimer. Latimer would later say that he learned more in the space of that conversation than he had had in all of the years of his studies at Cambridge.[25] This then was his conversion, which can be dated to around the spring of 1524.[26] As he stated in a sermon years later: "All the Papists think themselves to be saved by the law, and I myself was of that dangerous, perilous, and damnable opinion till I was

---

20. For discussion of the date, see *Clare College 1326–1926*, 1:133. See also Demaus, *Hugh Latimer*, 14–15; Darby, *Hugh Latimer*, 9–10.

21. Darby, *Hugh Latimer*, 20.

22. *Clare College 1326–1926*, 1:132; P. C. H. Lim, "Latimer, Hugh" in Timothy Larsen, ed., *Biographical Dictionary of Evangelicals* (Downers Grove, Ill.: InterVarsity Press, 2003), 360.

23. Hugh Latimer, *First Sermon on the Lord's Prayer* in *Works*, 1:334.

24. *Clare College 1326–1926*, 1:133; Demaus, *Hugh Latimer*, 38: "I understand no Greek," he stated at his trial in Oxford in 1555.

25. Latimer, *First Sermon on the Lord's Prayer* in *Works*, 1:334; *Clare College 1326–1926*, 1:133. See also Darby, *Hugh Latimer*, 26–28.

26. Demaus, *Hugh Latimer*, 47.

thirty years of age."[27] More generally, he stated of this great change in his life:

> It were too long to tell you what blindness I have been in, and how long it were ere I could forsake such folly...; but by continual prayer, continual study of Scripture, and oft communing with men of more right judgment, God hath delivered me.[28]

And as he said on another occasion, "I am a Christian man,... the child of everlasting joy, through the merits of the bitter passion of Christ."[29]

Within a year of these events he was accused of being a Lutheran and that by his bishop, Nicholas West (1461–1533), the Bishop of Ely, who came to hear Latimer preach in Great St. Mary's in Cambridge.[30] With boldness, Latimer took the occasion to set forth Christ as a model for bishops. Afterwards West asked Latimer if he would refute the views of Martin Luther. When Latimer told him that he could not refute what he did not know (Latimer had not read any of Luther to this point), West said, "Well, Mr Latimer, I perceive that you somewhat smell of the pan; you will repent this gear one day."[31] In other words, his sermons had the flavor of Lutheran doctrine. Years later, in 1552, when Latimer had had the time to read Luther, he described him as a "wonderful instrument of God, through whom God hath opened the light of his holy Word unto the world, which was a long time hid in corners and neglected."[32]

West forbade Latimer to preach in the entire diocese of Ely as well as in the university. A little later, however, Latimer was arraigned before Thomas Wolsey (1473–1530), the papal legate. Latimer made such a favorable impression upon Wolsey that the papal legate gave him freedom to preach throughout England and declared, "If the Bishop of Ely cannot abide such doctrine as you have repeated, you shall have my license and shall preach it unto his beard, let him say

27. Hugh Latimer, *Sermon Preached at Grimsthorpe on Twelfth Day, 1553* in *The Works of Hugh Latimer* (Cambridge: Cambridge University Press, 1845), 2:137.

28. Hugh Latimer, Letter to Edward Baynton in *Works*, 2:333.

29. Hugh Latimer, *Sermons on the Card* in *Works*, 1:7.

30. On West, see Darby, *Hugh Latimer*, 31.

31. *Clare College 1326–1926*, 1:133–34.

32. Hugh Latimer, *The Second Sunday in Advent* in *Works*, 2:52.

what he will."[33] And so Latimer was able to continue preaching in Cambridge.

When the matter of King Henry VIII's (1491–1547) marriage came to the fore in the late 1520s—he desired a divorce since it appeared that his wife, the Spanish princess Katharine of Aragon (1485–1536), could not bear him a living son—it was suggested by Thomas Cranmer that the matter be discussed by the university theologians at Oxford and Cambridge. At Cambridge, Latimer supported the King in his determination to divorce Katherine and marry Anne Boleyn (c. 1501–1536), which probably led to his being invited to preach before the King at Windsor on March 13, 1530. Henry VIII continued to favor his preaching so that even after Latimer had been appointed as the parish minister in the pocket village of West Kington, Wiltshire, for instance, he would be commanded to preach before the King from time to time.

"True preachers should be persecuted and hated"

It may have been these opportunities to preach before the king in 1530 that emboldened Latimer to write a courageous letter to the king that year, pleading with him to allow William Tyndale's (c. 1494–1536) translation of the New Testament to freely circulate in England.[34] Latimer does not mention Tyndale by name, but simply refers to having "the Scripture in English."[35] Since Tyndale's translation was the only one available at this time, the Reformer must have been defending his countryman's famous translation.

Latimer began by emphasizing that it was utterly necessary for him to speak truthfully to the king:

> The holy doctor St. Augustine, in an epistle which he wrote to Casulanus, saith, that he who for fear of any power hides the truth, provokes the wrath of God to come upon him, for he fears men more than God. And the holy man St. John Chrysostom saith, that he is not only a traitor to the truth who openly for truth teaches a lie, but he also who does not freely

---

33. Cited *Clare College 1326–1926*, 1:134; Demaus, *Hugh Latimer*, 66.

34. For this letter, see *Select Sermons and Letters, of Dr. Hugh Latimer*, ed. W. M. Engles (London: The Religious Tract Society, n.d.), 383–92.

35. Hugh Latimer, Letter to Henry VIII, December 1, 1530, in *Select Sermons and Letters*, ed. Engles, 384.

pronounce and show the truth that he knows. These sentences (most redoubted king) when I read now of late, and marked them earnestly in the inward parts of my heart, they made me sore afraid, troubled, and vexed me grievously in my conscience, and at the last drove me to this strait, that either I must show forth such things as I have read and learned in scripture, or else be of those who provoke the wrath of God upon them, and are traitors unto the truth; the which rather than it should happen, I had rather suffer extreme punishment.[36]

Equally strong as this fear of being found a traitor to the cause of God, was Latimer's desire to glorify God. As he told Henry:

My purpose [in writing to you] is, for the love that I have to God principally, and the glory of his name, which is only known by his word, and for the true allegiance that I owe unto your grace, and not to hide in the ground of my heart the talent given me by God, but to chaffer [i.e. speak] it forth to others, that it may increase to the pleasure of God....[37]

Latimer then pled with the king not to give way to those who would prevent the free circulation of the Word of God in English. He urged Henry VIII to read various passages from the Scriptures, where he would plainly see that the truth always stirs up opposition, and suffering persecution was one of the marks of a true servant of God:

In the tenth chapter of St. Matthew's gospel, saith our Saviour Christ also, "Lo, I send you forth as sheep among wolves" [Matt. 10:16]. So that the true preachers go like harmless sheep, and are persecuted, and yet they revenge not their wrong, but remit all to God: so far are they from persecuting any other but with the word of God only, which is their weapon. And so this is the most evident token that our Saviour Jesus Christ would that his gospel and the preachers of it should be known by, that it should be despised among those worldly wise men, and that they should repute it but foolishness and deceivable doctrine, and the true preachers should be persecuted and

---

36. Hugh Latimer, Letter to Henry VIII, December 1, 1530, in *Select Sermons and Letters*, ed. Engles, 383. Augustine's letter to Casulanus, an African elder, is *Letter 36* in his corpus. A perusal of the letter does not reveal any statement similar to the one Latimer attributes to Augustine.

37. Latimer, Letter to Henry VIII, December 1, 1530, in *Select Sermons and Letters*, ed. Engles, 391.

hated, and driven from town to town, yea, and at the last lose both goods and life....

Wherefore take this for a sure conclusion, that where the word of God is truly preached, there is persecution, as well of the hearers as of the teachers: and where is quietness and rest in worldly pleasure, there is not the truth.[38]

The persecution of those preachers who wanted Tyndale's New Testament available for the common man in England was a mark of their being truly sent by Christ. Since Latimer himself had experienced opposition for preaching God's Word, he was also clearly revealing his conviction that he had been called to be a preacher of the gospel.[39]

"Meat, not strawberries"

In September of 1535 Latimer's preaching gifts led to his being appointed Bishop of Worcester, which was probably the most neglected diocese in England. It had been occupied by Italian bishops for the forty years prior to Latimer becoming its bishop and not one of them had ever set foot in England.[40] Latimer's immediate predecessor was Girolamo Ghinucci (1480–1541), who had never been to England. Not surprisingly, there were ministers in the diocese who did not even own a copy of the Latin Bible and Latimer frequently encountered people who were completely ignorant of the Word of God, for these ministers rarely preached. In his famous *Sermon on the Plough* (1548), Latimer compared the rarity of such preaching to strawberries that came but in the summer:

The preaching of the word of God unto the people is called meat. Scripture calleth it meat, not strawberries, that come but once a

38. Latimer, Letter to Henry VIII, December 1, 1530, in *Select Sermons and Letters*, ed. Engles, 387.

39. At the close of the letter, Latimer made a remarkable assertion as he prayed for the king. He specifically asked that his sovereign "may be found a faithful minister of his [i.e. God's] gifts, and not a defender of his faith, for he will not have it defended by man or man's power, but by his word only" (Latimer, Letter to Henry VIII, December 1, 1530, in *Select Sermons and Letters*, ed. Engles, 392). The phrase "defender of his faith" is, of course, an allusion to the title given to Henry by Pope Leo X in 1521 for the book that he wrote in defence of the sacramental system of the Church of Rome, *Defence of the Seven Sacraments*.

40. Loane, *Masters of the English Reformation*, 108.

year, and tarry not long, but are soon gone. But it is meat, it is no dainties. The people must have meat that must be familiar and continual, and daily given unto them to feed upon. Many make a strawberry of it, ministering it but once a year; but such do not the office of good prelates.[41]

Once he came to a town where he had made arrangements before-hand to preach on the Lord's Day, and found the church locked up. He waited for half an hour for someone to show up, but no one did and when he went into the village to find out the reason why no one was at the church, he was told by one of the town's inhabitants, "Sir, this is a busy day with us, we cannot hear you; it is Robin Hood's day." Later, when recounting this incident, Latimer said that this

is no laughing matter, my friends, it is a weeping matter, a heavy matter; a heavy matter, under the pretence of gathering for Robin Hood,...to put out a preacher, to have his office less esteemed; to prefer Robin Hood before the ministration of God's Word; and all this hath come of unpreaching prelates.... If the bishops had been preachers, there should never have been any such thing.[42]

To Latimer's way of thinking, the great calling of the bishops of England was to be preachers of the Word.[43] Without preaching, Lati-mer was assured that there was no hope for England.[44] In his words that have been already cited: "take away preaching, and take away salvation."[45] Again, when faced with the following argument, "What need we preachers then? God can save His elect without preachers," Latimer replied, "I must keep the way God hath ordained.... This

41. Hugh Latimer, *The Sermon on the Plough* in *Works*, 1:62. See also Hugh Lat-imer, *The Sixth Sermon preached before King Edward, April 12, [1549]* in *Works*, 1:202: "The devil...hath set up a state of unpreaching prelacy in this realm this seven hun-dred year...."

42. Hugh Latimer, *The Sixth Sermon preached before King Edward, April 12, [1549]* in *Works*, 1:208; Loane, *Masters of the English Reformation*, 113.

43. Hughes Oliphant Old, *The Reading and Preaching of the Scriptures in the Wor-ship of the Christian Church* (Grand Rapids: Eerdmans, 2002), 142.

44. Chester, *Hugh Latimer*, 171. See also Hugh Latimer, *The Seventh Sermon preached before King Edward, April 19, [1549]* in *Works*, 1:234: "I am...sure that this realm of England...is allowed to hear God's word, as though Christ had said a thou-sand times, 'Go preach to Englishmen: I will that Englishmen be saved.'"

45. Hugh Latimer, *The Fourth Sermon preached before King Edward, March 29, 1549,* in *Works*, 1:155.

office of preaching is the only ordinary way that God hath appointed to save us all by."[46]

Latimer was well aware that it was not merely the act of preaching that saved sinners, but God opening hearts as the Word was preached. To quote from one of Latimer's later sermons, preachers

> can do no more but call; God is he that must bring in; God must open the hearts, as it is in the Acts of the Apostles. When Paul preached to the women, there was a silk-woman,..."whose heart God opened." None could open it but God. Paul could but only preach, God must work; God must do the thing inwardly.[47]

Latimer was Bishop of Worcester for only four years, however, as he retired in 1539 upon the promulgation of the Act of the Six Articles, which affirmed, among other things, transubstantiation, clerical celibacy, and the legitimacy of private masses.[48] For the next six years, not much is known about Latimer's life.[49] He was commanded not to visit either Oxford or Cambridge, or his old bishopric of Worcester. He was also placed in prison for a period of time during this period. Things radically changed again with the accession of Edward VI, though, in 1547. Latimer was offered back his bishopric in Worcester, which he refused, choosing rather to stay in London with Thomas Cranmer, the Archbishop of Canterbury, and assist Cranmer in reforming the church. He also spent time at Grimsthorpe Castle in Lincolnshire, where, as the guest of Katherine Willoughby (1519–1580), the Duchess of Suffolk, one of the wealthiest women of her day, and an ardent supporter of the Reformation,[50] Latimer generally preached two sermons every Sunday and during weekdays

---

46. Hugh Latimer, *Residue of the same Gospel declared in the Afternoon [at Stamford, November 9, 1550]* in *Works*, 1:306. See also Hugh Latimer, *Third Sermon upon the Lord's Prayer* in *Works*, 1:358: "The instrument wherewith we be called to this kingdom [of God,] is the office of preaching. God calleth us daily by preachers to come to this kingdom."

47. Hugh Latimer, *A Sermon preached at Stamford, November 9, 1550* in *Works*, 1:285.

48. Lim, "Latimer," 360.

49. Loane, *Masters of the English Reformation*, 116.

50. Willoughby helped finance the publication of a key book by her best friend, Katherine Parr, entitled *Lamentation of a Sinner*, and also supported England's leading Protestant publisher, John Day (*c.* 1522–1584), who has been called "the master printer of the English Reformation."

rose in the middle of the night so as to be at his studies by two in the morning.[51]

His commitment to the Scriptures and their truth is well seen by a comment he made in 1552 in one of his Grimsthorpe sermons. He was speaking about the Roman Catholic concern for unity and the implicit critique that the Reformation was wrong since it had split the Church. Latimer's response was simple: desiring unity was certainly biblical—he referred to the Apostle Paul's exhortation to "be of one mind" (1 Cor. 1:10)—but he stressed: "We ought never to regard unity so much that we would, or should, forsake God's word for her sake."[52]

"To suffer for God's holy word's sake"

Latimer preached hundreds of sermons, but there are only forty-one extant, of which twenty-eight were preached at Grimsthorpe to the servants of Katherine Willoughby or country congregations near to her castle in 1552.[53] These sermons, along with the others that are extant, were copied down as Latimer preached, which proved to be quite difficult, as the copyists struggled to keep up with what Allan G. Chester has called "the torrent of the preacher's eloquence" and fluency.[54] The Grimsthorpe sermons especially reveal a preacher who was able to adapt himself to his audience: he explicates a biblical text in its context, explains points of doctrine, emphasizes moral lessons, warns against the errors of the Roman Catholic Church, and all the while the sermons are suffused with what Allan Chester has called a "heartfelt earnestness."[55]

Here, for example, is Latimer speaking about the necessity of knowing Christ for salvation in a sermon he preached on December 27, 1552, the day assigned to St. John the Apostle in the liturgical calendar of the Western Church:

---

51. Allan G. Chester, "Introduction" to his ed., *Selected Sermons of Hugh Latimer* (Charlottesville, Va.: The University Press of Virginia for The Folger Shakespeare Library, 1968), xxvi.

52. Hugh Latimer, *Second Sermon on the Gospel of All Saints* in *Works*, 1:487.

53. Chester, "Introduction" to his ed., *Selected Sermons of Hugh Latimer*, xxvi–xxvii. On the reliability of the texts of these sermons, see Elizabeth T. Hastings, "A Sixteenth Century Manuscript Translation of Latimer's *First Sermon Before Edward*," *Publications of the Modern Language Association*, 60 (1945): 959–1002.

54. Chester, "Introduction" to his ed., *Selected Sermons of Hugh Latimer*, xxviii.

55. Chester, "Introduction" to his ed., *Selected Sermons of Hugh Latimer*, xxvii.

By [Christ's] passion, which he hath suffered, he merited that as many as believe in him shall be as well justified by him, as though they themselves had never done any sin, and as though they themselves had fulfilled the law to the uttermost. For we, without him, are under the curse of the law; the law condemneth us; the law is not able to help us; and yet the imperfection is not in the law, but in us: for the law itself is holy and good, but we are not able to keep it, and so the law condemneth us; but Christ with his death hath delivered us from the curse of the law. He hath set us at liberty, and promiseth that when we believe in him, we shall not perish; the law shall not condemn us. Therefore let us study to believe in Christ. Let us put all our hope, trust, and confidence only in him; let us patch him with nothing: for, as I told you before, our merits are not able to deserve everlasting life: it is too precious a thing to be merited by man. It is his doing only. God hath given him unto us to be our deliverer, and to give us everlasting life. O what a joyful thing was this![56]

Latimer was thus critical of Rome for arguing that salvation could be attained by our merits:

The papists, which are the very enemies of Christ, make him to be a Saviour after their own fantasy, and not after the word of God; wherein he declareth himself, and set out and opened his mind unto us. They follow, I say, not the Scripture, which is the very leader to God, but regard more their own inventions; and therefore they make him a Savior after this fashion. They consider how there shall be, after the general resurrection, a general judgment, where all mankind shall be gathered together to receive their judgment: then shall Christ, say the papists, sit as a judge, having power over heaven and earth: and all those that have done well in this world, and have steadfastly prayed upon their beads, and have gone a pilgrimage, etc., and so with their good works have deserved heaven and everlasting life, — those, say they, that have merited with their own good works, shall be received of Christ, and admitted to everlasting salvation. As for the other, that have not merited everlasting life, [they] shall be cast into everlasting darkness: for Christ will not suffer wicked sinners to be taken into heaven, but rather receive those which

---

56. Hugh Latimer, *Sermon on St. John Evangelist's Day* in *Works*, 2:125–26.

deserve. And so it appeareth, that they esteem our Savior not to be a Redeemer, but only a judge; which shall give sentence over the wicked to go into everlasting fire, and the good he will call to everlasting felicity.

And this is the opinion of the papists, as concerning our Savior; which opinion is most detestable, abominable, and filthy in the sight of God. For it diminisheth the passion of Christ; it taketh away the power and strength of the same passion; it defileth the honor and glory of Christ; it forsaketh and denieth Christ, and all his benefits. For if we shall be judged after our own deservings, we shall be damned everlastingly. Therefore, learn here, every good Christian, to abhor this most detestable and dangerous poison of the papists, which go about to thrust Christ out of his seat: learn here, I say, to leave all papistry, and to stick only to the word of God, which teacheth thee that Christ is not only a judge, but a justifier; a giver of salvation, and a taker away of sin; for he purchased our salvation through his painful death, and we receive the same through believing in him; as St. Paul teacheth us, saying,… "Freely ye are justified through faith." In these words of St. Paul, all merits and estimation of works are excluded and clean taken away. For if it were for our works' sake, then it were not freely: but St. Paul saith, "freely." Whether will you now believe St. Paul, or the papists?[57]

During one of the Grimsthorpe sermons that Latimer preached on the petition "Thy kingdom come" from the Lord's Prayer (Matthew 6:10), he made a statement that, from the perspective of later events, can be regarded as almost predictive. "Happy is he," he said, "to whom it is given to suffer for God's holy word's sake."[58]

Three years later, during the bloody reign of Mary I (1516–1558), Latimer and his fellow bishop Nicholas Ridley (c. 1500–1555) were called to indeed suffer death for the sake of their commitment to God's Word and its authority over all of life. Latimer had been committed to the Tower of London in September 1553, and then, in April

---

57. Hugh Latimer, *Sermon preached on the First Sunday after Epiphany* in *Works*, 2:146–47. Elsewhere Latimer described saving faith as "a faith that embraceth Christ, and trusteth to his merits; a lively faith, a justifying faith; a faith that maketh a man righteous, without respect of works" (*The Sermon on the Plough* in *Works*, 1:61).

58. Hugh Latimer, *The Third Sermon upon the Lord's Prayer* in *Works*, 1:361.

1554, he was taken with Ridley to the Bocardo prison in Oxford where they, and Thomas Cranmer, underwent examination of their theological beliefs. All three were found guilty of heresy and condemned to death. While in the Bocardo, Latimer wrote the following in a lengthy letter dated May 15, 1555:

> Soap, though it be black, soileth not the cloth, but maketh it clean: so doth the black cross of Christ help us to more whiteness, if God strike with the battledoor. Because you be God's sheep, prepare yourselves to the slaughter, always knowing, that in the sight of God our death is precious....
>
> Die once we must; how and where, we know not. Happy are they whom God giveth to pay nature's debt (I mean to die) for his sake. Here is not our home; let us therefore accordingly consider things, having always before our eyes that heavenly Jerusalem, and the way thereto in persecution.[59]

On October 16, 1555, Latimer and Ridley were taken out of Oxford through the Bocardo Gate where they were tied to a stake in what is now Broad Street. Wood was piled around the two bishops, and before the fire was lit, Ridley asked if he could say two or three words. He was told that if he was prepared to deny his "erroneous opinions," then he would be allowed to speak. If not, he was told, "you must suffer for your deserts." "Well," replied Ridley, "so long as the breath is in my body, I will never deny my Lord Christ, and his known truth!"[60]

The wood piled around Ridley was freshly cut and thus only smoldered. Ridley was in conscious agony till the very end and at one point was heard to pray: "I cannot burn! Lord have mercy upon me!" Latimer, though, died fairly swiftly, but before he did so he uttered the following words in response to this cry by Ridley. These words, recorded by the English martyrologist John Foxe (1516–1587), form a fitting conclusion to this study of Latimer as a preacher, for in a sense they have a sermonic quality: "Be of good comfort Master

---

59. Hugh Latimer, *Letter* LI in *Works,* 2:442, 444.

60. John Foxe, *The Acts and Monuments of the Church* (1570 ed.; "John Foxe's The Acts and Monuments Online," Book 11, page 1976; https://www.johnfoxe.org/index .php?realm=text&gototype=&edition=1570&pageid=1976; accessed April 19, 2017).

Ridley, and play the man! We shall this day light such a candle by God's grace in England, as I trust shall never be put out."[61]

---

61. Foxe, *Acts and Monuments* ("Acts and Monuments Online," Book 11, page 1976; https://www.johnfoxe.org/index.php?realm=text&gototype=&edition=1570 &pageid=1976; accessed April 19, 2017); Peter Newman Brooks, *Cranmer in Context: Documents from the English Reformation* (Minneapolis: Fortress Press, 1989), 93–94; Andrew Atherstone, *The Martyrs of Mary Tudor* (Leominster, England: Day One, 2005), 93–99; David Horan, *Oxford: A cultural and literary companion* (New York: Interlink Books, 2000), 129–30; Pasquarello, *God's Ploughman*, 199.

CHAPTER 3

The Reformers' Commitment to the Propagation of the Gospel to All Nations: A Historical Consideration

Elias Medeiros

The Reformers of the late sixteenth and early seventeenth centuries are commonly characterized by several mission historians as having been indifferent, silent, doing very little, and even being opposed to the propagation of the gospel to all nations during the Reformation era.[1] Gustav Adolf Warneck (1834–1910), one of the most influential German missiologists of the nineteen century, stated that the Reformers were devoid of any "missionary action," lacked "missionary zeal," were "strangely silent" on the recognition of the "missionary obligation," darkened "the permanent missionary task of the church," did not speak of "foreign mission work," and "had no proper missionary ideas."[2] This general view has been disseminated in some measure throughout the Protestant world by Kenneth Latourette, Stephen Neill, Herbert Kane, Ralph Winter, Ruth Tucker, and others.

The purpose of this chapter, based on the primary and secondary sources available, is to argue that the Reformers, especially John Calvin, were intentionally and intensively committed to the propagation of the gospel to all nations.

---

1. Two preliminary remarks: 1) when I am critiquing any mission historian, I am not addressing their character or their literary production, but their writings on the work of the Reformers—particularly John Calvin and the seventeenth century Dutch Calvinists; and 2) there was a time when the Reformed movement in Brazil was part of the history of the church in Geneva and in the Netherlands. Today, the church of Geneva and the Reformed church in the Netherlands are a part of the history of the Reformed heritage in Brazil.

2. Gustav Warneck, *Outline of a History of Protestant Missions from the Reformation to the Present Time* (New York: Revell, 1903), 9ff.

Primary Sources Available but Not Carefully Considered

Due to the quantity of resources available today, we cannot speak about Calvin's work as being limited to Geneva or even Switzerland. Calvin himself never limited his ministry to the city of Geneva. While there, he carried out extensive correspondence with other ministers and leaders elsewhere. For example, on May 7, 1549, Calvin wrote to Henry Bullinger, who succeeded Zwingli in Zurich, pleading for the alliance of the Reformed cantons[3] with France: "If I wished to regard my own life or private concerns, I should immediately betake myself elsewhere. But when I consider how very important this corner [of Geneva] is for the propagation of the kingdom of Christ, I have good reason to be anxious that it should be carefully watched over."[4]

These letters were not tweets, short email replies, or Facebook posts. These were long, loaded, leading, God-glorifying, church-edifying letters concerning the lost. Besides his commentaries, sermons, theological treatises, booklets, consistory minutes, records of the Geneva Academy, the Register of the Company of Pastors, etc., what a source of study Calvin's correspondence is! In his letters we find Calvin's journal, his diary, his emotions.

A careful reading of some of these sixteenth century resources would convince anyone of Calvin's commitment and passion for the spreading of the gospel to the world. Unfortunately, it seems that most who criticize Calvin on this subject simply appeal to secondary and tertiary references without having read Calvin and considering other primary sources.

No one can write or speak about John Calvin and Geneva as just a localized phenomenon. John Knox described Calvin's Geneva as "the most perfect school of Christ which has been seen on earth since the days of the apostles."[5] Calvin's influence was felt, not just in Geneva and Switzerland, but in England, Europe, the Netherlands, Germany, Hungary, Poland, Czechoslovakia, Italy, and even South America.

---

3. There were thirteen Reformed cantons (territorial districts) at the time Calvin wrote this letter.

4. Jules Bonnet, *Letters of John Calvin* (Edinburgh: Thomas Constable, 1857), 2:213.

5. Philip Schaff, *History of the Christian Church* (repr., Grand Rapids: Eerdmans, 1958), 8:510.

John Calvin: Geneva and Europe

Doubtless, the time of Calvin in Geneva represents an exciting moment for the church in Geneva, among the Company of Pastors and students of the Academy (founded in 1559). Peter Jonathan Wilcox says in his doctoral thesis that "the series of Lectures on the Old Testament Prophets which Calvin gave in 'the school' at Geneva… were addressed to people caught up with him in a missionary enterprise and…are therefore to be read in this light."[6]

Based on information discovered in the records of the newly inaugurated Academy in Geneva, Wilcox argues, "For the period after 1559…the evangelistic enterprise was at its height…. These records indicate that Calvin delivered his Lectures to a mixed audience of students (the majority of whom were missionaries in training), ministers (most of whom were missionaries awaiting re-assignment), and other hearers (among whom were refugees from France, many of whom were responsible for financing the missionary effort, and emissaries from the nascent French reformed churches, who were visiting Geneva to negotiate over the appointment of a minister)."[7]

The sending of preachers throughout Europe began in 1555.[8] But it is known that "in the less than twenty-five years—between Calvin's arrival in Geneva and the outbreak of the civil wars in France from 1562–98—more than a million French men and women had been converted to Protestantism."[9] Alister McGrath says, "At the opening of the momentous year 1562, the number of consistories [elders and deacons] in France had risen to 1,785."[10] The reports presented by

---

6. Peter Wilcox, "Restoration, Reformation and the Progress of the Kingdom of Christ: Evangelisation in the Thought and Practice of John Calvin. 1555–1564." PhD diss., University of Oxford, St. John's College, Trinity, 1993, 11.

7. Peter Wilcox, "Restoration, Reformation and the Progress of the Kingdom of Christ," iv.

8. 1555 was the year Nicolas Durand de Villegaignon occupied an island in South Brazil near the Guanabara Bay.

9. Mack P. Holt, *The French Wars of Religion, 1562–1629: New Approaches to European History* (Cambridge: Cambridge University Press, 2005), 192. See also Robert M. Kingdon, an authority on the history of the expansion of Protestantism in France through the work of the pastors sent from Geneva, in Robert M. Kingdon, *Geneva and the Coming of the Wars of Religion in France, 1555–1563* (Genève: Librairie E. Droz, 1956). His work has become a reference for scholars such as Holt, McGrath, and others.

10. Alister E. McGrath, *A Life of John Calvin: A Study in the Shaping of Western Culture* (Cambridge, Mass: Basil Blackwell, 1990), 184. The Genevan church prepared

researchers are astounding: "A study of eighty-eight agents sent out on 105 missions during the period 1555–63"[11] highlights the "early successes of Calvinism" and confirms "the impression that the movement held a special appeal to the urban middle class."[12] In a letter to Bullinger on October 1, 1560, Calvin reports the following:

> Meanwhile, the truth of the gospel is breaking forth. *In Normandy our brethren are preaching in public,* because *no private house is capable of containing an audience of three and four thousand persons.* There is greater liberty in Poitou, Saintonge, and the whole of Gascony. Languedoc, Provence, and Dauphiny possess many intrepid disciples of Christ.[13]

By the year 1562, "there had been an explosion in the growth of Calvinist congregations and influence; the complete reformation of France seemed a real possibility." Imagine if the complete reformation of France had become a reality! Likely France, not Great Britain, would have become the primary sending agent of pastors to Africa, North America, South America, and Asia.

By March 1562, Admiral Gaspar de Coligny and the governor of one of the French provinces/states prepared a list of Huguenot churches in France at that time and sent the figures to Catherine de Medici. According to that list "there were 2,150 Huguenot churches in France at that point."[14] McGrath understands that it would be difficult to verify these figures. He states, however, that "it would seem reasonable to suggest that there were at least 1,250 such churches, with a total membership in excess of two million out of a national population of twenty million."[15] Let us not forget that all these accomplishments were happening in the context of persecution.

---

and sent the pastors but the ecclesiastical leaders (elders and deacons) were provided by each local congregation.

11. Calvin died in 1564.

12. McGrath, *A Life of John Calvin,* 191.

13. Calvin's letter to Bullinger on October 1, 1560, which sounds like a report from the Book of Acts. Emphasis added.

14. McGrath, *A Life of John Calvin,* 191.

15. McGrath, *A Life of John Calvin,* 192. McGrath seems to rely on the information found in Robert M. Kingdon, *Geneva and the Coming of the Wars of Religion in France (1555–1563),* 79–80. See also Samuel Mours, *Le Protestantisme en France au XVIIe siècle (1598–1685)* (Paris: Librairie Protestante, 1959), 2:183. Peter Wilcox collected other data found in Calvin's correspondence. A 1561 letter from L'Église de Bergerac à Colladon included the following information: "The church in Bergerac

The Reformers' missionary work, especially John Calvin's, throughout continental and non-continental Europe during the sixteenth century, is well documented. According to *The Register of the Company of Pastors of Geneva at the Time of Calvin*,[16] Jean Vernou and Jean Lauvergeat were the first two pastors commissioned by the Company "to go and preach the Word [to the brethren who were scattered in several valleys of Piedmont][17] in response to the request of three brethren who were sent from there for this purpose."[18] They were

---

boasted that 'there is, by the grace of God, such a movement in the district that the devil is already, for the most part, driven out, so that we are unable to provide [ministers] for ourselves. And from day to day we are growing, and God has caused his work to bear such fruit that at sermons on Sundays, there are to be found about 4000–5000 people'" ("L'Église de Bergerac à Colladon," May 28, 1561, Ms. L. 121, footnote 36). The other two examples quoted by Wilcox have to do with the church in Montpellier and in Toulouse. In Montpellier we read the following report: "Our church, thanks to the Lord, has so grown, and so continues to grow every day... that we are obliged to preach three sermons each on Sundays, to a total of 5000–6000 people" (Epistolae 3714, *CO*, 19:282). And in 1562, the minister of Toulouse wrote to Calvin about the growth of the flock in that location assuring Calvin that without lying, or *sans mentir*—Wilcox translates as "without exaggeration"—they had grown "to the astonishing number of about 8000–9000." Wilcox adds that "this exceptional state of affairs had come about because the Town Council had given him [the minister of Toulouse] their support, charging him 'to preach the Word of God purely and sincerely,' and providing him with an armed escort to enable him to preach outdoors" (Epistolae 3714, *CO*, 19:282).

16. The original manuscript of the *Registres de la Compagnie des Pasteurs de Genève au Temps de Calvin* is in the Archives d'État de Genève [the State Archives of Geneva]. We reference *The Register of the Company of Pastors of Geneva in the Time of Calvin*, edited and translated by Philip Edgcumbe Hughes (Grand Rapids: Eerdmans, 1966), hereafter *The Register*, and a copy of *Registres de la Compagnie des Pasteurs de Genève au Temps de Calvin (1553–1564)*, Tome 2, edited by Robert M. Kingdon, with the collaboration of Jean-François Bergier and Alain Dufour, (Archives d'État de Genève, 1962). *Registres de la Compagnie des Pasteurs de Genève au Temps de Calvin (1546–1553)*, Tome 1 (Genève: Librairie E. Droz, 1964), was edited by Jean-François Bergier.

17. Vernoul and Lauvergeat ministered in the Valley of d'Angrogne, Piedmont. See Wulfert de Greef, *The Writings of John Calvin: An Introductory Guide*, trans. Lyle D. Bierma (Louisville: Westminster John Knox, 2008), 55.

18. *Registres de la Compagnie des Pasteurs de Genève au Temps de Calvin* reads as follows: "Maistre Jehan Vernoul et M. Jehan Lauvergeat estans envoiez par les ministres de ceste eglise aux freres qui sont espars en plusieurs vallees de Piedmont, ont escript lettres dattees du 22ᵉ d'apvril, contenans comme le Seigneur avançoit là son œuvre, ainsy qu'il appert par lesdites lettres. Et fut la charge d'aller là annuncer la Parole commise auxdits Vernoul et Lauvergeat, à l'instance de trois freres qui furent envoiez de pardela icy à cest effect" (*Registres*, 1553–1564), 2:62.

sent in order to establish the believers and to evangelize unbelievers. This was just the beginning of an increase in recruiting, training, and sending of "underground" ministers throughout Europe, especially to France, Italy, and neighboring countries.

Hughes, the editor and translator of the *Registres de la Compagnie des Pasteurs*, noticed in his studies that the Register named "88 such men who were sent from Geneva between 1555, when it was first considered safe for their names to be recorded, and 1562 when the wars of religion commenced in France and it became expedient once again to cease minuting the names of such men, most of whom went into French territory; but there were many more who are not mentioned in these annals."[19] For instance, in 1561, the Register records twelve names. Other sources (letters, minutes) indicate the sending of no less than 142 preachers from Geneva in 1561.[20]

When everything is heard, said, and written, Joel Beeke is correct when he concludes that,

> A negative view of Calvin's evangelism is a result of:
>
> • A failure to study Calvin's writings prior to drawing their conclusions,
>
> • A failure to understand Calvin's view of evangelism within his own historical context,
>
> • Preconceived doctrinal notions about Calvin and his theology. Some critics naively assert that Calvin's doctrine of election virtually negates evangelism.[21]

John Calvin: French Calvinists in South America

The Reformers' attempts to establish the Reformed faith in South America—French/Genevan Calvinists in South Brazil in 1556 and Dutch Calvinists in Northeast Brazil between 1630–1654—are another

---

19. Hughes, *The Register*, 25. Hughes's counting refers only to the number of pastors sent from Geneva between 1555–1562. It can be verified by a careful reading of *The Register*, 305–59. In Robert M. Kingdon's French publication under the direction of the Archives of the State of Geneva, see pages 59–100.

20. Hughes, *The Register*, 25.

21. Joel Beeke, "Calvin's Evangelism," in *Mid-America Journal of Theology* 15 (2004): 68.

attestation of the Reformers' readiness and promptness to reach out to the nations when God opens the door.[22]

Unfortunately, many mission historians have simply dismissed these historical facts as valid "missionary endeavor" or as irrelevant in terms of evidence of the Reformers' commitment to world evangelization. Regarding the sending of sixteen Calvinists from Geneva to Brazil in 1556, there is an entry in the *Register of the Company of Pastors of Geneva,* some eleven letters in Latin (two of them written by John Calvin, but all the others passed though Calvin's hands in Geneva. These letters have already been translated into Portuguese), Jean de Léry's "History of a Voyage to the Land of Brazil," and Jean Crespin's historical report (on the tragedy and martyrdom of the Calvinists in Rio de Janeiro). Unfortunately, Warneck, Latourette, and the other historians did not consult nor carefully exegete such valuable primary sources.[23]

---

22. Calvin comments on Acts 14:27, "Moreover, it is said that the door of faith was set open to the Gentiles, not only because the gospel was preached to them with the external voice, but because, being illuminated by the Spirit of God, they were called effectually unto the faith. The kingdom of heaven is indeed set open to us by the external preaching of the gospel; but no man entereth in save he to whom God reacheth out his hand; no man draweth near unless he be drawn inwardly by the Spirit" (John Calvin, *Commentary on the Acts of the Apostles* [Edinburgh: T. & T. Clark, 1861], 37:28). In reality, Calvin never disregarded the initiative of the preachers in taking advantage of the opportunities to preach the gospel everywhere. Commenting on Colossians 4:3, Calvin indicates that God's sovereignty in opening doors is a great comfort to and motivation for His servants: "For he [Paul] here intimates, by all elegant metaphor, that it is in no degree easier for us to speak confidently respecting the gospel, than to break through a door that is barred and bolted. For this is truly a divine work" (John Calvin, *Commentaries on the Epistles of Paul the Apostle to the Philippians, Colossians, and Thessalonians* [Edinburgh: T. Constable, 1851], 42:224). Commenting on 1 Corinthians 16:9, Calvin writes that Paul "makes use of a metaphor that is quite in common use, when he employs the term *door* as meaning *an opportunity.* For the Lord opened up a way for him for the furtherance of the gospel. He calls this a *great* door, because he could gain many. He calls it *effectual,* inasmuch as the Lord blessed his labor, and rendered his doctrine *effectual* by the power of His Spirit. We see, then, how this holy man sought everywhere Christ's glory, and did not select a place with a view to his own convenience or his own pleasure; but simply looked to this—*where* he might do most good, and serve his Lord with most abundant fruit" (John Calvin, *Commentary on the Epistles of Paul the Apostle to the Corinthians,* vol. 2 [Edinburgh: T. Constable, 1849], 41:73).

23. Warneck depended on a nineteenth century history of missions published by the historian William Brown, *The History of Christian Missions.* 3 vols. (London: Thomas Baker, 1864).

Let us just consider the Calvinist Huguenots in South Brazil (1556–1558) and let Jean de Léry (1534–1611)[24] speak in this regard.[25] He was a good friend of John Calvin and an eyewitness of the missionary journey of the sixteen Calvinists to South America in 1557.

The Purpose of the Missionary Voyage

A careful reading of Léry's work will suffice to convince the reader of the missiological details, importance, and insights that Warneck and other mission historians have missed or have been silent about.

The French Huguenots made their first effort to bring the Reformation to Brazil in 1556. Under the protection of the French invaders, sixteen of them embarked to Brazil with the direct and intentional support of John Calvin and Admiral Gaspar de Coligny. They went there to help establish a French colony in Rio de Janeiro, but Léry's report makes it clear that it was more than that. In his dedication to Lord François Comte de Coligny (the Admiral's son), Léry makes sure his intentions and purpose are well understood:

---

24. Jean de Léry was born in Burgundy in 1534. He was an artisan (probably a shoemaker) who studied under John Calvin in Geneva. He was a layperson at the time but theologically minded and biblically literate. After leaving Brazil in 1557, he spent two years in Geneva with John Calvin. He was later ordained as a minister of the gospel in La Charité and died in Berna in 1611. For a 23-page, well-written, and well-documented summary of Léry's life and publications, I strongly recommend Whatley's Introduction of Jean de Léry's *History of a Voyage to the Land of Brazil*, (Berkeley: University of California Press, 1990), xv–xxxviii. For more information regarding Léry's life, see Géralde Nakam, *Au lendemain de la Saint-Barthelemy: Guerre civile et famine, Histoire memorable du Siege de Sancere (1573) de Jean de Lery* (Paris: Anthropos, 1975). According to Whatley, Nakam's work is "the most thorough biography of Léry." See also Janet Whatley, "Food and the Limits of Civility—The Testimony of Jean de Léry," in *Sixteenth Century Journal* 15 (1984): 387–400.

25. Léry's credibility and reliability are unquestioned. His main critic was André Thevet, a Franciscan friar and a traveler like Léry. Thevet spent about ten weeks in Brazil in 1556. According to Whatley, in *History of a Voyage*, xxi, "Thevet was known to be careless and credulous, and Léry, with his meticulous habits of memory, verification, and logic, demolished Thevet's garbled accusations." Some contemporary scholars have questioned Léry's use of the phrase "noble savage" as being pejorative. This is a case of trying to impose a twenty-first century meaning on a sixteenth century document. The truth is that Léry uses the phrase in the sense of "living in a state of nature." Throughout his book, Léry criticizes his contemporary French atheists as barbarian when compared with the Tupinambá Indians. This critique has also been demystified by scholars such as Whatley.

It is my intention to perpetuate here the memory of a voyage to America undertaken for the purpose of establishing the pure service of God, both among the French who had retreated there, and among the savages living in that land; therefore I have judged it my duty to make it known to posterity how greatly he who was the cause and motive of it all is forever to be praised.[26]

[My] intention and my purpose shall be just to report what I have practiced, seen, heard, and observed, whether in the ocean, going to [Brazil] and returning to [France], or among the American savages among whom I lived for about a year.[27]

The Genevan team went to Brazil to preach the gospel and to support Villegagnon as a "Reformed" ruler. Léry did not believe the Roman Catholics brought the gospel to Brazil, but that the team from Geneva was "the first to propagate it [the gospel] in Brazil."[28] He presupposes the planting of a Reformed church in Brazil that would include the natives whom they purposed to win for Christ through preaching of the gospel to them.

The Two Leaders Behind This Endeavor: Calvin and Admiral Gaspar of Coligny (1519–1572)

Calvin and Gaspar of Coligny were the minds and hearts behind this expedition. Coligny was acquainted with Calvin's life, work, and vision. He knew and corresponded with Calvin, read his works, and was influenced by the passion of the Genevan Reformer.[29]

The French Huguenot leader, Admiral Gaspar of Coligny (1519–1572), was a personal friend of John Calvin and maintained an active correspondence with him.[30] He was the one who, together

---

26. Léry, *History of a Voyage*, xli.

27. Léry, *History of a Voyage*, 49. Precisely ten months.

28. Léry, *History of a Voyage*, 45.

29. Calvin's incomplete commentary on the Book of Ezekiel was dedicated to Coligny on January 18, 1565 by Theodore Beza on behalf of John Calvin, who died in 1564. Theodore Beza wrote in the dedicatory: "If anyone should chance to ask, Why I have dedicated it to you rather than to any one else? I plainly tell him, that Calvin is responsible for it, on the principle of everyone deciding as he pleases in things which concern himself, and that for most just and important reasons I have purposely done the very same that he also wished."

30. The correspondence between Calvin and François d'Andelot (Coligny's brother) and between Coligny and his wife is extensive. See Calvin's correspondence between 1558–1562. See also Wulfert De Greef, *The Writings of John Calvin: An*

with Calvin, encouraged and supported the formation of a Huguenot team to go down to Brazil in 1556—with the two Genevan pastors authorized by the church in Geneva—to preach the gospel in the "French Antarctic," as they called it.[31]

According to Léry, Gaspar "carried out his enterprise through those whom he sent to America, [and] besides making a part of that land subject to the French crown, also *gave ample proof of his zeal to have the Gospel declared* [preached] not only throughout this kingdom, *but throughout the entire world.*"[32] Reformers such as Coligny were not just interested in seeing those nations under the crown of France, but under the crown of the Lord Jesus Christ, while the true Gospel would spread throughout all the world according to God's timing and will. Gaspar was martyred during the Saint Bartholomew's Day massacre (along with more than 3,000–5,000 in Paris and 70,000–100,000 throughout France) on August 24, 1572.[33]

The "Macedonian" Call to Send Laborers to Brazil
As soon as Villegagnon, the French invader and "governor," arrived in Brazil in November 1555,[34] he built a fortress which he named

---

Introductory Guide, trans. Lyle D. Bierma (Louisville: Westminster John Knox Press, 2008), 48–59.

31. The French called Brazil the "Antarctica Gallia" (French Antarctic). See the letter in Latin, Richerius (Richer) and Charterius (Chartier) to John Calvin on April 1, 1557, *Joannis Calvini Opera* (CO), vol. 16, Epistolae 2613. My reference follows the arrangements presented at *Calvini Opera Database 1.0*, by the Instituut voor Reformatieonderzoek (www.instituutreformatieonderzoek.nl), Apeldoorn, the Netherlands, 2005, whose editor is Herman J. Selderhuis. This letter is part of the *Corpus Reformatorum*, vol. xliv.

32. Léry, *History of a Voyage*, xlii (see also page 31). Emphasis added.

33. On the life and work of Coligny, including his work among the Huguenots, see Gaspar de Coligny, *Memoirs of Gaspard de Coligny, Admiral of France*, edited and trans. David Dundas Scott (Edinburgh: William Oliphant and Sons, 1844). This book can be downloaded from: http://books.google.com/books?id=f9YDAAAAQAAJ &printsec=frontcover&dq=Gaspar+de+Coligny#PPA1,M1.

34. Villegagnon left France in May 1555 and arrived in Brazil in November of the same year. Léry reports that Henry II, the king of France at that time, "gave Villegagnon two fine ships fitted out and furnished with aruntilery, and ten thousand francs for the voyage" (p. 4) and that "before leaving France, Villegagnon promised several honorable persons who accompanied him that he would establish the pure service of God in the place where he would reside" (p. 4). After sailing from France in May 1555, the trip "underwent many tempests and tribulations; but finally, in spite of all difficulties, he reached his destination the following November" (p. 4).

Coligny. Villegagnon then sent a messenger to Geneva requesting ordained ministers to help him in Brazil.

> [Villegagnon] asked [Calvin] to send not only pastors but also other lay people who were well instructed in the Christian religion [Reformed faith] in order to bring the reformation to himself as well as to those who were already with him [in Brazil] *and at the same time to proclaim the way of salvation to the savages.*[35]

How Did Calvin and the Genevan Church See Such a Call?

Remember that John Calvin and the Genevan church were very busy with the Reformation in Europe, the doctrinal controversies with other Protestant groups, were under persecution, and John Calvin constantly suffered from health issues (stomach pain, migraines, colic/diarrhea, and kidney stones). Yet despite all of these things,

> When the Church of Geneva received his [Villegagnon] letters and heard his news, it first *rendered thanks to God for the extension of the realm of Christ into so distant a country*, even into so strange a land, and among a nation that was indeed completely ignorant of the true God.[36]

A Leader Chosen to Be in Charge of the Mission to Brazil

Who did the church put in charge of this mission to Brazil? The person solicited by Coligny and by the church and ministers of Geneva "to undertake the voyage" to Brazil, and "to lead those who wanted to join Villegagnon" was a *retiree*, "Philippe de Corguilleray, Sieur du Pont (who had retired near Geneva, and who had been his [Coligny's] neighbor in France near Châtillon-sur-Loing)."[37]

How did the Sieur du Pont receive the request?

> [A]lthough he was already old and feeble, the Sieur du Pont, out of the strong desire that he had to employ himself in *so good a work*, agreed to do what was asked of him, *postponing all his other business*, even *leaving his children and his family* to go so far away.[38]

---

35. Léry, *History of a Voyage,* 51. Emphasis added.
36. Léry, *History of a Voyage,* 4–5. Emphasis added.
37. Léry, *History of a Voyage,* 5.
38. Léry, *History of a Voyage,* 5. Emphasis added.

Recruiting Ministers to be Sent

It was easier and faster, it seems, to find such workers in sixteenth-century Geneva to send to South America than it is for contemporary mission agencies to recruit pastors today. Again, it is worth reading Léry's report regarding this crucial step in the sending of ministers (missionaries) to such a distant land.

> That being done [acceptance by Sieur du Pont to lead the group], it was next a question of finding ministers of the Word of God. Du Pont, and other friends of his, spoke of this to a number of students of theology in Geneva, and *several of them*, including Pierre Richier [a former Roman Catholic, more than fifty years old, with a doctorate in theology] and Guillaume Chartier [thirty years old], promised him that if *they were recognized according to the ordinance of the Church* to be fitted to that charge, they were ready to take it.[39]

The Examination of the Two Ministers to Be Sent

The church and the ministers of Geneva under Calvin's leadership examined the two ministers.

> After these two [Richier and Chartier] had been *presented to the ministers of Geneva*, who heard them *expound on certain passages of the Holy Scripture*, and *exhorted* them *concerning the rest of their duty*, they *willingly accepted*, with the leader Du Pont, *to cross the sea* to join Villegagnon, and *undertake to spread the Gospel in America.*[40]

The church in Geneva was not just counting workers. It was weighing them—their maturity, caliber, and so forth. The whole process was conducted with seriousness and consciousness of the privilege, responsibility, and obligation of crossing the ocean in order to preach the gospel of the Lord Jesus Christ. For Calvin, only

---

39. Léry, *History of a Voyage*, 5. Emphasis added.

40. The Company of the Pastors of Geneva made no major references to making a distinction between the ministers sent to preach the gospel in Brazil from those they sent to preach the gospel in Italy, France, Poland, Scotland, etc. Geography, or the location where a minister worked, did not make him more honorable or praiseworthy. Richier and Chartier were supposed to do in Brazil what every minister of the gospel was doing in Geneva and throughout Europe: preach the gospel, strengthen the local churches, reach out to the unconverted, plant new churches, and establish the local ecclesiastical leadership.

ordained male pastors who were tested as expositors of God's Word and exhorted by the "presbytery"[41] had the biblical and ecclesiastical authority to preach the gospel wherever the Lord would send them.[42]

Considering the Cost and Consequences for the Team
The recruiting did not end with the Sieur du Pont, Richier, and Chartier. They also chose lay persons to accompany these leaders and specified that such persons ought to be theologically minded and aware of the risks.

> Now there still remained to be found some *other persons instructed in the principal articles of the faith,*[43] and also, as Villegagnon had ordered, *artisans expert in their craft.* But so *as not to deceive anybody, Du Pont told of the long and tedious path to be taken:* that is to say, about a hundred and fifty leagues [about 375 miles] by land and more than two thousand leagues [more than 5,000 miles] by sea. He added that upon arrival in that land of America, *one would have to be content to eat,* instead of bread, *a certain flour made from a root;*[44] and as for wine, not a trace, for no grapevines grow there. In short, just as in a New World (as Villegagnon intones in his letter) *one would have to adopt ways of life and nourishment completely different from those of our Europe.*[45]

---

41. The Company of the Pastors in Geneva would correspond to a Presbytery.

42. Throughout the *Register of the Company of Pastors in Geneva,* we do not find any females being sent to pastor or plant churches anywhere. On November 20, 1541, the General Council promulgated the "Ecclesiastical Ordinances" for the church of Geneva. It listed the four orders in the church: pastors, teachers, elders, and deacons. These orders were to be exercised by elected males. The Register was started in 1546, but the text of the Ecclesiastical Ordinances was immediately annexed at the head of the Register. The ordinances established principles concerning the duty of pastors, the examination of pastors, the election of pastors, the day of the week for assembling, ministerial discipline, establishment of a college, the manner of the election of elders, the work of deacons, principles concerning the sacraments, marriage, hymns, burial, and so forth. The College would be "instructing children to prepare them for the ministry as well as for civil government" (John Calvin: *Selections from his Writings,* revised ed. [Missoula, Mt.: Scholars Press, 1975], 234).

43. Léry was an artisan who was well instructed in the principal articles of the Reformed faith. Reading through Léry's report, one immediately perceives how theologically and biblically astute he was.

44. Brazilians still eat this kind of "flower" — cassava flower — mixed with rice and beans. They were not ignorant regarding some cultural aspects of the natives among whom they hoped to minister.

45. Léry, *History of a Voyage,* 5. Emphasis added.

Were not such instructions in accordance with Jesus's teachings when He sent out the seventy? "And into whatsoever city ye enter, and they receive you, eat such things as are set before you" (Luke 10:8). No questions asked. Just eat it. If they eat it, it is edible. They really were aware of the challenges involved but it does not mean they thought it would be easy to minister in a different culture.

They did not encourage or appeal to everyone to go but selected and weighed those who were willing, motivated, examined, and prepared to die in the place they were going. Du Pont, however, did not stop with these requirements. According to Léry's description, they did not romanticize this missionary enterprise but made realistic demands:

> Therefore anyone preferring theory to practice in these things, and unwilling to undergo a change of air, or to endure the waves of the sea and the heat of the Torrid Zone, or to see the Antarctic Pole, would by no means choose to accept such a challenge, or to enlist and embark on such a voyage.[46]

Persecution and the First Reformed Martyrs in South America
Once they arrived in Brazil, the Genevan pastors organized the first Reformed Church on March 10, 1557, and held the first Reformed worship service in the Baía da Guanabara, in the State of Rio de Janeiro.[47] It was the first evangelical Calvinist gathering held in Roman Catholic Brazil.

---

46. Léry, *History of a Voyage*, 5–6.

47. John Calvin undoubtedly corresponded with those ministering and working in Brazil during that time. See, for instance, Calvin's letters 2530, 2609, 2612, 2613, 2826, 2838, 2841, and 3229, in *CO*, vol. 16 (pages 277–78, 433–34, 437–43), vol. 17 (pages 80–83, 107–109, 114–18), and vol. 18 (pages 149–51). Sixty years before the English pilgrim fathers came to North America, John Calvin was supporting Coligny and Villegagnon's plan to establish a South American refuge for the persecuted French Huguenots and to reach out to the native population of the country (see Léry, *History of a Voyage*, 33). The first words of Villegagnon recorded by Léry were these: "As for me I have long desired this, with all my heart, and I receive you very willingly under these conditions: because I want our Church to be renowned as the best reformed of all, from now on I intend that all vices be repressed, that sumptuousness of apparel be reformed, and, in short that everything that could prevent us from serving God be removed from our midst. Everything that I mean to do here is for you, and *for all those who come here with the same purpose as yours.* For I intend to make here a refuge for the poor faithful who are persecuted in France, in Spain, and elsewhere across the sea, so that, fearing neither king, nor emperor, nor

Villegagnon's enthusiasm for the Reformers and their theology did not last long. He slowly, but surely, turned toward his old confession and began to reject the teachings of the Genevan ministers at Coligny's fort.[48] Persecution started from within. In January of 1558, Villegagnon expelled the Huguenots sent from Geneva and France. Villegagnon strangled three of them[49] (these were the first Protestant Reformed martyrs in Brazil), after obliging them to confess their faith. Their written confession of faith became known as "Confissão Fluminense,"[50] written by Jean du Bourdel. Jacques le Balleur escaped and preached among the Tupinambás Tamoios Indians in São Vicente (São Paulo) until he was captured and imprisoned in the city of São Salvador (Salvador de Bahia). By 1567/1568 he was condemned and strangled under the incitement of the Roman Catholic Church. The Jesuit, Padre Anchieta, helped the Portuguese execute Balleur.[51]

---

any other potentates, they can serve God purely according to his will" (Léry, *History of a Voyage*, 33–34). Emphasis added.

48. There were spiritual pressures from within and political pressures from without. Léry offers a detailed description of the circumstances. After a celebration of the Lord's Supper, "Villegagnon declared openly that he had changed the opinion concerning Calvin that he had formerly claimed to have; and, without waiting for the answer that he had sent the minister Chartier to France [on June 4, 1557] to obtain [the opinions of the theologians and especially that of John Calvin], he said that Calvin was a wicked heretic who had strayed from the faith. From then on it was a hostile face that he turned to us" (Jean de Léry, *History of a Voyage*, 45).

The political pressure was from the Roman Catholic French rulers at the time. On June 7, 1557, the Catholic Queen Mary Tudor of England declared war against France. Henry II, son of Francis I, was the Roman Catholic king in France at that time.

49. Jean du Bordel, Pierre Bourdon, and Matthieu Verneuil. The other two martyrs were André La Fon and Jacques Le Balleur. Cf. Léry, *History of a Voyage*, 200. See also Léry, "La persécution des fidèles en terre d'Amérique," in Jean Crespin, *Historie des choses memorables advenues en la terre du Bresil* (Genève, 1564). Three of them (Bourdel, Bourdon, and Verneuil) were tortured and killed by Villegagnon after they wrote a Confession of Faith, known as Confissão Fluminense (or Confissão de Fé Guanabara—a confession that is now part of the Reformed Churches in Brazil).

50. A Portuguese translation of this Confession in seventeen articles was published by Domingos Ribeiro, *Origens do Evangelismo Brasileiro* (Rio de Janeiro: Graf. Appolo, 1937), 39–47.

51. Cf. the historical account by the French Historian, Olivier Reverdin, *Quatorze Calvinistes chez les Topinambous. Histoire d'une mission genevoise au Brésil (1556–1558)*, (Genève-Paris: Journal de Genève, 1957). See also Álvaro Reis, *O Martyr Le Balleur (1567)* (Rio de Janeiro: Comemoração do Quarto Centenário da Reforma, 1917), and Vicente Themudo Lessa, *Anchieta e o Supplício de Balleur* (São Paulo: Livraria Record Editora, 1934). Anchieta's version of the story is that Balleur was sent to Bahia

Léry and Crespin wrote concerning these less familiar episodes in their histories of the Reformed work in Latin America. Jean Crespin, the Flemish preacher, minister from Antwerp, and Geneva printer, published a historical report of that tragedy.[52] According to Léry, the true purpose of the journey of the Genevan team to Brazil was to establish "the pure service of God" [53] in the New World.

Léry almost prophetically anticipated the arguments of the future critics who would not consider this labor in Brazil as "missionary work" because it did not result in a permanent church planting movement. Léry wrote: "Some may say that given how short a time these things lasted, and that at present [1578?] there is no more news of the true religion in that land than there is name of Frenchman living there, this enterprise merits little esteem."[54]

We cannot simply agree with Warneck that the pastors and the group of laity sent to Brazil by Calvin to evangelize the heathen French in Brazil and the Brazilian Indians does not count as "missionary" activity because the Genevan brethren in Brazil recognized the difficulty of learning the native language and were martyred. Philip Hughes views this apparently "failed" attempt to evangelize South America this way: "Abortive though this excursion proved to be, it testifies strikingly to the far-reaching vision which Calvin and the Church of Geneva had of their missionary task."[55]

(a State in Northeast Brazil) as a prisoner. From Bahia, the Roman Catholic bishop D. Pedro Leitão sent him to Portugal, then to India, and he was never heard of again. José de Anchieta, *Informações e Fragmentos Históricos (1584–1596)* (Rio de Janeiro: Imprensa Nacional, 1886), 11. José de Anchieta died in 1597.

52. Jean Crespin, *Histoire des vrays tesmoins de la verité de l'Evangile, qui de leur sans l'ont signés depuis Jean Hus iusques au temps present , comprinse en VIII livres contenans actes mémorables du Seigneur en l'infirmité des siens ; non seulement contre les forces et efforts du monde, mais aussi à l'encontre de diverses sortes d'assauts et hérésies monstrueuses* (Liège: Centre national de recherches d'histoire religieuse, 1570). The first edition was published in Geneva in 1564. See especially pages 442–65 and 506–19, where Crespin gives a history of the persecution against the Calvinists in Brazil.

53. Léry, *History of a Voyage*, xli.

54. Léry, *History of a Voyage*, xli.

55. Philip Edgcumbe Hughes, "John Calvin: Director of Missions," in *Columbia Theological Seminary Bulletin* 59 (December 1966), 21. For the Register of the Company of Pastors of Geneva of August 25, 1556, concerning the sending of Pierre Richer and Guillaume Chartier, see Philip E. Hughes, editor and translator, *The Register of the Company of Pastors of Geneva in the Time of Calvin* (Grand Rapids: Eerdmans, 1966). This book was reprinted in 2004 by Wipf & Stock Publishers.

Conclusion

The work of the Reformers in Europe was an incomparable example of missionary work during the sixteenth century.[56] To dismiss such work as non-missionary is ludicrous and nonsense. To assume that Europe was "Christianized" and that the spiritual needs in Europe during the sixteenth century were not as urgent or as relevant as the heathen situation in Africa, Asia, and America, is disappointing in the light of biblical teaching and the historical reality of that time as well as our time. To suggest that the Reformers were only concerned with their immediate survival and not actively engaged in the expansion of the kingdom of God throughout the world, starting in their own "Jerusalem," is also a gross historical mistake.[57]

When Calvin's actions, writings, preaching, correspondence, minutes, and other historical documents are carefully considered, and when we ask, "Were the Reformers silent about 'missions' (the propagation, the preaching of the gospel and the planting of

---

56. The word "missionary" and the phrase "missionary work" are not found in the Reformers' writings during the sixteenth century. The issues of terminology and definition of terms have been discussed by other Reformed researchers. The Reformers frequently, not sporadically, used scriptural words and phrases. Calvin's letters to ministers in Italy, France, Switzerland, England, Poland, and other places, are filled with words such as "ministers," "work," "workers," "laborers," "fellow-workers," and "harvest," among others. For example, in a letter to Charles Utenhoven (a Dutch elder in one of the French Protestant churches in London, whose brother, John Utenhoven, had followed Laski to Poland) regarding the work in London, Calvin wrote: "I trust that the French Church in your parts, for which you had so anxiously solicited us, has been well provided for. To us, indeed, it was a severe trial to be deprived of Nicholas des Gallars, who has hitherto proved himself a faithful colleague and fellow-worker with us, but since you are of opinion that among you he will reap a more abundant harvest of his labors, we dared not let pass this opportunity" ("Letter from Geneva, May 1560," in *Calvin's Letters 1559–1564*). In a letter from F. Morellanus, probably a Genevan emissary in Paris, dated from "Nonis Iunes 1559," and addressed to Calvin, Morellanus mentions a minister called Aurelian Arnaldo sent to Orléans by the church in Paris: "*quia tam copiosa illic seges est ut eam sine auxilio nostro metere non possint* [because *the harvest is so plentiful* that they are not able to gather it without our help]" (Epistolae 3065, *Ioannis Calvini: Opera Quae Supersunt Omnia*, 17:540). Texts with such terminology abound throughout Calvin's correspondence.

57. Many scholars have expressed their views and published their research regarding this matter. Wilcox's doctoral dissertation (1993) is an especially impressive, well-documented work. See Peter Jonathan Wilcox, "Restoration, Reformation and the Progress of the Kingdom of Christ: Evangelisation in the Thought and Practice of John Calvin, 1555–1564" (Ph.D. diss., Oxford: University of Oxford, 1993).

churches) during the Reformation period as stated by many mission historians?" The answer is: absolutely not. I have concluded that—concerning their commitment to the propagation of the gospel to all nations—the Reformers of the sixteenth and seventeenth centuries were biblically,[58] theologically,[59] and practically[60] committed to—and directly involved in—the preaching of the gospel through the ministers of the Word to all men everywhere. The mission historians who have categorically denied this fact are mistaken. Their error can be attributed to 1) the limited availability of sources researched/explored at the time of their research (especially minutes, correspondence, archives, and so forth); 2) their preconceived and prejudiced assumptions due to some aspects of Reformed theology;[61] 3) a lack of assessment of the data; and 4) mere disregard of crucial historical data. Therefore, many of the beliefs sustained against the Reformers today regarding this matter are due to hearsay.[62]

---

58. They used the biblical language to refer to and describe what missiologists today would call "missions," "missionary," "missionary work," and "mission field."

59. The Reformation period theologians were God-centered, Christ-centered, Spirit-centered, Scripture-centered, Church-centered, and eschatologically focused. They expected God to revive His people in due time and in such a way that the earth would be "full of the knowledge of the LORD as the waters cover the sea" (Isa. 11:9) and "filled with the knowledge of the glory of the LORD, as the waters cover the sea" (Hab. 2:14). Such motivation, based on God's sovereignty, led them to an active (never passive) dependence. They were truly propagating the gospel and caring for the planting of churches in all the places they were able to assist. The doctrines of grace—especially the doctrine of predestination—were central in their optimism regarding the success of the work of God throughout the world until the end of time.

60. Historical evidence abounds regarding the explicit and visible concern and actions of the Reformers concerning this matter. They explored all proper means (written and verbal), all sources (human, political, economic, and material), and all circumstances (seasonal and non-seasonal) in order to advance the Kingdom of God in all the corners of the earth in accordance with their human limitations.

61. Especially the doctrine of predestination.

62. With the exception of Warneck and Latourette, other influential mission historians do not make such bold statements against the Reformers.

CHAPTER 4

Lessons for Today from Lesser Known Reformers: The Company of Pastors in Geneva

William VanDoodewaard

Our world celebrates celebrities, and we also have an innate tendency to admire the prominent and prolific. But our Lord has a different economy, a different weighing of importance, than we often do. While He does at times raise His servants to great public prominence, using them in mighty ways, many of His great and gracious works occur less visibly. In fact, some of His greatest works in the history of redemption, the history of the church, are those worked in humility and obscurity.

Scripture reminds us of this in a variety of ways: Our Lord Jesus Christ was born of an unknown, poor virgin. He taught His disciples to have the sight to see that the great ones of the kingdom of heaven were those like the poor widow (Luke 21) with her mites, the unnamed woman who poured perfumed ointment on Jesus's head (Matt. 26:7–8). Little children are of great esteem in the kingdom of heaven (Matt. 18; 19:13). Speaking of our calling by Christ, the apostle Paul reminds us that few of us were wise or powerful or noble from the vantage of this world: God chooses what is foolish to shame the wise, what is weak to shame the strong, so that it would be plain that all glory is due to Him (1 Cor. 1:26–31).

As we consider the Reformation, perhaps no individual is more familiar to us than John Calvin. The recent 500th anniversary of his birth was marked by conference after conference: publishers produced a steady stream of new volumes dedicated to his life and theology. Yet, as mightily as he was used by the Lord, Calvin was never a lone Reformer. Through his time in Geneva, many others surrounded him, serving equally, if not in more profound ways at times. The work of those who labored alongside Calvin was essential to the Reformation of the church in Geneva. Collectively, the

Reforming ministers of Geneva were known as the "Company of Pastors." Along with John Calvin, this Company included some who are still known to us, like Guillame Farel, Pierre Viret, Theodore Beza, but also a good many whom we have largely forgotten, like Nicholas des Gallars, Michael Cop, Pierre Blanchet, and Mathieu de Geneston.

The Company of Pastors of Geneva numbered some ten to twenty ministers serving three city churches and a dozen rural parishes during the Reformation era. They functioned as a subset of the Consistory of Geneva, which included lay elders who held a shepherding and governing role, as well as deacons, who were devoted to mercy ministry. While influential in their midst, Calvin was simply one of them—bearing an equal and shared authority in the ministerial life of the church. Together, they worked towards reformation in the specific area of the recovery of shepherding and pastoral care for the flocks entrusted to them.

The standard of shepherding and pastoral care in the late medieval church was bleak. Not only was Europe at a place of endemic loss of the knowledge of Christ, doctrines of grace, pulpit ministry, and corporate worship, but also a resulting loss of faithful shepherding, pastoring, and discipline. In some ways the long, slow decline—which had taken place over centuries—was hidden. Incredible church buildings, soaring architecture, rich artistic beauty, drama, pageantry, ritual, and crowds of people masked the loss of true spiritual life. People could not see the loss of a true care of souls. At the same time, the veneer of medieval "Christendom" was thin: bishops' and priests' sexual immorality was rampant. Even the worst cases merely led to a temporary suspension, followed by a quick reshuffling to a new church location. Added to this were bribery, greed, gluttony, misuse of church funds, and manipulation of church offices for power and cash. A late fourteenth century English writer, William Langland, records his encounter with the "gospel ministers" of his day:

> A heap of hermits with their hooked staves went to Walshingham on pilgrimage, with their wenches following after. These great long loafers, who loathed work, were clothed in clergy's capes to distinguish them from laymen, and behaved as hermits for the sake of an easy life. I found the friars there too—all the four orders [Franciscans, Domincans, Augustinians, and Carmelites]—preaching to the people for what they could get

for their bellies. In their greed for fine clothes, they glossed the gospel to suit themselves...their money and their merchandise of preaching march together.... Ever since charity has become a business matter, they have become confessor-in-chief to absolve wealthy lords...the worst mischief on earth is mounting up fast....

There also preached a pardoner [a church officer who sold indulgences]. He brought forth a document with bishops' seals on it, and said that he had power to absolve all the people from broken fasts and broken vows. The laymen believed him and liked his words. They came up kneeling to kiss his documents. He blinded their eyes with his letters of indulgence thrust into their faces, and with his parchment raked in their rings and broaches. Thus you give your gold to help gluttons, and lend it to louts who live in lechery.[1]

Calvin, a century or so later, described it as a church filled with "monstrous abuses" led by priests and bishops who outdid all men in their

notorious...excess, effeminacy, voluptuousness, in short, in all sorts of lusts; in no order are there masters more adept or skillful in every deceit, fraud, treason and treachery; nowhere is there a greater cunning or boldness to do harm. I say nothing of their arrogance, pride, greed and cruelty. I say nothing about the dissolute license of their entire life...there is scarcely a bishop, and not one in a hundred priests, who, if his conduct were to be judged by the ancient canons, would not be subject either to excommunication or at least to deposition from office.[2]

As it was, Calvin said, the Roman Catholic Church dealt more severely with the man who ate meat on a Friday, than "the one who has spent a whole year in a constant course of lewdness. Is it not deemed a more capital offence in a priest to marry than to be caught a hundred times in adultery?"[3] The late medieval church was in the

---

1. For the original source from which this selected adaptation is drawn see William Langland, *Piers Ploughman: Critical Text* (Piers Ploughman Electronic Archive), http://piers.chass.ncsu.edu/. Accessed September 12, 2017.

2. John Calvin, *The Institutes of the Christian Religion* (Philadelphia: Westminster Press, 1986), 4.5.7; 4.5.14.

3. Calvin, "Reforming the Church," in *Tracts and Letters* (Carlisle, Pa.: Banner of Truth, 2009), 1:177.

condition of the Old Testament church of Judges or Jeremiah. Clergy and people "loved the darkness rather than the light, because their deeds were evil" (John 3:19).

This was the cultural context in which the holy, triune God worked reformation, transforming first one, then another, then another of these priests, bringing them out of slavery to sin, to new life in Christ, calling them into gospel ministry, and commencing a mighty work of grace in bringing out of this an increasingly faithful church. This was also the personal background and daily context for the pastors in Geneva.

Early Beginnings of the Effort to Recover Pastoral Care

"Becoming Protestant" during the Reformation was not necessarily evidence of the Lord's grace. In fact, it appears that cities that became Protestant in the Reformation often did so for political or economic reasons. In Edinburgh, for example, one year after the great Reformation Parliament of 1560, only about 10 percent of the population was attending Sunday worship. Yet, a city or region's "becoming Protestant" did allow an open door for gospel proclamation and the recovery of the church and its ministry. Much of the late medieval culture remained pervasive, even where papal dominance ended. The calling before the Reformers was hard and slow, often overwhelming and painful.

Not too far from Geneva, in Strasbourg, Martin Bucer and other ministers worked hard to try to implement a real Reformation transformation of the church, not only in pulpit ministry, but also in pastoral practice. But city magistrates, who attended the church, proved a constant hindrance. They did not mind a reformation of the pulpit or even of worship, but worked hard to prevent a reformation of their comfortable pews. Unable to achieve governing support for a full reformation, Bucer wrote the book *Concerning the True Care of Souls*.[4]

The company of pastors in Geneva faced much the same difficulty as Bucer. John Calvin and Guilliame Farel, who had taken the initial lead to recover a right administration of the Lord's Supper, met stiff resistance—to the point of their exile from Geneva. While it was a

---

4. Martin Bucer, *Concerning the True Care of Souls* (Carlisle, Pa.: Banner of Truth, 2009), ix–xxvi.

disheartening time, the Lord worked through it all. Martin Bucer invited Calvin to Strasbourg, giving Calvin a room in his home, sharing meals with him, and encouraging him to join in the work of Reformation in the city. Not long after Calvin's arrival, Bucer helped Calvin secure a home—the backyard adjoined his own. It was in 1538—the time of Calvin's arrival in the city—that Bucer's book on pastoral care went to print. Calvin undoubtedly discussed the content with his friend and mentor. In God's surprising providence, Calvin found that he was the first who was able to put Bucer's vision for the recovery of shepherding and pastoral care into practice through his call to serve the French refugee congregation in Strasbourg. City magistrates did not bother much about what the French refugees did in the French church.

Back in Geneva, spiritual transformation through Pierre Viret's pulpit ministry, political shifts, and Roman Catholic attempts to lure the city back to Romanism, opened the way for Calvin to go back. Bucer and Viret were profoundly influential for the Genevan Reformation. Through their preaching, teaching, and opening ministry doors for Calvin, they advanced the gospel cause. Deepened and better equipped, Calvin returned to join the Company of Pastors. Scott Manetsch, author of *Calvin's Company of Pastors*, notes that "it was only after Calvin's return from his Strasbourg exile in 1541 that the constructive work" of the Reformation of the church in Geneva began in earnest.[5] Not only was Calvin back: his return also indicated positive movement towards the removal of hindrances to Reformation for the Company of Pastors. With renewed energy, they pursued a holistic recovery of faithful shepherding.

The Recovery of the Offices of the Church

By the time that Calvin returned to Geneva in 1541, the Company of Pastors were convinced, by past events, present needs, and Calvin's experience in Strasbourg, that the doctrine of the church needed to be clearly established. This had to be done in principle and practice in Geneva. It was especially essential for the city magistrates and council to recognize and enshrine this. Without that, the foundational problems which had led to Calvin and Farel's exile would still

---

5. Scott Manetsch, *Calvin's Company of Pastors: Pastoral Care and the Emerging Reformed Church, 1536–1609* (Oxford: Oxford University Press, 2013), 30.

be there. "The Geneva council—which previously, like the council of Strasbourg had hindered a full Reformation of the church (and still would in the area of discipline of members!), now agreed to the formation of an ecclesiastical order written jointly by the Genevan pastors and several members of the council," resulting in the *Ecclesiastical Ordinances* of 1541.[6] As the pastors pursued faithfulness, the Lord inclined a favorable ruling of the Geneva city council, bringing approval of this church order as the governing document for church order in the city.

The opening paragraph of the *Ordinances* made plain that the authority of Scripture impelled, directed, and defined this movement for ecclesiastical recovery:

> It has seemed advisable that the spiritual government of the kind which our Lord demonstrated and instituted by his Word should be set out in good order so that it may be established and observed among us. Accordingly we have made it a fixed rule to observe and maintain in our city and territory the ecclesiastical polity which follows, since we see that it is taken from the Gospel of Jesus Christ.[7]

The beginning point for change was in the recovery of "the four orders in the church": pastors, teachers, elders, and deacons. The definition of these offices was rooted in the recovery of the teaching of Scripture found in passages such as Ephesians 4, 1 Timothy 3, and Titus 1, already expressed in Calvin's *Institutes*. There was marvelous mystery in the Lord's creation of these offices. Some asked, "Why doesn't the Lord rule his church immediately and directly?" Calvin's answer was: "Because this is the way the LORD has willed...and because he does not dwell among us in visible presence...he uses the ministry of men...as a sort of delegated work, not by transferring to them his right and honor, but only that through their mouths he may do his own work—just as a workman uses a tool to do his

---

6. David Hall, "John Calvin's View of Church Government" in *Theological Guide to Calvin's Institutes: Essays and Analysis*, 391.

7. "Ecclesiastical Ordinances" in Philip Edgecumbe Hughes, trans. and ed., *The Register of the Company of Pastors in Geneva in the Time of Calvin* (Grand Rapids: Eerdmans, 1966), 35–49.

work."[8] God was pleased to save and sanctify sinful men for use as His instruments in the salvation and sanctification of others.

The office of deacon fell under the scriptural parameters of *diakonos*; these men had the calling from Christ to care for the poor and sick in the church. In the *Ordinances*, this calling of deacons to steward the resources of the church, especially in relation to the poor and sick, emphasized their calling to care for and remember them. Diaconal ministry was expected to be carried out in person, and included spiritual and physical care for the church's poor and sick. Interestingly, in the sixteenth century, the work of the deacons also included the work of running the local hospital in cooperation with the city. It gave accommodation, meals, and care not only to sick, but also to poor elderly people, widows, and orphans. In other words, the hospital functioned as a ministry of the church.

In exegeting and applying Scripture's teaching, the *Ordinances* placed the three church offices of pastors, teachers, and elders under the scriptural definition of *presbyteros/episkopos*. Men in these offices had a leading, governing role in the church.

In relation to the presbyters, the Genevan view was that the teacher was an officer given solely to the teaching/interpretation of the Word; the *Ordinances* described them "teaching theology, the scope of which includes both the Old and New Testaments."[9] Meanwhile, the pastor's duty included teaching and more—preaching, administration of the sacraments, and shepherding and discipline. Minister and elders, who also shared in a governing role with the ministers in the consistory, jointly shared shepherding and discipline work. Thus ministers, elders, and deacons each served the church in Christ-ordained offices in God-appointed realms of ministry—all of which contributed to aspects of the pastoral care of the flock.

The work of the Company of Pastors in delineating church offices meant that none of the officers of the church, including Calvin, was ever alone in pastoral ministry. They saw that Scripture clearly laid out a plurality of ministry leadership in the church, both in plurality

---

8. Hall, 394; Calvin, *Institutes*, 4.3.1.

9. "Ecclesiastical Ordinances," 41. Calvin, Beza and others in Geneva functioned as teacher-pastors, combining these two offices into one. The Church of Scotland, in its *Presbyterial Form of Government* (1645), would state that the office of teacher is a ministerial office, the teacher being one "who is also a minister of the Word, and has power of the administration of the Sacraments."

of offices and also of office-bearers. Every church should have at least one minister serving alongside elders and deacons. Scripture testified this was the Lord's ordinance for His church.

The Recovery of the Shepherding of Church Officers

Calvin and the other ministers and elders of Geneva realized that a recovery of faithful ministry, including pastoral care and shepherding, meant more than simply recapturing biblical categories of church office. People could make this kind of a reorganization and fill it with the same notorious men who were papal bishops and priests. The Reformers realized that a biblical reformation, rooted in recovery of scriptural patterns, required a recovery of scriptural qualifications for those in office. This required mutual spiritual encouragement and real accountability before the Lord for those in office. They pursued the goal of godly, faithful devotion to Christ and leadership with great intentionality. Manetsch describes Calvin and his fellow ministers as fully engaged in this transformation:

> Calvin not only championed, but institutionalized a form of church government that promoted pastoral equality and collegiality. The caricature of John Calvin as the "dictator of Geneva" deserves to be put to rest once and for all.... Calvin cultivated a spirit of collegiality.... Calvin [and his fellow ministers] had a deep aversion to forms of church government that were hierarchical and autocratic. They believed that Scripture taught that, though pastors' roles might vary from parish to parish, the pastoral office was a single office, and all pastors were equally servants of Christ and ministers of the Word of God.[10]

Authority isolated from meaningful accountability was dangerous to both leaders and the church as a whole. Both hierarchy and isolation were dangers to be avoided: the biblical paradigm that the Reformers rediscovered was the plurality and equality of office and authority. The reality of the late medieval church deeply impressed the necessity of this recovery for a healthy mutual encouragement and mutual accountability. The Company of Pastors, "recognized

---

10. Manetsch in Matthew Claridge, "Calvin's Company of Pastors: An Interview with Scott Manetsch," in *Credo Magazine* (July 22, 2015), http://www.credomag .com/2013/12/11/calvins-company-of-pastors-an-interivew-with-scott-manetsch/. Accessed July 28, 2017.

the need for ministers to [both encourage one another in the Lord, and hold one another] accountable...to preserve the health of the church."[11] Mutual encouragement, accountability, and the growth in qualification for office were pursued through two main avenues.

First, while it was expected that ministerial fellowship would occur informally, weekly and quarterly meetings were established. The Company of Pastors implemented "the weekly Congregation... where the city's pastors met to study Scripture together and evaluate one another's exposition of biblical texts."[12] Manetsch notes that among the reasons that they

> valued collegiality among pastors [was] because [they] recognized the dangers of individual interpretations of Scripture. Right doctrine depended on a community of pastors studying Scripture together. In a letter to a colleague in Bern in 1549, Calvin defended the work of the Congregation as "not only useful but necessary" for the health of the church. Calvin further stated that "The fewer discussions of doctrine we have together, the greater the danger of pernicious opinions...for solitude leads to great abuse."[13]

But sound doctrine was not enough: right living and faithfulness in office also depended on a community of pastors coming together. Every three months, the men met on "a day of censure" to "give special attention to see whether there is anything open to criticism among themselves, so that as right, it may be remedied."[14] Calvin and the other pastors knew that mutual shepherding could not occur without mutual fellowship. Just as shepherding church members could not take place without the pastors knowing the sheep personally, so the ministers and elders needed to know one another in order to shepherd each other's souls.

The second aspect of the recovery of the shepherding of office-bearers was through the establishment of clear, scriptural parameters on how to care for ministers and elders, maintaining a biblical integrity of church office where there was error in life and doctrine. The *Ordinances* presented clear direction as to how elders were to

---

11. Claridge, "Interview."
12. Claridge, "Interview."
13. Claridge, "Interview."
14. "Ecclesiastical Ordinances," 40.

address varied cases of ministerial offence. There was no doubt that the Company of Pastors realized the urgency of faithful engagement with sin and scandal, for God's glory and the church's good:

> In order to obviate all scandals of conduct it will be needful to have a form of discipline for ministers, as set out below, to which all are to submit themselves. This will help to ensure that the minister is treated with respect and the Word of God is not brought into dishonor and scorn by the evil fame of ministers. Moreover, as discipline will be imposed on him who merits it, so also there will be need to suppress slanders and false reports that may unjustly be uttered against those who are innocent.[15]

The Company of Pastors, and consistory as a whole, carefully noted that there were both "crimes which are altogether intolerable in a minister," requiring deposition from the ministry, and "faults which may be endured provided that a fraternal admonition is offered," leading to repentance and the pursuit of spiritual growth.[16] The list of vices which required deposition from office, preventing future ministerial service, included "heresy, schism, rebellion against ecclesiastical order, blasphemy which is open and deserving of civil punishment, simony and corruption by bribes...leaving one's church without lawful permission and genuine vocation, fornication, larceny, assault punishable by the laws, usury...[and] offences which in another would merit separation from the church."[17]

Faults that allowed a continuance in ministry as long as there was genuine repentance and effort towards growth, included, "Negligence in study and especially in reading the Holy Scriptures. Negligence in reproving vices. Negligence in performing all the duties of one's office. Buffoonery. Deceitfulness. Dissolute language. Rashness. Evil scheming. Avarice and niggardliness. Uncontrolled anger. Brawling and quarrelling. Dissoluteness unbecoming a minister, whether in clothing or conduct or in any other way."[18]

Where these were found in a minister or elder, the admonition was not a private, individual matter, but was to be brought to the attention of the full consistory of Geneva for investigation. If found

---

15. "Ecclesiastical Ordinances," 38.
16. "Ecclesiastical Ordinances," 38.
17. "Ecclesiastical Ordinances," 38–39.
18. "Ecclesiastical Ordinances," 39.

true, the consistory would give admonition and call to repentance. "Lesser vices" than these were to be corrected by simple admonition within the Company of Pastors, and only brought to the consistory by necessity, and in last resort, brought publicly before the church.[19] The Company of Pastors drew their categories of negative offences from descriptions of Christian character and the standards for office-bearing found in Ezekiel, Acts, Timothy, Titus, 1 Peter, and elsewhere. The Reformation's rediscovery of the Word brought the Company of Pastors to a renewed understanding of the relationship of law and gospel, including the essential place of church discipline and biblical qualifications for church office.

The minutes of the Company of Pastors and consistory of Geneva, along with the letters of the Genevan pastors, illustrate how mutual shepherding and accountability among office-bearers was put into practice. The *Register of the Company of Pastors* quickly makes it clear that the pursuit of faithfulness in shepherding the shepherds was not limited to Geneva. Gex, a town ten miles from Geneva, was politically and ecclesiastically connected with the city of Bern. Some ministers who had been disciplined and deposed in Geneva wanted to stay in the ministry, and so moved along to what they viewed as opportunity in a more welcoming region.[20] From the vantage of the Genevan ministers, however, the nominally Protestant Gex was in a state of spiritual declension—partly because of the men who had taken up ministry there. Rather than ignoring the situation, the Company of Pastors wrote a remarkable letter in June 1547, displaying courageous love for Christ and His church in advancing holistic reformation:

> We are constrained by a necessity greater that we would wish, in that there are many scandals in [Gex] which we see and cannot overlook, in consequence of which the Word of God is held in great contempt and, what is worse, the Gospel is quite commonly blasphemed. Concerning these scandals, we for our part are well aware who are the cause of them. But since our brethren from Berne are here to remedy them we pray them to

---

19. "Ecclesiastical Ordinances," 39.

20. Hughes states, "The Company is protesting against the welcome which had been given in the territory of Gex to certain pastors who had been deposed because of misconduct and compelled to leave the city, namely, Champereau, de la Mare, and some others." Hughes, *The Register of the Company of Pastors in Geneva*, 61.

investigate them carefully, hoping that they will find out more than we are able to tell them here....

We trust they will take steps against the negligence of those who instead of being watchful over the flock in the parish to which they are appointed, do nothing but gad about hither and thither after their pleasures, and instead of living peacefully in their homes will always be found in some tavern, spending more on themselves than they have for sustaining their whole family, and indulging in all sorts of misbehavior....

There are those who beat and ill-treat their wives, and even are not free from the strong suspicion of adultery, having at least a bad reputation for it, to the great prejudice of the Word of God.... It is a great disgrace and scandal for ministers to molest and devour each other by having recourse to lawsuits...matters that ought to be brought before the [church] are dragged into the courts...these men even boast...in the taverns of their lawsuits and litigations....

We therefore pray them to examine carefully all these and similar matters which ought to be remedied; and if they find it a tiresome and annoying duty they should consider that it is no small thing to purge the Church of God of all disorders and scandals, and, moreover, that, inasmuch as ministers ought to be an example to all the people, they should take great care that ruin does not come from their side. And we bring all this to their attention because of the love which we should bear towards them in our Lord, and indeed do bear towards them, in such a way that we likewise are ready to receive the admonitions which they shall offer us, if there should be anything to criticize in us.[21]

While the letter evidenced the Company of Pastors' commitment to wider Reformation, they also pursued integrity in dealing with scandals in ministry in Geneva. In April, 1549, Jean Ferron, a member of the Company of Pastors who had signed the letter to Gex, was accused of having engaged in sexual immorality, inappropriately

---

21. "Memorandum for the Brethren Who are Being Sent to the Chapter Which is to be Held at Gex by the Delegates (Commis) of the Seigneurs of Berne on Thursday 9 June" in Philip Edgecumbe Hughes, trans. and ed., *The Register of the Company of Pastors in Geneva in the Time of Calvin* (Grand Rapids: Eerdmans, 1966), 60–62.

touching a young woman who was a family servant.[22] The case was made complex through contradicting testimonies and the involvement of a civil court.

How did the Company of Pastors navigate scandal in their own midst? Initially, while trying to establish the facts of the case, the Company of Pastors removed Ferron from service in the city churches, temporarily moving him to a rural parish location. Though they were careful not to treat him as guilty before the case had been clearly ascertained, they were clearly already concerned by the harm this was doing to the ministry and its reputation, as well as the potential damage this had caused to a woman who was a member of the flock and his household. At this stage, Ferron displayed anger for what he saw as an unfair pursuit of discipline against him. After some months of trying to sort out the matter, when the truth became clear through Ferron's own penitent admission that what the servant girl stated was in fact true, "the brethren resolved not to investigate the case further, but to summon…the Consistory together…and proceed in accordance with ecclesiastical order."[23] Ferron was now immediately suspended from all ministry and the Lord's table. With the testimony inescapable, Ferron professed to have come to a sincere repentance and begged to be allowed to resign his office instead of being deposed from it.

On 5th September of 1549, Ferron was summoned before the Consistory "who confronted him with the girl. She proffered several other dishonorable charges against him."[24] Though he had not committed a fully consummate act of adultery, and despite his stated willingness to resign, Mr. Ferron's in-office violation of the qualifications of being a one-woman man through the sin of sexual harassment of his servant girl, who was also his parishioner, brought the consistory to depose him. He was permanently banned from ministerial office.

At this point, Mr. Ferron acceded to removal from the ministry in Geneva, but was clearly unwilling to step away from it altogether.

---

22. "Charges Against M. Jean Ferron" in Philip Edgecumbe Hughes, trans. and ed., *The Register of the Company of Pastors in Geneva in the Time of Calvin* (Grand Rapids: Eerdmans, 1966), 109–112.

23. "Charges Against M. Jean Ferron," 111.

24. "Charges Against M. Jean Ferron," 111.

The *Register* records: "He requested testimonial letters...but these were refused him.... Meanwhile it became clear that Mr. Ferron, and his wife, had been spreading false reports through the city regarding the case and the Consistory.... Having been reproved for these Mr. Ferron arose and when he had walked three or four steps he turned and asked that at the very least he might have some certificate [enabling him to serve elsewhere in ministry]; after discussing this request, the brethren declared they could not grant him this."[25]

The account of the *Register* reveals the care with which shepherding and discipline were pursued: Ferron's fellow Genevan ministers remained faithful to Scripture, even while they grieved the loss of a fellow minister. The same testimony is found across the varied cases of the *Register*. Discipline was pursued in love and care so that "the hearts of sinners would be touched" that "they might turn away from their sins and bear the fruit of repentance."[26] "All [discipline] was to be so moderated that no severity should have the effect of overwhelming the offender, but rather that the disciplines imposed should act as medicines to bring sinners back to our Lord," honor God, and preserve the integrity and health of the church.[27]

Like today, sexual immorality was one of the leading causes for ministerial removal in Geneva during the Reformation era. By the standards laid out in the *Ecclesiastical Ordinances*, fornication, and the greater offense of adultery in a pastor disqualified men from ministerial service. Between 1541 and 1600, the company of pastors permanently removed five of their number from office for sexual immorality. Scott Manetsch records that including other issues listed in the *Ordinances*, "16 percent of the ministers (22 out of 135) who served Geneva's churches from 1536 to 1609 were removed from

---

25. "Charges Against M. Jean Ferron," 112.

26. Manetsch, 215.

27. "Ecclesiastical Ordinances," 49. John Knox, who served for a time with the Company of Pastors in Geneva, was instrumental in drafting the First Book of Discipline, which stated that where by grace in Christ discipline bore the fruits of repentance, "the minister ought to exhort the church to receive that penitent brother in their favour, as they require God to receive themselves when they have offended; and in sign of their consent, the elders and chief men of the church shall take the penitent by the hand, and one or two in name of the whole shall kiss and embrace him with all reverence and gravity, as a member of Christ Jesus." Adapted from "The Buke of Discipline" in David Laing, ed., *Works of John Knox* vol. 2 (Carlisle, Pa.: Banner of Truth, 2014), 232.

office...while ministers suspended from the Lord's Supper were usually restored to the sacrament following repentance and reconciliation, this process of reintegration did not include restoration to their pastoral offices...none of the ministers deposed from office... were permitted to resume pastoral work."[28] As sober and disappointing as these depositions were, they also displayed marvelous beauty: the recovery of faithful, scriptural shepherding care for those ordained to ministry, and the recovery of the integrity in the ministerial office. Profound love for Christ and His church had been restored in Geneva, resulting in a willingness to believe that Christ and His church were far more important than any man's ministry. The Company of Pastors committedly held that pursuing Christ's call in this would bring Him glory and bless His church. Not only did the vast majority of Genevan ministers (84%) serve in steady ministerial fidelity, their mutual shepherding was profoundly influential in the recovery of a popular respect for clergy—Protestant clergy—in contrast to the corruption of clerical offices in Roman Catholicism.

While mutual shepherding included discipline, the collegiality of the ministry in Geneva included much besides. The kind of fellowship and encouragement found in laboring together as a team and shared study of Scripture was evident in the day to day encouragement of ministers for each other. Writing to Pierre Viret, who had recently moved away from Geneva, Calvin shared both the joys and trials of ongoing Genevan ministry, while encouraging Viret in his own.[29] The relationships of the ministers, at times impacted by disputes and disagreement, were often warm: they prayed together, labored together, enjoyed each other's hospitality, and when apart, wrote each other, staying connected in mutual, loving care.

The Recovery of the Shepherding of the Flock

With qualified, examined, accountable, and encouraged officebearers there was the recovery and retention of sound doctrine and faithful public worship. That including preaching of the Word and a right administration of the sacraments—baptism and the Lord's

---

28. Manetsch, 196.
29. Calvin, "Letter to Viret, 19 August 1542" in Jules Bonnet, ed., and David Constable, trans., *John Calvin: Tracts and Letters*, vol. 4 (Carlisle, Pa.: Banner of Truth, 2009), 340–44.

Supper. Calvin saw feeding the people's souls, instructing, rebuking, encouraging corporately from the pulpit, as essential to faithful ministry. The Genevan ministers were deeply committed to the centrality of sound doctrine and public worship. The expectation of both ministers and magistrates was that every resident of Geneva would attend at minimum the Sunday morning and afternoon worship services, along with the Wednesday morning prayer service—during which shops were also to be closed.[30] Above this, there were also three week day morning services, at which it was expected that one member of every household would attend.

The Company of Pastors realized that more than a recovery of pulpit ministry, sacraments, and worship was needed for a scriptural reformation. In the *Ordinances* they made it clear that the ministers were called to proclaim the Word of God, instructing, admonishing, exhorting and reproving, not only in public, but also in private.[31] Calvin stated that "the office of a true and faithful minister is not only to teach the people in public, which he is appointed to do as a pastor, but also, as much as he is able, to admonish, exhort, warn, and console each person individually."[32] Another member of the Company of Pastors, Theodore Beza, cast the same in shepherding terms:

> It is not only necessary that [a pastor] have a general knowledge of the flock, but he must also know and call each of his sheep by name, both in public and in their homes, both night and day. Pastors must run after lost sheep, bandaging up the one with the broken leg, strengthening the one that is sick…. In sum, the pastor must consider his sheep more dear to him than his own life, following the example of the Good Shepherd.[33]

This was practically demonstrated not only through regular household visits, where ministers and elders discussed spiritual life and growth with couples, children, and servants, but also the expectation that ministers would visit the sick and minister the Word to them.[34] With many fatal sicknesses, there was a certain urgency: no one

---

30. Manetsch, 149.

31. "Ecclesiastical Ordinances," 36.

32. Calvin, "De La Visitation des Malades," in *La forme des prieres et chantz ecclesiastiques*, M3v–M4, cited in Manetsch, 256.

33. Manetsch, 281.

34. Manetsch, 281.

in the city was allowed to be sick in bed for more than three days without notifying the ministers so that pastoral care could happen.[35] Thoughtfully, the *Ordinances* included the request that sick parishoners or their relatives call the minister to come "at a convenient hour, so as not to distract him from that office in which he and his colleagues serve the church in common"—that is, his ability to preach.[36]

Ministry to the sick was not only cast in terms of urgency, though, but also need and opportunity, "because many are negligent to console themselves in God with His Word when they find themselves in necessity through illness."[37] Calvin added to this encouragement, writing a treatise on the importance of the calling of ministers to lovingly and compassionately minister the riches of the Word to the souls of sick congregants.[38]

This was not an easy task: during plague outbreaks many of the ministers were reticent to do so, especially after Pierre Blanchet, a member of their Company, died doing this in 1543.[39] A number of the Company of Pastors were now found pleading that though the duty of visiting the sick belonged to their office, "God has still not given them the grace of strength and constancy needed to go to the said hospital."[40] The magistrates argued that Calvin was too valuable to lose, and the church should not let him visit plague victims and potentially die for the sake of one sick person. The records of the Company of Pastors indicate that, "finally a young minister named Mathieu de Geneston broke the impasse by stepping forward and volunteering to offer spiritual consolation to the sick at the plague hospital.... Geneston began making periodic visits to plague victims...like Blanchet, he soon contracted the diseases and died."[41] While Calvin stands large in our record of the Reformation, perhaps in the Lord's economy it is Pierre Blanchet and Mathieu de Geneston who are actually some of the greatest figures of the Genevan Reformation. They were willing to lay down their lives in

---

35. "Ecclesiastical Ordinances," 46.

36. "Ecclesiastical Ordinances," 46.

37. "Ecclesiastical Ordinances," 46.

38. Calvin, "The Visitation of the Sick" in Henry Beveridge, ed. and trans., *John Calvin: Tracts and Letters* vol. 2 (Carlisle, Pa.: Banner of Truth, 2009), 127–29.

39. Manetsch, 285.

40. Manetsch, 286.

41. Manetsch, 286.

love for Christ, and for the sheep who were suffering and struggling the most.

Alongside pastoral visitation of families and the sick, ministers were also expected to rotate through a weekly chapel service in the Geneva jail, bringing the Word to the prisoners. The men went in pairs, never alone. These visits not only showed care for the souls of lost or straying souls, but also resulted in a greater accountability for the prison wardens; with ministers at times bringing complaints to the magistrates over situations or conditions, they needed to give appropriate measures of care to the prisoners.[42]

While they labored in a full-time, dedicated capacity, the ministers were not alone in the call to engage in shepherding in Geneva. The office of elder in Geneva was defined by the calling "to watch over the life of each person, to admonish in a friendly manner those whom they see to be at fault and leading a disorderly life, and when necessary to report them...for the administration of fraternal discipline in association with the pastors and elders."[43] Watching over the life of each person, necessitated a recovery of individual and family shepherding at a level that required regular conversation and visits with the members of the parishes. Records of the manner of these visits is limited. A member of the Company of Pastors, Nicholas des Gallars, provides this reflection on Calvin's pastoral care:

> No words of mine can declare the fidelity and prudence with which he gave counsel, the kindness with which he received all who came to him, and the clearness and promptitude with which he replied to those who asked his opinion on the most important questions, and the ability with which he disentangled difficulties and problems which were laid before him. Nor can express the gentleness with which he could comfort the afflicted and raise the fallen and distressed.[44]

Ronald Wallace, reflecting on Calvin's letters as an example of pastoral care in Geneva, states that, "even the diplomatic gives way

---

42. Manetsch, 283–84.
43. "Ecclesiastical Ordinances," 47.
44. Nicholas des Gallars, as cited in Ronald Wallace, *Calvin, Geneva and the Reformation: A Study of Calvin as Social Reformer, Churchman, Pastor and Theologian* (Grand Rapids: Baker, 1988), 180–81. See also Ray Van Neste, "The Care of Souls: The Heart of the Reformation" in *Themelios* 39 (2014) 1:53–63.

entirely to an evangelistic motive and we find his first concern is with his correspondent as a person. Is he or she keeping close to God, listening to his word continually, and likely to continue to resist foe temptations of Satan in order to running well in the Christian race—in other words, how is it with your soul?"[45]

A significant question is how this kind of pastoral care by ministers and elders could be practically engaged in a way that would reach all of the members of the flock. With the swell of refugees beginning in the 1540s, there were as many as 25,000 people in the city—thousands in the Cathedral of St. Pierre and hundreds in the other churches of the city. One practical help was found in the expectation that ministers and elders would live in the parish area of their congregants alongside their people, enabling greater interaction in ordinary life. But the primary means remained ministers and elders visiting every household annually; by 1561 this had been upped to visiting every household every three months.[46] Through these interviews and times of spiritual counsel and encouragement, ministers could privately engage with families and individuals, enabling a very personal pastoral ministry.

The consistory met weekly—Thursdays at noon—to oversee the shepherding by reviewing visitations and, where necessary, admonish and discipline those guilty of flagrant sin. There were long-standing challenges in this area, particularly as the power of suspension and excommunication was hindered by the magistrates for some time. Calvin and the pastors believed it was rightly the prerogative of the church court, the consistory. But the civil magistrates of the city council battled long and hard to try to keep their authority over it. It was not until 1555 that the consistory received the freedom to practice excommunication—fourteen years after Calvin's 1541 return to ministry in Geneva.

Despite the fact that the consistory did not fully hold the keys of discipline for a time, the fruits of faithful worship, pulpit ministry, right administration of the sacraments, and dedicated pastoral care to every sheep had a marked effect in the city. While some remained unconverted and went to church as little as possible, the overall change was dramatic. At the time of his visit to Geneva in 1554, just

45. Wallace, *Calvin*, 170.
46. Manetsch, 190.

over a decade after the implementation of this new pastoral care, John Knox wrote: "In other places, I confess, Christ is truly preached, but in manners and religion so sincerely reformed, I have not yet seen in any other place."[47] In sovereign, gracious power, the Lord was pleased to save sinners and transform them into a company of pastors, elders, and deacons—many whose names we do not know—and use them as His instruments in gathering and restoring His flock in Geneva and beyond. Looking to Christ and His Word, they pursued the humanly impossible, receiving divine blessing on their hard and sometimes deeply painful work for His glory.

---

47. Manetsch, 182.

THE EXPERIENTIAL FLAME
OF THE REFORMATION

CHAPTER 5

Soli Deo Gloria: Why There Was a Reformation

Ian Hamilton

The Reformation was a seismic moment in the history of the world. But why was there a Reformation at all? The instinctive answer of many Christians would be, "To recover the biblical doctrine of salvation. Wasn't Martin Luther's great discovery that salvation is not achieved by a mixture of faith, love, and good works, but by self-abandoning faith alone in Jesus Christ alone?" It is absolutely true that the Reformation heralded the glorious gospel truth, "Upon a life I have not lived, upon a death I did not die; Another's life, another's death, I stake my whole eternity."[1] The Reformation did recover for the church and the world this glorious, Christ-exalting, man-humbling truth. But this is not the fundamental reason why there was a great reformation.

In 1543, John Calvin wrote a masterly tract entitled *On the Necessity of Reforming the Church.* In his dedication to the Holy Roman Emperor, Charles V, Calvin plainly told the Emperor why there needed to be a reformation: "If it be inquired, then, by what things chiefly the Christian religion has a standing existence amongst us, and maintains its truth, it will be found that the following two not only occupy the principal place, but comprehend under them all the other parts, and consequently the whole substance of Christianity, viz., a knowledge, *first*, of the mode in which God is duly worshipped; and, *secondly*, of the source from which salvation is to be obtained."[2]

Notice where Calvin begins. The first concern of the Reformers was a knowledge of the mode in which God was to be duly worshiped,

---

1. Horatius Bonar, *Communion Hymns* (Edinburgh: James Nisbet, 1881), 73.
2. John Calvin, *The Necessity of Reforming the Church* (Philadelphia: Presbyterian Board of Publication, 1843), 13–14.

and secondly, a knowledge of the source from which salvation is to be obtained. God first, men and women second. It is somewhat artificial to separate these two. You cannot worship God as He has commanded until you are born again and brought by the God of grace into a right relationship with Him. But Calvin (and he was speaking for all the magisterial Reformers) is making a fundamental and foundational point: The glory of God comes before the salvation of men and women. Paul expresses this magnificently in Romans 8:29: "For whom he did foreknow, he also did predestinate to be conformed to the image of his Son, that he might be the firstborn among many brethren." Our salvation is God's proximate purpose. His ultimate purpose is the glory of His Son.

We live today in a church culture where almost anything goes in a service of Christian worship. If the Bible does not forbid it, we are completely free to do it. This mindset is diametrically opposed to that of the Reformers. In this little tract, Calvin expresses his frustration that so many were reluctant to have a service of worship wholly shaped and informed by the Word of God: "I know how difficult it is to persuade the world that God disapproves of all modes of worship not expressly sanctioned by His Word. The opposite persuasion which cleaves to them, being seated, as it were, in their very bones and marrow, is, that whatever they do has in itself a sufficient sanction, provided it exhibits some kind of zeal for the honor of God."[3]

This is exactly where the evangelical church, by and large, is today. There truly is nothing new under the sun. However, the conviction Calvin expresses has nothing to do with personal and preferential "taste." In 1539, the Pope sent his emissary, Cardinal Sadoleto, to try to persuade Geneva to return to the Roman fold. Geneva had banished Calvin the year before but now turned to him to respond to Sadoleto's letter of entreaty. In his response Calvin wrote, "There is nothing more perilous to our salvation than a preposterous and perverse worship of God."[4]

For Calvin, as for all the other Reformers, how we worship God transcends matters of taste or culture. To worship God in any other way than He has prescribed in His Word imperils our salvation.

---

3. Calvin, *The Necessity of Reforming the Church*, 17.

4. John Calvin, *A Reformation Debate*, ed. J. C. Olin (New York: Harper and Row, 1966), 59.

Why? Because when we worship God as we please, we are in danger of worshipping a God of our own imagining.

I have often thought it strange that evangelical Christians should be so passionate in defending and contending for the biblical truth of justification by grace alone, through faith alone, in Christ alone, and yet be so indifferent to the biblical truth that God is to be worshiped according to His Word alone, and not according to our fertile imaginations. In Leviticus 10, Moses records for us an incident that is intended to impress on us the seriousness with which God takes His worship: "And Nadab and Abihu, the sons of Aaron, took either of them his censer, and put fire therein, and put incense thereon, and offered strange fire before the LORD, which he commanded them not. And there went out fire from the LORD, and devoured them, and they died before the LORD" (Lev. 10:1–2).

Lest you be tempted to think, "But this was under the old covenant," remember what Paul wrote to the church in Corinth concerning the way the Lord's Supper was being abused: "For he that eateth and drinketh unworthily, eateth and drinketh damnation to himself, not discerning the Lord's body. For this cause many are weak and sickly among you, and many sleep" (1 Cor. 11:29–30). God takes how we worship Him seriously.

The great sixteenth-century Reformation happened because men like Luther and Calvin were brought to see that God's Word alone was to shape and define both our worship of God and how we appropriate the salvation of God. We should, however, understand that *sola scriptura,* Scripture alone, is not *nuda scriptura,* naked Scripture. *Nuda scriptura* says, "We only need the Bible. We do not need the wisdom of the church throughout the ages. No creed but the Bible." On first reading, this seems admirable, but appearances can be, and often are, deceptive. Jehovah Witnesses practice *nuda Scriptura.* A JW will tell you they believe the whole Bible to be true. They are, so they claim, believers in the infallibility of Scripture—but then so did the Pharisees. Ask JWs if they believe John 1:1 and their answer will be "Certainly." But if you ask them, "Do you believe that Jesus is the eternal Son of God made flesh?" they will immediately say "No." *Sola scriptura* means that God's Word alone is "our only rule of faith and life" (Isa. 8:20). It does not mean that we do not listen to and learn from the accumulated wisdom of the church throughout the ages. This is why creeds (like the Nicene Creed), confessions (like the Westminster Confession), and catechisms (like the Heidelberg Catechism), are so important. They help keep the church "on track," and from falling victim to the latest theological fads and fashions.

With this in mind, consider our Lord Jesus Christ's words in John 4:24, "God is a Spirit: and they that worship him must worship him in spirit and in truth." Jesus is evangelizing a Samaritan woman. Step by step He leads her into the truth. At the crucial moment He probes her heart, "Go, call thy husband" (John 4:16). Jesus wants this woman to know that there will be no salvation while she remains in the darkness. She needs her life to be exposed to the searching scrutiny of God's holy law. Jesus truly is the model evangelist. As Jesus reaches the near climax of His evangelizing of the woman, He tells her that God is to be worshipped in Spirit and Truth. What did Jesus mean? John's Gospel is punctuated with "double meanings," and this is one of them. "Spirit and Truth" could mean true worship is inward worship, from the heart, according to God's revealed truth (that is, spiritually and biblically); or it could mean true worship is worship energized by the Holy Spirit and mediated by Jesus, who is Himself the Truth (John 14:6). We don't need to choose. It is not either/or, but both/and. In John 2:19–22, John has spoken of Jesus as the true temple. True worship can only take place in and through Him. Because God is a Spirit, that is invisible, we only know Him in and through His self-revelation in His incarnate Son (John 1:18). True worshippers worship "in Christ" and "through Christ" who is himself the Truth. Who *God* is—not who and what *we* are—is to shape and style our worship! This has special significance because Jesus had earlier told His disciples that when the Spirit came, "He shall glorify me: for he shall receive of mine, and shall shew it unto you." (John 16:14). Worship worthy of the name Christian is Christ-centered, Spirit-inspired, and God-glorifying.

True worship is "in spirit" *and* "in truth." It is striking to notice that the preposition "in" governs both nouns. That is, there are not two separable aspects of true worship—they are one. The Holy Spirit is the Spirit of truth and He is the Spirit of the Lord Jesus Christ who is the Truth (John 14:17; 15:26; 16:13).

None of this means that God's worship should be static or mono-cultural or independent of tradition. In a justly famous passage in

The Institutes, Calvin discusses the trans-cultural and trans-temporal nature of God's worship. He understands that times change, and cultures vary greatly. So, while absolutely committed as he was to "the regulative principle," that God's Word alone is to shape and inform our worship, Calvin nonetheless concludes the section with the words, "Let love be our guide and all will be safe."[5] He is not in any sense saying that we are to turn a blind eye to forms of worship that are contrary to Holy Scripture. He is saying that while the biblical elements of true worship will always be the same; the cultural form they take, and the times in which the worship is carried out, necessarily mean that the expression of those fundamental elements will differ. This is why the practice of Christian love is so important. There is always the prideful danger of absolutizing the way our church or denomination practices the regulative principle, expecting everyone else to do as we do. This is spiritual hubris. Far from being a recipe for encouraging worship mayhem, Calvin's wise words reflect both the breadth of Reformation worship and, more importantly, the catholicity of biblical religion: "Let love be our guide and all will be safe."

So, what will this mean for God-honoring worship? What does worship in Spirit and Truth look like?

First, *God's worship will be scriptural.* What I mean is that true worship (worship that is in Spirit and Truth) will be filled with the truth of God's written revelation. Such worship will be shaped and filled by what God has revealed of Himself and His ways in His inerrant Word. This means that the following elements will shape a God-honoring service of worship: There will be *singing,* there will be *praying,* there will be *preaching,* there will be *confession of sin,* there will be *confession of faith,* and there will be *the regular practice of the new covenant sacraments.* God's Word does not specify how often, or at what time services of worship should happen. These and other "incidental" matters are left to the wisdom and oversight of the churches' appointed leaders. However, the "essential elements" of worship *are* specified. God has not left us to wonder how we are to worship Him.

---

5. John Calvin, *Institutes of the Christian Religion,* ed. John T. McNeill, trans. Ford Lewis Battles (Philadelphia: Westminster Press, 1960), 4.10.30.

Second, *our sung worship will be patterned after the songs of the Old Testament and the songs of the New Testament.* As such, our sung worship will blend objective truth and heartfelt experience. A church's sung worship will not be shaped by tradition or culture, but neither will it ignore tradition or culture. The principle of *sola Scriptura* requires that we do not isolate ourselves from the life of the church throughout the ages. All of our singing (and our praying and preaching no less) should be saturated with the truth of God's Word; not just its language, but its doctrine, its proportion, and its passion. There are many reasons why God-honoring worship should be punctuated with the main old covenant song book, the Psalms. In the Psalms we encounter the variegated character of true religion; its highs and its lows; its delights and its perplexities; its soaring doxologies and its plummeting despairs. It is little wonder that John Calvin described the Psalms as "An Anatomy of all the Parts of the Soul."[6] Few things would do more good to the evangelical church today than a reinstatement of the Psalms into our services of worship.

Third, *God-honoring worship will be Trinitarian.* Christian worship is uniquely and supremely marked by its Trinitarian shape. In his *Institutes,* Calvin quotes some words from the Greek early church Father Gregory Nazianzen that, he says, "vastly delights me."[7] Gregory's words are from his Baptismal Oration 40.41: "No sooner do I conceive of the One than I am illumined by the Splendor of the Three; no sooner do I distinguish Them than I am carried back to the One. When I think of any One of the Three I think of Him as the Whole, and my eyes are filled, and the greater part of what I am thinking of escapes me. I cannot grasp the greatness of That One so as to attribute a greater greatness to the Rest. When I contemplate the Three together, I see but one torch, and cannot divide or measure out the Undivided Light."[8]

---

6. John Calvin, *The Author's Preface* to the *Commentary on the Book of Psalms,* vol. 1. In *The Commentaries of John Calvin on the Old Testament,* 30 vols. (Edinburgh: Calvin Translation Society, 1843–1848), xxxvii.

7. John Calvin, *Institutes of the Christian Religion,* ed. John T. McNeill, trans. Ford Lewis Battles (Philadelphia: Westminster Press, 1960), 1.13.17.

8. Gregory Nazianzen, *On Holy Baptism,* Oration 40.41. In *A Select Library of Nicene and Post-Nicene Fathers of the Christian Church,* 2nd Series. 14 vols. (1898–1909; repr., Grand Rapids: Eerdmans, 1994), 7:375.

Christian prayers, songs, confessions, and preaching should have a Trinitarian shape to them. Even when we are singing to our Lord Jesus Christ, we sing to Him as the sent One of the Father and the One who has the Spirit without measure. This is not to say that in worship there will not at times be a particular focus on the Father or the Son or the Spirit. But we must never worship as if any One of the Three were isolated, separated, or distant from the others. Gregory's words should be pondered every time a pastor prepares to lead a congregation in the worship of God.

Fourth, *God's worship will be supremely, if not only, communal.* What I mean is that the high point of worship will not be our quiet times, but the corporate worship of the saints. It is only together with "all saints" that we discover how high and wide and deep and broad is God's love (Eph. 3:18). The exhortation of the writer to the Hebrews not to neglect to meet together, "as the manner of some is" (Heb. 10:25), was written to Christians who were in danger of turning away from Jesus Christ. Nothing will give more stability to our Christian lives than an undeviating commitment to the corporate gathering of the church for worship. Personal quiet time and family worship are very important, but public worship takes precedence over everything else.

Fifth, *God's worship will not be tied to a holy place, but it will focus on a holy day, the Lord's Day.* It is true that all of life is worship (Rom. 12:1). But when Christians gather on the Lord's Day, yes, we gather for fellowship and teaching, but first we gather together to worship our great and glorious triune God. The sanctifying of the Lord's Day is not for the holy few; it is a privilege God has given to all His people. God has embedded a rhythm in the heart of the cosmos, the rhythm of rest and work. We see the rhythm in the account of creation in Genesis 1–2. We see it engraved in the fourth commandment. We see it in the life of our Savior.

Sixth, *God's worship will be from the heart.* Nothing appalls God more than rote religion (Isa. 1:10–20; Mark 7:6–7). God looks on the heart and is not deceived by our forms no matter how orthodox and Reformed. "My son, give me thine heart" (Prov. 23:26). So, God-honoring worship will come from redeemed and reconciled hearts, from hearts invaded by God's grace and love in His Son. This will mean, and should mean, that God-honoring worship will overflow with joy and delight.

Seventh, *God's worship will be joyfully reverent* (Ps. 95:1–3; Heb. 12:28–29). Christian worship will always be marked by intimacy and awesomeness. Jesus taught His disciples to pray, "Our Father, who art in heaven" (Matt. 6:9). He is not merely our Father, but our exalted, ineffably glorious Father, before whom the unfallen angels veil their faces. Let us be careful not to disdain the worship Christians give who are not in our church tradition. We can easily fall into the sin of denominational pride and spiritual censoriousness. Of course, exuberance in worship can be "of the flesh," but no less can grim solemnity also be "of the flesh." "Our God is a consuming fire" (Heb. 12:29) and therefore should be worshiped with "reverence and godly fear" (Heb. 12:28). But He is also the God who causes His people to "rejoice with joy unspeakable and full of glory" (1 Peter 1:8). Reverence and awe does not mean joylessness. And it is no excuse to say that the joy is deep in our hearts, hidden from sight. What is truly deep within will show itself in our faces and general demeanor. This will vary from person to person because the Lord has made us all uniquely different. But manifesting joyful reverence should be a distinguishing mark of all true Christian worship.

So, what is the distinguishing mark of a life which confesses *soli Deo gloria*? A life of wonder, love, and praise that is informed and shaped by the Word of God. Reformed Christians, above all, should be known for their joyful, thankful, praise-filled lives. Commitment to orthodoxy is a commitment to rejoice in God, as well as a commitment to defend the faith once for all delivered to the saints.

It was because God was not being worshiped according to His Word that there was a Reformation. God's honor was paramount. If we are passionate about Scripture alone shaping our doctrine and understanding of justification, ought we not with equal passion to be concerned that Scripture alone should shape and inform how our great and gracious God should be worshiped? May it be so. *Soli Deo gloria*.

CHAPTER 6

Solus Christus: The Preaching that Defined the Reformation

Ian Hamilton

The Reformation of the sixteenth century was many things: It was the recovery of the biblical truth about worship and salvation, the true meaning of the sacraments, the true identity of the church, and the recovery of godly pastoral care. But no less, the Reformation signaled the recovery of the centrality of preaching in the life of the church. The passion of the magisterial Reformers was to re-center the life of the church, its worship, its nurture, and its mission, in the Word of God. They sought to de-sacramentalize the church and recover for the church the life-giving, God-glorifying ministry of God's inspired Word. The Reformers grasped that it is the Holy Scriptures—not the church's sacraments–that make us wise for salvation through faith in Jesus Christ (2 Tim. 3:15). They understood that God had ordained the foolishness of what is preached to save those who believe (1 Cor. 1:21). They had come to know personally that while the gospel is a stumbling block to Gentiles and sheer foolishness to Jews, it is the power of God for salvation to everyone who believes (1 Cor. 1:21–24). Priestly drama, spectator worship, and adorned church buildings were out; gospel proclamation, congregational participation, and unadorned worship were in.

At the heart of this recovery of preaching the Word of God was the preaching of Jesus Christ and Him crucified (1 Cor. 1:23). Above all else, the Reformers sought in their preaching to show from God's Word that Christ alone, *solus Christus*, accomplished salvation. Not Christ plus the church. Not Christ plus the intercession of the saints. Not Christ plus the seven Roman sacraments. Not Christ plus the Roman-supposed treasury of merits. Not Christ plus Mary. Not Christ plus my good works of faith and love. Christ alone: *solus Christus*.

John Calvin, the great French Reformer, whose life and ministry God used to make Geneva, according to John Knox, "the most perfect school of Christ on earth since the days of the apostles,"[1] made the point memorably in his response to Jacopo Sadoleto's (the Pope's emissary) letter to the citizens of Geneva in 1539: "Wherever the knowledge of it (that God justifies sinners by faith alone, in Jesus Christ alone) is taken away, the glory of Christ is extinguished, religion abolished, the Church destroyed, and the hope of salvation utterly overthrown."[2]

When you add anything or anyone to Christ, you teach a deficient and defective Christ, a Christ who is less than He claimed to be, a Christ whose representative life and sin-atoning death and resurrection were not sufficient to reconcile judgment-deserving sinners to God.

This was unthinkable and abhorrent to the Reformers. Like Paul, their first and foremost concern was not the salvation of sinners but the glory of the Savior of sinners. Notice Calvin's words, "the glory of Christ is extinguished." This is why Paul writes as he does in Galatians 1:8–9, "But though we, or an angel from heaven, preach any other gospel unto you than that which we have preached unto you, let him be accursed. As we said before, so say I now again, if any man preach any other gospel unto you than that ye have received, let him be accursed."

James Denney strikingly comments on Paul's piercing words: "If God has really done something in Christ on which the salvation of the world depends, and if He has made it known, then it is a Christian duty to be intolerant of everything which ignores, denies, or explains it away. The man who perverts it is the worst enemy of God and me."[3]

Paul is not being dyspeptic. He is not being narrow-minded. He is not being gratuitously rude. He is simply appalled that the teaching of the Judaizers both imperiled the salvation of sinners and robbed

1. John Knox, *The Works of John Knox*, ed. David Laing (Edinburgh: James Thin, 1855), 4:240 (spelling modernized).
2. John Calvin, *A Reformation Debate*, ed. J. C. Olin (New York: Harper and Row, 1966), 66.
3. James Denney, *The Death of Christ*, 5th edition (London: Hodder and Stoughton, 1905), 110–11.

Christ of His saving glory. It is a truism that the early church feared heresy more than martyrdom.

Solus Christus then is not simply a Reformation era, Protestant slogan. On the contrary, it is the pulse-beat of biblical religion. Peter spoke for the early church when he proclaimed, "Neither is there salvation in any other: for there is none other name under heaven given among men, whereby we must be saved" (Acts 4:12).

Even more, *solus Christus* was the compelling pulse-beat of Jesus's own ministry. When our Lord Jesus Christ came into the world, He was self-consciously aware of His unique and universal mission. Think of the repeated "I am" declarations in John's Gospel: "I am the bread of life." "I am the light of the world." "I am the door." "I am the good shepherd." "I am the resurrection, and the life." "I am the way, the truth, and the life." "I am the true vine." Consider especially Matthew 11:28–30: "Come unto me, all ye that labor and are heavy laden, and I will give you rest." The egocentricity is breathtaking: "Me, Me, Me, it's all about Me." *Solus Christus.*

Why was Jesus so self-consciously exclusive? How was it possible for Him to say, "I am the way, the truth, and the life. No one comes to the Father except through me" (John 14:6)?

For two reasons:

First, *because He knew who He was*. "For the bread of God is he which cometh down from heaven, and giveth life unto the world...I am the bread of life: he that cometh to me shall never hunger; and he that believeth on me shall never thirst" (John 6:33–35). The divine identity of Jesus was a truth that the apostle John placarded at the beginning of his Gospel: "In the beginning was the Word, and the Word was with God, and the Word was God" (John 1:1). The writer to the Hebrews begins his letter with the identical conviction that Jesus is God incarnate, God's last and consummating Word to humanity: "God...in these last days [hath] spoken unto us by his Son, whom he hath appointed heir of all things, by whom also he made the worlds; Who [is] the brightness of his glory, and the express image of his person" (Heb. 1:1–3). Jesus is not just another in a long line of prophets. He is a prophet, but He is "God the Word." Jesus, not Muhammad, is *the* prophet, God's ultimate and final revelation to His creation. He is unique. He is unrivaled. He is not the first of many. He is radically removed from the many. The concluding words of John's Prologue beautifully, if unfathomably, expresses what the whole Bible teaches: "No man hath seen God at any time, the only begotten Son, which is in the bosom of the Father, he hath declared [exegeted] him" (John 1:18). This is the truth doubting Thomas finally grasped after Jesus's resurrection (John 20:28).

Jesus is both the glory and the mystery of Christianity. John Owen understood this great truth when he wrote, "this glory is the glory of our religion, the glory of the Church, the sole Rock whereon it is built, the only spring of present grace and future glory."[4]

In His own eternal Son, God has come into His broken, rebellious, sin-cursed world to seek and to save the lost. It took Jesus's disciples some time before the proverbial penny dropped. When Jesus calmed the storm on the lake, "they feared exceedingly, and said one to another, What manner of man is this, that even the wind and the sea obey him?" (Mark 4:41). But the resurrection blew away all their doubts and fears. It was not only Thomas who bowed down and said, "My LORD and my God" (John 20:28).

In His own Son, God has joined our frail flesh to His glorious deity. Is it any wonder our forebears were willing to give their very lives to proclaim and defend this astounding truth? We equally need to understand that those who best grasp this gospel wonder are those who bow down and worship.

Second, *because He knew what He had come into the world to do.* At a significant moment in His earthly ministry, Jesus said to His disciples, "the Son of man came not to be ministered unto, but to minister, and to give His life a ransom for many" (Mark 10:45). Jesus understood from the Scriptures that as the Lamb of God He had come to lay down his life for his sheep (John 10:15). We could multiply the New Testament references.

The day I was converted to Christ, I heard for the first time the words of John 3:16. What I heard that wet Sunday afternoon in Glasgow persuaded me of the truth of words I would later read—*crux probat omnia*—the cross is the test of everything. Martin Luther had himself come to understand that the saving gospel of God centered in, and was wholly shaped and styled by, what God had done in His Son on Calvary's cross. No one other than Jesus has

---

4. John Owen, *The Works of John Owen*, 16 vols., ed. William H. Goold (London & Edinburgh: Johnstone & Hunter, 1850), 1:310.

become a sin-bearing sacrifice. *Solus Christus*. No one other than Jesus has paid in full the awful price of sin. *Solus Christus*. No one else has provided for all who believe in him a judgment-proof righteousness. *Solus Christus*. No one other than Jesus has conquered death and the powers of darkness. *Solus Christus*. No one other than Jesus is "the way, the truth, and the life" (John 14:6). *Solus Christus*.

Some years ago, while ministering in Cambridge, I met with two Mormons. They had stopped me in the street and I invited them to have coffee with me. As they were about to launch into their pre-programmed presentation, I asked if I could pose a question to them. They agreed. I asked, "In the Bible I read that Jesus Christ, God's own Son, lived and died and rose from the dead for me. I read that through faith alone in Him, God freely and fully forgives all my sins, adopts me into His family, sends His Holy Spirit into my life, gives me the sure and certain hope of eternal glory, and promises never to leave me nor forsake me. Here now is my question, 'What more can Joseph Smith do for me?'" I remember that they looked at one another somewhat embarrassed.

Is it any wonder that when the Word of God was recovered from the avalanche of man-made traditions and ceremonies in the early years of the sixteenth century, the men and women of the Reformation preached and lived *solus Christus*? Not Christ plus anything or anyone. Christ alone. The church exists to proclaim Him and worship Him, not to add anything to Him. God's so great and gracious salvation is exclusively and alone found in Christ. Not Christ plus my good works. Not Christ plus my evangelical obedience. Not Christ plus the church's absolution. Not Christ plus Mary or the saints. *Solus Christus*!

But having said this, it would be a huge mistake to think, "Well, if it is all *solus Christus*, then I don't need anything or anyone in order to live a truly Christian and godly life." This would be a huge error and one that will dramatically stunt and even destroy your Christian profession. Faith alone in Jesus Christ alone brings you into Christ *and* at the same time into the fellowship of His church, His body (Eph. 4:15–16). It is only in union and communion with "all the saints" that we are able to comprehend "the breadth, and length, and depth, and height; and to know the love of Christ" (Eph. 3:18–19).

Perhaps the main reason why many professing Christians make little progress in their faith and commitment, is their failure to join themselves to Christ's body, His church. They end up living as practical disembodied limbs, and it shows! Christ "loved the church" (Eph. 5:25). Do you love your Savior's church, particularly? Does your life show that you do? It was inconceivable to the early church and to the Reformers that you could be a Christian, confess *solus Christus* and not be a baptized member of a church, living under its ministry and pastoral care. We honor our Savior by living our lives in communion with God's people in a particular congregation, worshipping our great God, hearing His Word, sharing in His ordained sacraments, growing together with them in the grace and knowledge of Christ. *Solus Christus* is not simply a Reformation slogan, it is the corporate confession of the body of Christ, His church.

THE PRACTICAL LESSONS OF
THE REFORMATION FOR TODAY

CHAPTER 7

What Augustine Teaches Us Today

Carl Trueman

My task for this evening is to talk about St. Augustine. It might seem a slightly odd topic to be giving at a conference devoted to the Reformation, so I'm going to give a little bit of background as to why I have chosen this figure from the fourth and fifth centuries—over a thousand years before the Reformation—to speak about this evening.

I was in Manhattan on Monday this week for lunch with a Roman Catholic friend—a very well-read theological friend—and he asked me, if I had to recommend one book for him to be able to understand historic Protestant theology, what would it be? It's one of those deceptively simple questions to which there is no really simple answer. And after I paused and thought for a moment or two, I actually said, "I don't think I can recommend a single book; what I'd do is I'd recommend to you a series of what I would consider classic Christian books through the ages which culminate in the great writings of the Protestant Reformers of the sixteenth century." I told him I would start with the writings of St. Augustine, particularly the book, *The Confessions of St. Augustine*.

I will come back to the *Confessions* and talk about it in more detail in a few moments, but first, I want to quote the great Princeton theologian, B. B. Warfield, to give some background as to why I gave my friend the answer I did. Warfield, writing on Augustine, said this: "The Reformation, inwardly considered, was just the ultimate triumph of Augustine's doctrine of grace over Augustine's doctrine of the church."

Like all great memorable sayings, it's probably about sixty-five percent true. But it sounds great and it captures something important. What it does is it points us to the fact that the Reformation was, to a large extent, the debate over the meaning of the writings of St. Augustine.

I remember when I was doing my PhD; the post-graduate students in Scotland from Aberdeen, Glasgow, Edinburgh, and St. Andrews would gather together once a year for a reading party. I remember hearing one of the academics who was present—a professor from Glasgow University—making the off-hand comment at a seminar that as far as he was concerned, "the Reformation was simply a footnote to the writings of St. Augustine." And it grips my imagination! I think that is probably about forty-five percent true but it captured something of the importance of Augustine for the great theologians of the sixteenth century.

Calvin famously commented on Augustine, that *"Augustinus... totus noster est,"*[1] which translates as, "Augustine is completely ours." I would say that is probably fifty to fifty-five percent true. But again, it points us to the importance of Augustine as a source for the Reformation. The Reformation was a battle over the correct interpretation and application of the writings of St. Augustine.

Why was that? Well, Augustine had written works touching on pretty much every important aspect of Christian theology. I think his great work on the Trinity remains the greatest work in the history of the church on the doctrine of the Trinity. I did a reading class at Westminster last year and the first half of the semester we just read through Augustine's work on the Trinity, chapter by chapter. I think it has never been surpassed as a treatment of the topic.

He wrote major works on the church. He wrote foundational works on grace. And he wrote what I think is the single greatest religious autobiography in the history of the church, and that is *The Confessions.* I suspect there are those in this room that may dispute that and say it is *Grace Abounding* by John Bunyan. Augustine's *Confessions* remains, in my mind, however, the greatest Christian autobiography in the history of the church.

Why is that? Two reasons: First, I think that the great writings of Augustine on grace that he produces at the beginning of the fifth century—that would become absolutely foundational to the church's later understanding of the apostle Paul, absolutely foundational to Luther, Calvin, and the Reformers—were part of a controversy,

---

1. John Calvin, *Institutes* (Philadelphia: Westminster Press, 1960), 2.4.33.

the anti-Pelagian controversy, which was triggered by a statement that occurs several times in the *Confessions*. The statement was this: "Command what you will, and give what you command." Augustine's *Confessions* is an autobiography but is really written as an extended prayer to God. And at various points he just explodes into doxology. Several times he calls out, "Grant what you command, and command what you wish,"[2] which captures, I think, intuitively, in a nutshell, what Christian grace is. Pelagius heard the book being read and was deeply offended because he thought that it gave place to laxity in Christian observance.

The second point, I think, that makes the work so great—and what Pelagius did not realize—was that Augustine, in the *Confessions*, understood and analyzed the tragedy of the fallen human condition in a way unparalleled in Christian history before that time (after the apostle Paul) and probably unparalleled until the time of the Reformation.

Augustine's *Confessions* was written in the 390s. In it, he reflects on events touching on his conversion in the city of Milan some ten years earlier. I think it's a peculiarly useful book for Christians. It's an intuitive reflection upon the nature of grace. More than that, it is a compelling study of the psychology of fallen man, in a fallen world, as he stands before God. That is one of the things that makes it a peculiarly useful book for the present age.

We live in a peculiarly, strangely *psychological* age. When you consider how we think of lives today, so often we think in terms of psychological categories, don't we? If I had ever said to my grandfather, "Do you get satisfaction out of your job?" Or, "Do you find your job satisfying?" I wonder if he would have even understood the question. But had he done so, he probably would have answered it in this way: "Yes, because my job allows me to put food on the table and shoes on my children's feet." If you ask me—or if I ask many of you if you get job satisfaction today—I suspect you will give me a psychological answer. You'll tell me, "Well yes, I enjoy teaching. It gives me great personal satisfaction to teach." Or, "I find my job intrinsically interesting and satisfying." These are signs of an age where we think in psychological categories. And in such an age, I

---

2. Augustine, *Confessions, A New Translation by Sarah Ruden* (New York: The Modern Library, 2018), 320.

think a book like Augustine's, which addresses the psychology of humanity in the presence of God, is peculiarly important.

Think about the categories of our age. I am starting to preach at my own church through the Book of Jude—I preached on Jude 1 and 2 last week—and it struck me as I thought about the world to which Jude is writing and the world to which we write, that we live in a world where we have more creature comforts, more security, better health care, higher average salaries than at any point in human history. And yet, if there is anything that characterizes our age compared to previous ages it's anxiety. Anti-depressants are at an all time high. It is the pathology of a psychological age when it is not our *material* condition that is the most important thing; it's our *psychological* condition. And that is exactly where Augustine starts his *Confessions*.

In Book 1, Chapter 1, Augustine says this: "The heart is restless above all things until it finds its rest in Thee." Augustine starts with that fallen human condition that ultimately manifests itself in restless anxiety. We live in an era, I think, where that is more characteristic, perhaps, than ever before.

And so, when students ask me, "What is a good book I could look at with a non-Christian friend where they might be able to take seriously, from the get-go, what is being said?" Augustine's *Confessions*. That's the one! Think of who publishes it. If I say to a student, "Do you read a lot of Calvin?" Who publishes Calvin? Presses that are well known to *us*, but by and large they are pretty obscure in the wider world. Penguin publishes Augustine's *Confessions*. Oxford World Classics publishes Augustine's *Confessions*. I have here a translation that came out just a month ago in the Modern Library. People are still translating it. Why do these publishers publish Augustine? Because they can sell it. Because people read it. It is a classic Christian book still being read by people who are not Christians. Maybe it's *Pilgrim's Progress*. Maybe it's Augustine's *Confessions*.

Why is Augustine's *Confessions* so important?

My big burden, as a teacher of church history, has always been to try to teach the students who sit in my class to read the great texts of church history for themselves. I am not a teacher who cares to produce followers or clones of myself. I am conscious that I only have students for a relatively short period of time. What I want to do is enable students to read the great texts of church history for themselves so they can go away and benefit from them.

I was given the brief of "What can we learn from Augustine today?" I am conscious also that I am not to engage here in an exercise of nostalgia or antiquarianism. I am not teaching just a great piece of literature which you will be entertained by. I want to show you a couple of points in Augustine's *Confessions* where, if you read and think, you will be transformed; you will learn more about the human condition in general, and your own condition, in particular.

There are two incidents. The first one involves a *pear tree*; the second involves a *gladiatorial display*.

a. A pear tree
Augustine's *Confessions*, Book 2, contains his narrative of what we might call his teenage years. In Book 1, he talks about himself as a newborn infant—a great argument for original sin there. He cries, and he demands "even as a child," he says. And then he takes the story through to Book 2 where he is a teenager. I'm going to read a small section from the newest translation by Sarah Ruden in the Modern Library. But I'll say in advance, I think this is one of the passages of greatest literary simplicity and theological sophistication in the history of post-biblical literature. Augustine says this in Book 2:

> There was a pear tree in the neighborhood of our vineyard, but the fruit weighing it down offered no draw either in its look or its taste. After playing in vacant lots clear 'til the dead of night—that was the behavior we visited on the town as our habit—we young men, full of our endless mischief, proceeded to this tree to shake it down and haul away the goods. We filched immense loads, not for our own feasting but for slinging away to swine, if you can believe it. But in fact, we did devour some pears. Our only proviso was the potential for liking what was illicit.[3]

You get the scene. A gang of youths headed off into town as was their usual practice, causing trouble, clamber over a wall of a neighboring garden, steal a bunch of pears, maybe eat a couple of them themselves. They not really very attractive to look at. They're not

---

3. Augustine, *Confessions*, 42.

very tasty. They end up giving them away to pigs. Twenty years later, one might say Augustine is haunted by this incident. Why does he include it in the *Confessions*?

I think when we reflect on this incident, we learn something deep and powerful about the tragedy of the fallen human condition—something that is recovered in the Reformation—and which helps trigger the Reformation's great recovery of Augustine's understanding of grace.

There are several things that strike us about this passage.

First, its *utter triviality*. If you go to your typical Christian bookshop and you look for those true life testimonies, generally speaking, you will not find people writing Christian testimonies that become bestsellers about stealing a few pears or apples from a neighbor's garden. Generally speaking, we are looking for something more spectacular, such as, "I was a murderous biker, and then I found Jesus." Or, "I was a crazy villain, an ex-con, and somebody gave me a tract, and I repented of my sins, and came to Jesus." And they are wonderful stories; I don't want to belittle them. They are great stories when somebody who is a notorious villain or evil doer is converted by the grace of the Lord Jesus Christ. But one of the things that happens when we read books like that is this: If I read a book like that, if I'm honest, I'm probably not reading it in order to find out about the person's conversion. More likely, I'm reading it to find out what it was like to be a murderous biker, because I have no idea. If I wrote my own testimony, it would be: "I was a boring, law-abiding white guy and then I met Jesus. And I'm still a boring, law-abiding white guy, but now I'm united to Christ by faith." Again, not to belittle the grace of God at all, but it doesn't make for a very interesting story. And Augustine is sort of writing something of the equivalent of that here, isn't he? Most of us, I think, when we look back to our youth, can remember times when we did something like this. Where I grew up in England we had a technical term for it. We called it "skrumping." It's actually a word that means "stealing fruit from somebody else's garden." It was a relatively commonplace bit of *criminality* for the youth—it was trivial—and nobody is going to do a long stretch in jail for that.

As we read this we might think, "Well, why is he writing this, because I can remember doing that myself." *That's the point.* If

Augustine had written something spectacular—if he had written, "We murdered somebody and buried the body, and we got away with it"—you would read it, and it would be an interesting story, but you would never identify with it. But by choosing something so trivial, Augustine draws the reader into the story. And that's important, because one of the things that Augustine is going to try to do in the *Confessions* is, as he tells his story, it's going to be the story of every man. As Augustine tells his story it's precisely its nondescript nature that draws us into the narrative in what will be an extremely important way, as we shall see in just a few moments.

Second, notice that Augustine goes out of his way to underline *the sheer pointlessness of the crime.*

Again, go back to those Christian biographies that are often popular. They were certainly popular in the 1980s when I was converted. *The Cross and the Switch Blade* would be a great example. *Run Baby Run*, by Nicky Cruz, would be another. These were the sort of books that I read as a young Christian, and they were exciting reads and were encouraging because you saw the power of God's grace. What is often interesting about the sins described in those books though is one could see a kind of rationale for them. If you think about it, if I were to go out tonight from the conference and rob a bank, that would be a deeply wicked thing to do, but you could see a kind of rationale to it. Why do people rob banks? They rob banks to get big quantities of money more easily than earning it. It may be wicked— we may not sympathize with it—but we can see there is a kind of internal logic to the sin. There is something extrinsic that is gained as a result. If you rob a bank, you are richer than you once were. What Augustine does here is go out of his way to highlight the fact that this crime is utterly pointless. He's got better fruit in his own garden. They steal the fruit and what do they do? Well, maybe they take a few bites out of this fruit, but it's revolting. They give it to pigs, and they run away laughing. It's the pointlessness of the crime, I think, that allows Augustine to draw out an important lesson about the pointlessness of sin.

Often we can think of extrinsic rationales for sin. There is something we gain as a result of our sin. But what Augustine is trying to do here is push us right back and say, "No, the real essence of sin does not lie in anything you gain as a result of sin. Look at what I did with those pears." He makes the point right at the end of that passage that the reason he broke the law was that *it was breaking the law!* That's what gave him the kick! That's why he enjoyed doing it! There is no other reason for stealing these pears than the fact that it had been forbidden. And that raises all manner of interesting questions, doesn't it? Why is it that breaking the law is so exciting? Why does it make him feel so good? Why does he get this rush?

Well, he will go on to expound the answer in the next paragraphs and coming pages. There are various aspects to this, but one of the points he makes is this: It's God who makes the law, and therefore God stands above the law. And when you break the law what do you do? You make yourself feel like God. That's why sin feels so great, because you're throwing off the yoke of your Creator, and you're feeling like you're the Creator yourself. The problem, of course—as Augustine will go on to explain—is that it makes sinning rather like taking drugs. Now this is not an analogy that Augustine would use today, but I think all of us here are all familiar enough with it to use it today. We all know this from the perspective of pain killers. You've got a splitting headache so you take an aspirin or an Ibuprofen and the pain goes away. But then the drug wears off and then you need to take another one. You could look at that in a very bleak and negative way as it relates to drug addiction. I'm told that those who are addicted to drugs, when they take the drug, they feel "high" and they feel fantastic. But then the high wears off and they feel terrible, so what do they do? They go off and do it again because they need to get the same feeling again. I think Augustine, in this passage, penetrates to one of the puzzling problems of the psychology of sin. And that's why people keep doing it.

Some years ago, there was an interesting case in New York where the warrant officers—we call them bailiffs in the UK—broke into the apartment of a lady who was a high-flying New York lawyer—a very wealthy lady who had gone bankrupt through buying things online. I remember watching the news report. She bought so much on line and ran up such credit card debts that she was declared bankrupt and the bailiffs broke in to take away property to sell in order to pay off the debt. But that's not the really interesting part of the story. The *really interesting* part of the story is what the bailiffs found when they broke into her apartment. They found all of the stuff that she had purchased *still in their boxes.* She had bought, and bought, and bought stuff, but never bothered to open it. This raises the question: Why did she buy all this stuff? She wasn't buying *stuff*—she was *buying* stuff. It was the *buying*, the *doing* of something she knew she shouldn't do that gave her the kick. And she did it again and again and again, ultimately to her own terrible harm. She didn't use this stuff at all—it was pointless, a bit like the pears—but it made her feel like God when she did it.

Augustine goes on to talk about other aspects of this story as well. He talks about the role of the crowd. We often underestimate that, but he wonders why it was that they all went away laughing. And then he points out that—well, generally speaking—we only laugh in groups.

I've inherited this from my grandfather, much to my wife's disgust, but I'm one of those people who is actually able to laugh all by himself, and I will keep her awake at night lying in bed remembering funny things I've seen and bursting out laughing. And as you all know, there is nothing more annoying than somebody else laughing and you not knowing what they are laughing about. So Augustine's argument wouldn't quite work for me or my grandfather, but I think it works for 90 percent of the human race, and that is this: The roar of the crowd—*sin has a profoundly social dimension.*

I'm not thinking *social sin*, or the *structures of sin* here, but I'm thinking, why was it when my boys were growing up—and they were good kids, and their friends were good kids—that I never really worried when my boys went out by themselves, but I always worried when they went out in a group, even with their good friends? The moral sum of the whole of a group of young men is *always* less than the moral sum of the parts, isn't it? Something happens when they get into a group.

Augustine is analyzing it and saying, "I wouldn't have stolen those pears if I had been on my own, but it was such a laugh to do it with a bunch of other lads, even though there was no point to it." That simple paragraph brings out so much about human psychology and human sin.

And then, finally, go back to what I said at the start: Why does he choose something so simple, something that we can all identify with? It's to draw us into the story, and that's vitally important for the following reason: Now I don't mean this in a trivial or disrespectful way, but what is the first act of "skrumping" in human history? It is the stealing of the fruit from the Tree of the Knowledge of Good and Evil! When you read that paragraph by Augustine—and when you identify with Augustine as he steals those pears from a tree—what Augustine does is draw you into that giant biblical narrative. The sin of Augustine becomes the sin of Adam, and it becomes the sin of *everyone*.

That's why, I would say—with all respect to John Bunyan—I think the *Confessions* is in some ways a greater work than *Grace Abounding* because the literary and theological genius involved is breathtaking. That's just a single paragraph! How much Pauline theology and psychology is compressed into that one paragraph?

b. Gladiatorial combat

The second passage I want to read to you is from Book 6. Augustine has a good friend and ultimately they will be converted together in a garden in Milan. Interestingly enough, they will be converted under a tree. Some have said that that's so convenient it can't possibly be true. I'm pretty confident there are a lot of trees and gardens in Milan. If you were converted in a garden in Milan, chances are there was a tree there somewhere. But you see the fall on the one tree, and then redemption on the other tree.

Augustine's friend, Alypius, is his constant companion. The two of them go through this journey to Christianity together. And one of the things about Alypius that Augustine notes is that although he was not yet a Christian, we might say he was quite a pious pagan. He was quite strict in terms of how he lived his life. And one of the things that Alypius abhorred was gladiatorial combat, because of the bloodshed and violence involved. And Augustine is shocked when he meets up with Alypius at one point to discover that Alypius has completely changed his opinion about gladiators and gladiatorial games. And the reason is described in Book 6. It's a slightly extended paragraph, and you'll have to bear with me, but I want to make some powerful and, I hope, some very contemporary points out of this.

Alypius is surrounded by a bunch of his friends who love the gladiatorial combat and they say to him that they're going to take him along to the circus to see what's going on. Here I pick up the narrative as Augustine describes it:

> He [Alypius] said, "Even if you haul my body to that place and sit me down there, you can't aim my mind and my eyes at the show, can you? Though I'm there I *won't* be there, and that's how I'll be the victor over what is going on, and over you too." When they heard this, they took him along just the same, now maybe with the added motivation of testing whether he could achieve what he'd said he would.
>
> They arrived and took their places in the seats available, and everything was seething with the most barbaric kinds of entertainment. He closed the doors of his eyes and forbade his mind to go outside into such terrible wickedness. If only he'd plugged his ears! One of the combatants fell, and a booming shout from the whole crowd struck him forcefully. Curiosity overcame him and, on the pretext that he was ready to condemn and overcome whatever he saw, he opened his eyes.[4]

Then an almost poetic passage follows:

> He was run through with a wound in his soul more lethal than the physical wounding he'd longed to look at, and he fell more pitifully than the one whose fall the shouting was about. The yells came in through his ears and unlocked his eyes, so there was access for assaulting and bringing down a mind that was daring but not yet strong, and was weaker in that it relied on itself when it should have relied on you. When he saw the blood, he guzzled the cruelty at the same time. He didn't turn away but instead riveted his gaze there; he gulped down the demons of rage, though he didn't know it. He was delighted at the criminal contest and got drunk on the gory diversion. He was no longer the person he'd been when he came, but was now actually part of the mob he'd come to, and he was a true confederate of those who brought him along.[5]

That is a powerful passage. And if the pears, if you like, were the fall of Augustine, this is the fall of Alypius. This young man who despised the gladiatorial combats and the pornography of the violence they involved, goes along and, at this critical moment when

---

4. Augustine, *Confessions*, 151.
5. Augustine, *Confessions*, 151–52.

one of the gladiators is slain and the crowd roars, he opens his eyes and immediately, says Augustine, "his soul is slain." He was dealt a more deadly blow than that which had hit the gladiator in the circus below.

There are things to notice here. One of the things that fascinates me—certainly in my pastoral work at an OPC Church outside of Philadelphia—in talking to other pastors, is that every single one of them tells me the same story. A couple of weeks ago at Moore Theological College in Sydney, Australia, Katrina and I were staying with Mark Thompson, the Principal there. Mark interviews every student who comes to Moore College and he always asks the male students three things: "Do you struggle with homosexual temptation?" Pretty much all of them say no. Then he asks, "Do you struggle with pedophilia temptation?" They always say no. He asks, "Do you struggle with Internet pornography?" And almost every single one says yes. Almost every single one. It is an absolute plague in the church. And I think—though Augustine clearly doesn't predict the Internet world in which we live—I think what he describes here is phenomenologically the same thing. And I think he describes it more truly than even he could know.

First of all, *the power of the visual is very striking here.*

One of the things that we are learning about the scourge of Internet pornography is the power of the visual to shape our minds and our thinking. I might add that Christians are, by and large, far more sensitive to the pornography of sex than the pornography of violence, which is what Augustine was talking about here. But the visual is very powerful. Part of the tragedy of the human condition is the way that the visual has been perverted.

I have sort of taken a Nazarite vow this year that when I am traveling I am just going to read poetry. It sounds kind of pretentious, but I feel that I haven't read enough poetry over the last few years so I've decided to read all of those poems that I've never had time for; you know, the long boring ones.

The first one I chose was Milton's *Paradise Lost,* and there's that beautiful speech where Adam opens his eyes, and he sees Eve for the first time, and he waxes lyrical about her beauty, God's last and greatest gift to him. The visual imagery is powerful and beautiful.

How the visual has been twisted and perverted for us in the fallen world—Augustine touches on that here.

Second, he understands that *the visual transforms the person.*

Here, I could sound really geeky, I suppose. One of the things I did when I became a pastor—when Internet pornography came up as a problem in the church—is I did some reading on it, not just on the phenomenon, but also on the physiology: neuroplasticity. One of the most amazing things about the human brain is that it literally rewires itself. That is why people brought up speaking two languages find it much easier to learn a third, a fourth, a fifth, or a sixth language, because from a very young age their brains have been wired to think in more than one language. It's why the older you get the harder it becomes to learn a language because the brain kind of hardens and becomes more difficult to rewire. One of the things we've discovered about Internet pornography is that it rewires the brain. That is why it is so hard to break. Because, when you're heavily into pornography your brain has changed.

And that's what fascinates me about the language that Augustine uses here: "He was no longer the person he'd been when he came." Augustine is just observing here. You know, he has no access to neuroscience or brain physiology. He is just observing; but he is saying that after this experience he was not the same man. He was completely different.

So it's the second passage in the *Confessions* that I bring to your attention. I press this book on you because there's a lot of debate about what makes a great book; what makes a great piece of literature. It is not arbitrary, but my personal take on it is this: A great book is one that you read, and you understand yourself and your world better at the end of it than you did when you started. And a *truly great book* is one that, after the second, and the third, and the fourth time you read it, you learn more and more about yourself. Augustine's *Confessions* is one of those books. I make it a compulsory read for all students in the Ancient Church course at Westminster. They have to read Augustine's *Confessions* because there is always a question on it in the exam. They can forfeit 25% of the exam if they wish, but so far nobody has done that. One student once said, "Dr. Trueman makes reading the *Confessions* annually a basic mark of a credible Christian profession of faith." I am not going to go quite that far, but maybe once every two years one would have to do it.

Third, another thing about Augustine that is significant is that *his thinking has continued throughout the ages to inspire the best Christian thought.*

A few years ago, after the Twin Towers attack, there was an interesting sort of surge in the entertainment industry. Video rentals went up, and people went out shopping. And I was reminded of a comment that Augustine makes in his great work, *The City of God*, where he is reflecting on the fact that Rome, the eternal city, has fallen to the gods, and he is trying to explain how it is that the city that was meant to be the meaning of history has fallen to the gods. But early on in that book, he makes an observation about the Roman citizens flooding across the Mediterranean into the town of Hippo where he is Bishop. And he says this: "They've lost everything and they come to Hippo and they go to the theatre but they do not come to the church." There Augustine points to something about the deep self-deception that is involved in human sin.

And that brings me up to the seventeenth century, because the last bit of Augustine I want to talk about actually comes from the hands of a Roman Catholic thinker, Blaise Pascal. He was not highly thought of as a Catholic thinker—the Catholic Church didn't like him, by and large, because he was a fairly consistent Augustinian—but Pascal, too, asked that question in his age, "Why is it that given the misery that surrounds man, he goes to the theater, and not to the church?"

I'm going to read you a little bit here from Pascal's great book, *The Thoughts*, where he draws on Augustine, and then I'm going to comment on it.

> It is in fact the greatest source of happiness in the condition of kings, that men try incessantly to divert them, and to procure for them all kinds of pleasures. The king is surrounded by persons whose only thought is to divert the king, and to prevent his thinking of self.[6]

---

6. Blaise Pascal, *Pascal's Thoughts* in *The Harvard Classics* (New York: P. F. Collier and Sons, 1910), 48:53.

What Pascal does here is he asks a question of his age that I think we should ask of *our* age. I started by talking about the restlessness of our age, given the massive amounts of comforts that we now have. And Pascal asks this very simple question: "Why do kings have jesters?" Remember, he is writing in seventeenth-century France, at a time when the French monarchy is consolidating its power like never before, and the French king is perhaps the most powerful man on the face of the earth. And he asks the question, "Why is it that the most important man in the king's retinue is a clown?" Why is it? He uses his Augustinian anthropology to answer that question. He says this: "For he is unhappy, king though he be, if he think of himself."[7] What is Pascal saying there? While building on Augustine, he's saying this: "The thing about a king is, he lives in absolute luxury and security. What is there to worry about? There is nothing to worry about except the only thing that is left to worry about—*death* itself and the *judgment* to follow."

Pascal, as a good follower of Augustine, knows that that thought— that the king himself is not God—is unbearable to him. So what does he do? He employs a clown to entertain him and to stop him thinking about that.

Why is that important and useful for us today? Why does that part of the Augustinian tradition speak to us today? Who are the most highly paid people in North America? It's not the President. I don't know what the President earns; last time I looked I think it was around $400,000 a year. The most highly paid men and women in North America are the movie stars and the sports stars. It's staggering what sports stars get paid. They play what are essentially schoolyard games. Now, I enjoy watching a game of rugby. But it's become an obsession in our culture, hasn't it? The amount of money spent on sport, and movies, and entertainment. And you've got to ask yourself, "Why?" Why do we pay the President less than a million dollars a year and a movie star gets more than that for a major role in one movie. Do we really consider the movie star to be doing something that's actually more important than the President?

If you take a step back, you'll say, "That's ridiculous! Whoever is President is doing a far more important job—he is the civil magistrate—he's tasked to protect the innocent and to put down the

---

7. Blaise Pascal, *Thoughts*, 48:53.

wicked. There is no more important job in the civil sphere than the President of the United States." But we pay him peanuts. And we would probably have a fit if they raised income tax by a cent in order to pay him more. And yet, year after year, people routinely shell out huge sums of money for season tickets, and for concerts, and never complain. Why not? Because they consider those people to be doing a more important job. Why? It takes me back to what I said at the start—it is precisely because we live in such a secure age that it is so ridden with anxiety. Because in an age when everything is secure, we have only one thing left to worry about, and that is our own *mortality*. And we will do anything to *avoid* reflecting on our own mortality.

Pascal has numerous paragraphs in his great book, *The Thoughts*, about the impossibility of sitting on one's own in silence. "It is unbearable," he says. And why is it unbearable? Because as soon as you do that you have to reckon with who you really are before God. And he doesn't just talk about entertainment; he'll say that it's why bureaucracies flourish. He has this whole kind of critique of French society. Why is there so much bureaucracy?

As an immigrant to the United States, I can tell you that there is a lot of bureaucracy out there in the United States. We have people in my church who won't do the child background checks because they don't want the central government to have their fingerprints. As a foreigner, the central government must have a dozen copies of my fingerprints for various reasons. Masses of bureaucracy! Pascal would say, "Why? Because we actually love it!" It keeps us occupied, and therefore prevents us from thinking about the really serious things in life.

Conclusion

What can we learn from Augustine today?

First, by reading his *Confessions* we can learn about *the power of sin*. The power of sin! There's good news, of course. Augustine has a very powerful view of grace as well, but I have no time to deal with that now. But the *power of sin*; the nature of what it is to be a fallen human being. Second, the *power of the visual*; the pornography of violence and sex. These are very contemporary things that Augustine is describing and wrestling with in his *Confessions*. Third, his understanding of human beings as *those who will not accept that they are not God.* And when forced to face that reality in the silence of their own rooms, will do anything other than to sit in silence—switch on the television, surf the Internet—anything other than face the reality of that.

If ever, I think, there is a Christian thinker who speaks to the contemporary modern malaise, it is Augustine. I would suggest that if you have non-Christian friends who are interested in reading a Christian book with you, Augustine's *Confessions* might be a good place to start. Even if they don't agree with his conclusions, I think they will recognize themselves in his description.

CHAPTER 8

What Luther Teaches Us Today: Theology of Preaching

Carl Trueman

It is good to be with you—speaking to you about another giant of the faith. I sometimes think I have the second best job in the world. I get to spend my days talking about interesting characters from church history. I think if you love telling stories but have no imagination, then being a historian is the job for you, because the stories are already written; you merely need to retell them.

Background

I want to speak to you about Martin Luther. I feel the topic is somewhat vast, but we will narrow it down to a fine strand of his thinking. I will share some things I've been pondering for a few years relative to Luther that derive from the intersection of three major areas of focus in my life. First, I'm a church historian, so historical questions interest me. Second, I am a Christian, so theological questions interest me. Third, I am a pastor, and therefore pastoral questions interest me.

One of the things about the Reformation is that it represents a moment in history when there was a remarkable theological and pastoral transformation of the church, and this is mainly due to a return to the primacy of preaching. There was preaching prior to Luther. If you read Augustine's *Confessions* you will note that he mentions the preaching of Ambrose—the great Bishop of Milan who lived at the end of the fourth century—and that Ambrose had a huge impact on Augustine. And if you know anything about the history of the church during the Middle Ages you know that there were numerous great preachers during that time. For example, Bernard of Clairvaux is frequently quoted by Calvin as being one of the great preachers of the Middle Ages. Bernard was a Dominican monk who lived during the thirteenth century. He established an "order of preachers" in an attempt to revive the practice of preaching within the medieval church.

But preaching took on a peculiarly central role during the Reformation. And I believe the reason is this: preaching took on more of a *theological* and a *pastoral* role in the church than it had during the Middle Ages—or really any time since the Apostolic Era—which is practically important for us today. And at the center stands the figure of Martin Luther.

If preaching during the Reformation was merely a convenient way of communicating God's truth at a particular moment in time, then as time changes and history moves on, we can reasonably expect that the practice itself will be modified, or perhaps even pass away. However, if preaching rests upon a specific theology that transcends a particular point in time, then preaching will remain an extremely important part of the church's life, regardless of the age we are living in, or even where we are living.

To cut a long story short, my own sympathies lie very much with the latter of these two scenarios. I believe that preaching arises as a theological necessity. In his book, *Positive Preaching and the Modern Mind*, P. T. Forsyth describes preaching as an act whereby "Christianity stands or falls."[1] And central to that is the figure of Martin Luther.

Today I want to talk about how Luther's theology served to bring preaching back to the center of the church's life in a way that was historically unprecedented since the time of the apostles.

God's creative speech
The first thing I want to do is argue that Luther rediscovers, or zeros in on, the idea of *God as a speaking God*. Creation is the linguistic action of God (Genesis 1 and 2). Divine speech is creative speech. There was nothing; God speaks; and then there is something: "By the word of the LORD were the heavens made; and all the host of them by the breath of his mouth" (Ps. 33:6). It is typical in Scripture to talk about God's speech as creative.

Luther latches onto this. He understands and begins his *Lectures on Genesis* with the power of divine speech: "This word is God; it is

---

1. P. T. Forsyth, *Positive Preaching and the Modern Mind* (Coromandel East, South Australia: New Creation Publications, 1907), 1.

the omnipotent word uttered in the divine essence. No one heard it spoken except God Himself, that is, God the Father, God the Son, and God the Holy Spirit. And when it was spoken, light was brought into existence, not after the matter of the word, or from the nature of Him who spoke, but out of the darkness itself. First the Father spoke inwardly, and outwardly light was made and came into existence immediately. In this manner other creatures too were made later. This, I say, is sufficient knowledge for us concerning the manner of the creation."[2]

Do you see what Luther is saying? He is pointing to creation as a "wordy" thing. Speech is creative and powerful. It is a differentiating, creative power as well. Luther talks about the word of the fifth day, and this is a fascinating statement on the power of God's speech: "Who could conceive of the possibility of bringing forth in the water a being which could not continue to exist in water? But God speaks a mere word, and immediately the birds are brought forth from the water. If the word is spoken, all things are possible. So that out of the water made are the fish or birds." Then he continues with this fascinating line: "Therefore any bird whatever and any fish whatever are nothing but nouns in the divine rule of language; through this rule of language those things that are impossible become very easy, while those that are very clearly opposite become very much alike, and vice versa."[3]

Notice the phrase, "Therefore any bird whatever and any fish whatever are nothing but nouns in the divine rule of language." God's speech is creative. As human beings we have a framework of what we think is possible, but that is trumped by God's speech. When God speaks, that which appears to us to be impossible—is made possible. This is because God's speech is not simply describing what is there; it is also bringing into being that which is there. Reality, we might say, is what God says it is.

Now I want you to hold that thought in mind because that will become important in our understanding of Luther's view of preaching. For Luther, as with all the Reformers, the preached word is the

---

2. Martin Luther, *Luther's Works* (Philadelphia: Muhlenberg, and Fortress; St. Louis: Concordia, 1955–), 1:57–58.

3. Luther, *Works*, 1:49.

Word of God, and therefore stands in close analogy to God's speech in creation.

Luther draws this out dramatically in his description of the fall. When he describes the fall in his *Lectures on Genesis* he describes it as a struggle over language. Whose speech will Adam and Eve believe? Will it be the speech of God or the speech of the serpent? He says, "Moses expresses himself very carefully and says: 'the serpent said.' That is, with a word the serpent attacks the Word. The Word which the Lord spoke to Adam was: 'Do not eat from the tree of the knowledge of good and evil.' For Adam this Word was Gospel and Law; it was his service and the obedience he could offer God in this state of innocence. These Satan attacks and tries to destroy. Nor is it only his intention, as those who lack knowledge think, to point out the tree and issue an invitation to pick its fruit. He points it out indeed; but then adds another and a new statement, as he still does in the church."[4]

Notice two things which we can draw from Luther here:

First, he shows the fundamental human struggle, as *a struggle over words*. The struggle between God and Satan in Genesis is a linguistic struggle because it involves two different accounts of reality. The challenge to Adam and Eve is—which one will they believe?

Second, it makes the issue of language—or we might say the issue of reality itself—*a moral issue*. I want you to hold that in your mind, because what I will do later is come back and say to you, "You know, that is what is happening in the pulpit every Sunday. The people are being presented with the speech of God, and the choice facing them is, do they believe that speech or do they believe the speech of their own hearts and the speech they hear every day of the week from every other outlet in this world?"

How God presences Himself in Scripture

For Luther, I think it is fair to say that he very much picks up on (besides God's creative use of language) the fact that speech is the way in which God presences Himself. For all of us, we have an intuitive understanding of this, because this is the way we use language ourselves.

---

4. Luther, *Works*, 1:146.

It is a delight to have my wife with me this week, but often she is not with me when I travel. I can send her a text or an email, but nothing beats speaking with her on the phone because the sound of her voice makes her that much more present to me, even though she is far away.

You may have those moments in your marriage when you may have forgotten something or done something, and as a result your wife doesn't speak to you for a time, and yet she is still there. There is a feeling of absence, although she is still physically present. That is analogous to the way God's speech functions in the Bible, and Luther certainly saw this. We see it at key points in the biblical narrative. Think of the Shunamite woman in 2 Kings 4. She has had a child and that child has died, and she runs to find the man of God (an important phrase that I will come back to later). In response, Elisha hands his staff to Gehazi, his servant, telling him to run back to the lady's house, greet no one along the way, to get there as quickly as possible, and to lay his staff on the child (v. 29). But she will not leave Elisha there. She insists that Elisha must come. Why? Because of who he is constantly referred to—as was his predecessor Elijah—as "the man of God." We shall see that "the man of God" is defined as *the one who speaks God's Word and it comes to pass*. She needs Elisha there because she wants God to be savingly present with her child. God could have done it through Elisha's staff, but she knows that God normally works through the speech of His servants.

Think of the baptism in Mark 1:9–10: "And it came to pass in those days, that Jesus came from Nazareth of Galilee, and was baptized of John in Jordan. And straightway coming up out of the water, he saw the heavens opened." That language of "opened" is very important in the Jewish tradition, from Isaiah 64:1: "Oh that thou wouldst rend the heavens, that thou wouldest come down…" God would not be present with His people until the heavens were torn open. Mark uses that original word for "opened" in only one other place in his gospel—when the curtain in the temple is torn asunder. When the heavens are torn open, Mark is consciously connecting the events of Jesus's baptism to the prophecy of Isaiah 64. What happens as soon as the heavens are torn open? The next thing is the Father speaking. We read, "…and the Spirit like a dove descending upon Him…" (Mark 1:10), and then the Father speaks. God is present with His people.

How do we know that? He speaks. His speech indicates His saving presence with His people.

Look at the book of Acts. Christ ascends, the Spirit descends, and what is the immediate sign? The apostles are marked by speech, and immediately communicate the gospel to the linguistically eclectic crowd around them in a way that they all understand. God is savingly present with those people. Of course, God is present all the time, but specifically, powerfully, and savingly present through His speech.

Luther understands this when he is commenting on Amos 8:11: *"I will send a famine in the land.* This is the last blow. It is the worst, the most wretched, of all. All the rest of the blows would be bearable, but this is absolutely horrible. He is threatening to take away the genuine prophets and the true Word of God, so that there is no one to preach, even if men were most eager to hear the Word and would run here and there to hear it. This happened to the Jews in the Assyrian captivity and in that last one."[5] Do you understand what Luther is saying? People will run all over the place looking for God but they will not find Him. Do you know why? Because He will not be speaking to them. Yes, metaphysically He will be their sustaining existence, but God will not speak to His people. Therefore, we might say He will be functionally absent from them.

All of that is really foundational background to what I want to say about Luther on preaching. But the thing we need to understand is for Luther, speech is vitally important. It is an attribute of God, we might say. What is the first thing we learn about God? He speaks. What do we learn about God's speech? It is powerful and creative; it is not descriptive so much as that which brings things into being. That understanding of God underlies all of Luther's theology.

Think about justification. What is the great innovation or the great breakthrough on justification during the Reformation? It is that justification is this: *You are justified when God says you are righteous.* It does not matter that you are not intrinsically saved. The speech of God declares you to be righteous, and therefore you are. God is not describing you at that point; He is bringing into being a state of affairs.

I officiated a wedding last week for a couple in my church and at some point in the ceremony I made the statement, "I now pronounce

---

5. Luther, *Works*, 18:182–83.

you man and wife." I am not describing a state of affairs; I am making them man and wife. That is analogous to the speech of God which doesn't describe—but brings into reality that which is stated.

All of this lies as background as we come to think about Luther and the importance of preaching. My favorite quotation from Luther on preaching, which has already been quoted to you by Ian Hamilton, comes from March of 1522. If you don't know much about the life of Luther, March 1522 is perhaps the moment in Luther's life when he is most vulnerable. We often think of the Diet of Worms—this one man standing against the might of empire and church—as being the moment when he was most at risk. Certainly, there was danger involved in the Diet of Worms. The precedent for rebel priests going to imperial councils and departing unscathed was not good.

In retrospect, we know that Frederick the Wise, Luther's princely protector, had a sort of semi-military plan to kidnap him and take him away to safety. But while he is living in the Wartburg Castle—during the period of the Diet of Worms—the Reformation in Wittenberg descends into chaos. The leadership passes to a number of other men and it moves in a much more radical direction. So the Elector, the Prince, who is very disturbed about what is going on, transfers Luther from Wartburg Castle to Wittenberg in early 1522. At this point Luther is really alone. The Elector is standing back to see what will happen. Luther's allies have all abandoned him; it is just down to him. It is a mark of the measure of the man that he is able to bring peace back to the streets of Wittenberg by preaching. He preaches this remarkable series of sermons which we call *Invocavit Sermons*. In one of them he makes this famous statement talking about the power of the Word over against worldly power. Luther says this regarding the Word: "I will preach it, teach it, write it, but I will constrain no man by force, for faith must come freely without compulsion. Take myself as an example. I opposed indulgences and all the papists, but never with force. I simply taught, preached, and wrote God's Word; otherwise I did nothing. And while I slept, or drank Wittenberg beer with my friends, Philipp and Amsdorf, the Word so greatly weakened the papacy that no prince or emperor ever inflicted such losses upon it. I did nothing; the Word did everything."[6]

6. Luther, *Works*, 51:77.

In some ways it is a classic piece of Luther. He was a bombastic sort of individual. He was never knowingly understated in any way. But it also rests upon a powerful but important understanding of the theological nature of preaching.

As an aside, one of the reasons why this topic is important to me is that one of the things I have been struck by, is that many seminaries don't produce many good preachers. One of the reasons for this is that we don't teach a theology of preaching. Much of the teaching in seminary on preaching is rightly on the technicalities of what is going on—proper exposition, exegesis, moving to doctrinal synthesis, and then to application. There are all these technical skills that we teach, but nothing beats actually understanding what preaching is *theologically* to set the imagination on fire for the task. It is why I love Martin Lloyd-Jones's book on *Preaching and Preachers*. I have described it as fifty percent genius, but it sets the imagination on fire for preaching for 100 percent. Even the terrible bits that may be wrong actually do get you excited about preaching. So it is an interesting book from that perspective. I would say to students, any book that uses the phrase, "That's an abomination," on every other page must be worth reading at some level.

But all of this is to say, as a background, that my interest in this arises out of wanting to understand what preaching is theologically for my own benefit, and hopefully for the benefit of students as well.

Theology of Preaching

Humans are linguistic beings

Theology of preaching for Luther is rooted in a theology of divine speech, but it is also rooted in an understanding of human beings as primarily linguistic creatures. It is fascinating, and as far as I can work out, two major things that mark human beings from every other creature on the earth are these: 1) our ability to use language, and 2) our ability to hear, produce, and appreciate music.

Again, as an aside, isn't it fascinating that the preaching of the Word and communal singing were the two things that were really restored during the Reformation? There was some good theology in the Middle Ages and the Reformers built on a lot of medieval theology. But the two things that they really broke with were: 1) they replaced the centrality of the sacraments with the centrality of the

Word, and 2) they replaced choral music—as performance by a priestly cast—with the whole church singing.

It just fascinates me that those are two major things that separate us from every other creature on the face of the earth and intuitively seem to touch upon the image of God in some ways. We reflect God, perhaps, in our ability to speak and in our ability to hear and appreciate music.

So human beings are linguistic beings. It marks us off from all creatures. Not only that, but speech is given a profoundly theological importance for human beings in Genesis 2:19 where we see that God has named man, so He brings every beast of the field to Adam, and Adam names the creatures. That surely is a sign of authority. The fact that we are able to use our language to name the creatures that God made is a sign of Adam's viceregency. God has placed Adam there as His viceregent in the Garden of Eden.

We might also say that *speech is that which allows us to participate, by analogy, in the creative power of God*. Why is it that a chimpanzee can never write a Shakespearean sonnet? Chimpanzees are not created to do that. That little example I just used of the marriage ceremony, when the minister creates a marriage there is an analogy, is there not, between the way human beings function with language, and divine language?

We can even see that in some of the things that we might despise. Think of all the trouble about political correctness, countless speech codes. On one level some people are very intolerant of what seems to be complete nonsense. On the other hand, political correctness points to something very deep and real, and this shows us that language is powerful. For example, if someone uses a racial epithet about someone they are not simply describing them, they are repeatedly putting them in their place. They are doing something to them. Our language has power, for good or for evil. Where does that come from? I think it is because we are created in God's image, and our language functions analogously to the language of God.

It is also a *means of human presence, and it is a means of human power*, again going back to Genesis 2. We see that Luther can move us from understanding God as a linguistic being, to seeing human beings as linguistic beings, and how language has power.

Now let's move back to Luther proper. I want to revisit *key moments in Luther's career in April 1518.*

It has always struck me that it is odd that we celebrate the beginning of the Reformation as October 31, 1517. It is odd because Luther said more radical things before October 1517 and nobody paid any attention whatsoever. He certainly said much more radical things very shortly after October 1517, and everyone paid attention.

One of these instances occurs in Heidelberg, April 1518, when Luther travels to one of the Chapter meetings, the Presbytery Meeting of the Augustinian Order, that is meeting in that city. Typically such meetings involved dealing with a certain amount of business of the Order. But also there would be some time spent discussing a theological topic. Luther composed a series of Theses, a series of points for discussion or debate. They were actually presented by his pupil, Leonard Baier, but Luther wrote them. These Theses contained in a nutshell the whole of Luther's later mature theology. Some say Luther is not a systematic theologian. Technically that is true; he never wrote a Systematic Theology. What people often mean by that is that he was not a consistent theologian. I think he was remarkably consistent. Did he contradict himself? Probably on occasion, yes. There exist at least 120 volumes of his German Latin Works. That is a lot of writing for a man to never contradict oneself. Even now I am asked, "What did you mean when you wrote this on such and such a page?" I was doing a radio interview once and was asked that question, and I said, "You will have to forgive me, but I need to go and get the book and look at exactly what I said and see if I can remember it." The words of Robert Browning to his then fiancé Elizabeth Barrett come to mind when she asked him about one of his poems, "What did you mean when you wrote that?" Robert Browning said, "When I wrote that, only God and Robert Browning knew what I meant. Now only God knows what I meant."

In 1518, in Heidelberg, Luther presents these Theses and he really lays out the great foundations of his later theology—law vs. gospel, faith vs. works. In Theses 19–21 he draws an interesting contrast. I will read them to you and then come back and offer a slightly different take than one normally gets from each one.

Thesis 19: "That person does not deserve to be called a theologian who looks upon the invisible things of God as though they were clearly perceptible in those things which have actually happened."[7]

Luther is saying that a person doesn't deserve to be called a theologian who looks at the way the world is and extrapolates up to God and assumes that God is like that. It is exactly what Ian Hamilton said last night when he said, "God is not a big version of you." Luther here is zeroing in and saying it in more technical language, but is essentially saying that a person who thinks God is just a big version of themselves does not deserve to be called a theologian.

Thesis 20: "He deserves to be called a theologian, however, who comprehends the visible and manifest things of God, seen through suffering on the cross."[8]

There is a very important point in Luther's theology that emerges here. We don't look at the way the world is to understand how God is towards us. We look at the cross, and the broken flesh of Christ on that cross.

Setting aside second commandment issues for a second, there is a very famous painting by Lucas Cranach which shows Luther preaching. He is standing in the pulpit with his left hand on the Bible, and his right hand outstretched, pointing to Christ hanging on the cross. That is Cranach's depiction of exactly what preaching was for Luther. You go from the Bible to the cross. That is the point being made.

Luther goes on to bring these two together in Thesis 21, saying, "A theologian of glory calls evil good and good evil. The theologian of the cross calls the thing what it actually is."[9]

Luther is saying, "Don't look at the way the world is and assume that is how God is. Look at the cross and see there, in some ways, the contradiction of all of our expectations of God." How do we understand God's righteousness? Look to the cross. How do we understand God's strength? Look to the weakness of the cross. How do we understand God's glory? Look to the humiliation involved in the cross.

7. Luther, *Works*, 31:40.
8. Luther, *Works*, 31:40.
9. Luther, *Works*, 31:40.

It is this last Thesis I am mainly interested in today: "A theologian of glory calls evil good and good evil; a theologian of the cross calls the thing what it actually is." The word "calls" is the word I want to focus on here. Luther is basically saying, "By their speech you will know them." What is the task of the theologian of the cross? To call the thing what it *actually* is—we might say—is to point to reality and describe it in terms of truth. Though Luther does not make this connection yet, this relates to the task of the preacher. The cross, we might say, disrupts language. The cross transforms language. The cross inverts language in the light of God's action.

Luther said, "How do you understand the glory of God? It is through the humiliation of the cross. How do you understand the power of God? In the weakness of the cross. Where does that come out? In the task of the church in the way she describes reality. What is the preacher? The preacher is the theologian of the cross par excellence. The preacher is to be the one who calls the thing what it actually is."

Track back to the Garden of Eden with Luther. What is going on in the garden? God is saying one thing; Satan is saying another. Adam and Eve have to choose which reality they will trust. In which reality will they put their faith? For Luther, that is sort of reenacted every time a man speaks from the pulpit. What is the man in the pulpit doing? He is speaking God's reality, presenting it to the people, and giving them the challenge to trust it or to reject it. I have to quote one more thesis because it is my favorite of them all.

Thesis 28: "God's love does not find but creates that which is lovely to it." In other words, the love of man comes into being through that which is lovely to it.

I play a cruel trick on students when I teach this in class. There is usually a married couple in the class and I will immediately pick on the husband and say, "Why did you fall in love with your wife?" The man always hesitates, and you can see the wife getting redder and redder as the husband can't remember. I always say to them afterwards, "Look, just say she was beautiful. Do what works." But the point is that I want to hear the response, "I saw something lovely or beautiful in my wife, and that drew out my love to her." Luther is saying here that if you think about God's love like that you are a theological bore. What Luther is saying here is God's love does not find but creates that which is lovely to it.

Again, that is where the Word of God comes in. What is the Word of God? We heard at the start of this lecture that it is a creative thing. So when the Word of God is proclaimed, God is creating those things which are lovely to Him.

So then, we have this theology behind Luther's thinking. We could connect it to the Protestant understanding of salvation. What is salvation for Luther? Salvation is based upon divine declaration grasped by faith. We might put it this way: For Luther faith is the acceptance of God's linguistic declaration of reality. Outward appearance and human expectation are no safe guide.

This is what Luther says on the freedom of the Christian man, talking about the power of the proclaimed Word to transform reality:

> One thing and only one thing is necessary for Christian life, righteousness, and freedom. That one thing is the most Holy Word of God.... Let us then consider it certain and firmly established that the soul can do without anything except the Word of God and that where the Word of God is missing there is no help at all for the soul (i.e., God Himself is functionally absent). If it has the Word of God it is rich and lacks nothing since it is the Word of life, truth, light, peace, righteousness, salvation, joy, liberty, wisdom, power, grace, glory, and of every incalculable blessing. This is why the prophet in the entire Psalm (119) and in many other places yearns and sighs for the Word of God and uses so many names to describe it.
>
> On the other hand, there is no more terrible disaster with which the wrath of God can afflict men than a famine of hearing His Word, as He says in Amos 8:11. Likewise there is no greater mercy than when He sends forth His Word, as we read in Psalm 107:20. Nor was Christ sent into the world for any other ministry except that of the Word. Moreover, the entire spiritual estate— all the apostles, bishops, and priests—has been called and instituted only for the ministry of the Word.
>
> You may ask, "What then is the Word of God, and how shall it be used, since there are so many words of God?" I answer: "The apostle explains this in Romans 1. The Word is the gospel of God concerning His Son who was made flesh, suffered, rose from the dead, and was glorified through the Spirit who sanctifies. To preach Christ means to feed the soul, make it righteous, set it

free, and save it, provided it believes the preaching. Faith alone
is the saving and efficacious use of the Word of God, according
to Romans 10:9."[10]

There may not be a finer couple of sentences describing what
preaching is in the whole of Christian literature. I love that sentence:
"To preach Christ means to feed the soul, make it righteous, set it
free, and save it, provided it believes the preaching. Faith alone is the
saving and efficacious use of the Word of God."

God speaks in creation, and it is so. God speaks through His
prophets in the Old Testament and things happen. When Christ
ascends and the Spirit descends, He preaches through His apostles,
and things happen. And now in the post-apostolic era for Luther,
God proclaims His Word through His chosen preachers, and things
happen too.

This brings me to another observation on Luther, and that is, for
Luther, *form and content go together.*

The theology of the cross brings with it a specific form. The key
verse here is 1 Corinthians 1:21: "For after that in the wisdom of God
the world by wisdom knew not God, it pleased God by the foolishness of preaching to save them that believe." The modern consensus
on that verse translates it somewhat differently, but I think incor-
rectly. The NSV says: "For since, in the wisdom of God, the world did
not know God through wisdom, it pleased God through the folly of
what we preach to save those who believe." There is an important
difference there. In the one it is the *mode*; in the other it is the *content.*
It is a tricky verse, so in tracing the history of the exegesis of that
verse it seems that C. H. Dodd is very influential. Dodd makes this
comment in his book, *Apostolic Preaching and its Developments.* Paul
said, "It pleased God by the foolishness of preaching to save them
that believe" (1 Cor. 1:21). Dodd's comment is: "The word here translated 'preaching,' *kerygma*, signifies not the action of the preacher,
but that which he preaches—his message—as we sometimes say."[11]
What is fascinating is that that is the sum total of Dodd's argument.
He just states it. And Dodd pretty much carried the day for sixty or
seventy years on that verse in a remarkable way.

---

10. Luther, *The Freedom of a Christian,* in *Works,* 31:345–46.
11. C. H. Dodd, *The Apostolic Preaching and Its Developments* (New York: Harper,
1936), 7.

The word *kerygma* has been more recently reassessed, and for those who are interested in more detail or argument, I definitely recommend Duane Litfin's book on Paul's preaching, *Paul's Theology of Preaching*.[12] It is an excellent study of the context, background, and language that Paul used to describe his preaching. What Litfin does is to show that *kerygma* is inextricably connected to the role of the *kerux*, the herald. Essential to the role of the herald were a couple of things: 1) his humble position, and 2) the fact that he faithfully and simply declared in words his Master's message. Litfin argues, I think correctly, that the idea of a *kerygma* separate from the idea of a *kerux*—the idea of a gospel or announcement separate from the idea of a herald—is essentially impossible. To be fair, perhaps through the modern translation tradition, we might say that the King James Version and the new translations both capture something of the truth. What Paul is trying to communicate here is that form and content are intimately connected.

It makes sense, of course, from a Reformation position. Why? If the essence of the gospel is promise, there has to be a linguistic component. There has to be a declared connection. First, if we build on Luther's theology we can certainly tie form and content together. If we accept his view of the creative nature of divine language—that the Word is, in a sense, that which it signifies—that the word of judgment is God's judgment—that the word of forgiveness is God's forgiveness—then we can see that form and content must necessarily exist in a tight connection.

Secondly, we can see in the Old Testament that there is a tight connection between God's speech and the speech of His servants. The commission of Isaiah is a wordy commission. He is given words to say, as we read in Isaiah 6:9, "Go, and tell this people." Think of the Old Testament prophets. What marked them out was often their humble, outsider status. Elijah is *the* great example of this. The fascinating thing we learn about Elijah is the thing we do *not* learn about him. He appears out of nowhere. We are given no patronymic for Elijah because, in the ancient world, it was vitally important to know who your father was. My wife is from Lewis, and the question is: "Who are your people?" You are nobody unless you connect

---

12. Duane Litfin, *Paul's Theology of Preaching* (Downers Grove: IVP Academic, 2015).

somewhere. You've heard the phrase, "If you're not Dutch, you're not much." Unless the surname ends in "stra" or "sma" you're kind of an outsider. Elijah, in the world of patronymics, has no patronymic. Why? His authority is what? He brings the Word of God. That is the only reason he has any authority. It is nothing intrinsic to his person. The humbleness of his person is one thing—the power of his message is quite another.

We move to the New Testament. How is the church described in the New Testament? In a number of ways, but one of them is surely this: *It is a new creation.* I think the language of creation, when applied to the church, should take us back to Genesis 1. How was the world created? By the speech of God. How was the church created? By the speech of God through His servants.

It is interesting and fascinating as I have been reading and thinking about this. In 1 and 2 Kings, that phrase, "the man of God" occurs again and again in relation to Elijah and Elisha. In 1 Kings 17:24, Elijah has raised the widow's son and she says this, which is very significant: "Now by this I know that thou art a man of God, and that the word of the LORD in thy mouth is truth."

If you were to say to me, "How would you go to the New Testament to make a case for preachers being the successors of the Old Testament prophets?" It would take a long time to produce an arbitrary case. I direct your attention to perhaps the key passage—a passage that in some ways we chop up because the chapter division does not help us at this point. In 2 Timothy 3:16–4:2 we read: "All scripture is given by inspiration of God, and is profitable for doctrine, for reproof, for correction, for instruction in righteousness: That the man of God may be perfect, throughly furnished unto all good works. I charge thee therefore before God, and the Lord Jesus Christ, who shall judge the quick and the dead at his appearing and his kingdom; Preach the word; be instant in season, out of season; reprove, rebuke, exhort with all longsuffering and doctrine."

That fascinates me! Often when we go to those verses today, because of all the higher critical assaults on Scripture, we focus upon those first few words: "All scripture is given by inspiration of God." Certainly that focus is thoroughly legitimate in that context. But we must not lose sight that it is actually part of a larger argument that Paul is making at this point about *the man of God.* He is picking up—deliberately it seems—on Old Testament prophetic language to identify Timothy as the man of God. And he goes on to do what? He describes the task of the man of God: "I charge thee therefore before God, and the Lord Jesus Christ.... Preach the word; be instant in season, out of season; reprove, rebuke, exhort with all longsuffering and doctrine." That is exactly what the prophets of the Old Testament did, now applied with prophetic language to Timothy in the New Testament.

There is, I think, justification for what I see was Luther's understanding of preaching as a prophetic task which brings the creative Word of God into the congregation Sunday by Sunday. You will have to trust me on that. But I think this passage is critical for understanding ministry in the New Testament.

Think of how that reshapes how one would think of the ministry. The ministry ceases to be social work; it ceases to be somebody who explains the Bible. I would say to students, "If you want the Bible explained, don't come and listen to me preach. Buy a commentary. Commentators know far more about the book of the Bible that I am preaching on than I do." You don't go to church primarily to have the Bible explained to you. Dr. Johnson was reputedly telling people in the eighteenth century, "Get a book; don't go to a lecture; it is a much better way of learning." You go to church to hear the Word of God proclaimed; to be rebuked, exhorted, reproved with all longsuffering and doctrine.

I would also point to the close connection Paul makes *between his ministry of preaching and the shape of his ministry as a whole,* in 1 and 2 Corinthians.

First, we say the cross determines the content of his ministry; second, the cross determines the form. And when Paul engages in those long defenses of the form of his ministry in 2 Corinthians, he is not engaging in self-justification. What he is saying to his critics is, "Those things you criticize about my ministry, the fact that you do criticize them shows you despise the cross of the Lord Jesus Christ— because there is an intimate connection between the form of my ministry and the content of my ministry."

Again I would use that as a way of indicating that people say preaching is weak today; it is foolishness. They said that in Paul's day about Paul's ministry, and it was somewhat essential to the nature of his ministry that that was the case.

We could push that to Luther's idea of the theologian of the cross. The contradiction of outward power—of what is outwardly plausible and that which is true—lies at the very heart of the cross for Luther, and therefore, at the very heart of the church's existence.

In 1539, Luther writes a great treatise on *The Councils and the Church* in which he gives seven marks of the church. The seventh mark is the cross. To summarize, he says, "Weakness and outward contradiction are an essential mark of the church relative to the wider culture."[13]

I had spoken on that recently, and a post-millennial friend was in the audience. He came up to me afterwards and said, "I appreciated what you had to say, with all the usual reservations." It made me laugh. But of course, for me, Luther gets it right. He gets Paul right. Outward contradiction is a fundamental part of what the church is to expect. And that means that the modes of the church's operation ought to be those that the world despises: the spoken word, and the sacraments. And yet they are powerful. Why? Because they are rooted in an understanding of God as a speaking God.

Conclusion

First, for Luther, *the importance of preaching and the centrality of the Word is rooted in his doctrine of God.* The question we need to ask ourselves is this: "Is Luther's doctrine of God as a speaking God a correct one?" If it is, then the case for the perennial importance of preaching becomes one that is easy to make. And for myself, his arguments about God as a speaking God are fundamentally sound.

Second, *Luther believes that preaching is important because of his understanding of the gospel.* If the gospel is primarily promise, then it has to be proclaimed. Promises have to be proclaimed. There is an ineradicably linguistic component to the nature of the promise.

Third, *Luther would find arguments ranged against the implausibility of preaching because it is a foolish medium in an era of high technology in an era very much preoccupied with aesthetics.* Luther would find those arguments less than compelling because he would see preaching as theologically grounded and he would see that our aesthetic

---

13. Luther, *Works*, 41:164–65.

sensibilities, such as they are, need to be shaped by the weakness of the cross, not the power of the surrounding culture.

Fourth, and this is a helpful way of thinking about preaching: *What is preaching? It is a redescription of reality in light of God's revelation of Himself in Christ crucified*—which challenges the era to accept the preacher's account; which—if he is faithful to Scripture—is God's account rather than the account of the world.

That is why I think preaching should have a sense of urgency to it. One of the striking things I find in certain Reformed traditions of preaching is the clinical manner in which preaching is conducted. The preacher seems to think that as long as he can trace every text to Christ the task is done. That does not seem to capture Paul's description of the task where he urges people to be reconciled. It is fascinating. He is speaking to Christians who are already reconciled and says, "I urge you to be reconciled." There is that powerful existential aspect that cannot be dispassionately delivered in the manner of a lecture. And that is because the theology that drives preaching should prevent that from happening.

We have students preaching in our church on occasion, and I say to them, "If it is not clear from the moment you open your mouth when you enter the pulpit that what you are about to say is the most important thing the people will hear that week, then you are not preaching. It has to be *that* clear, and *that* pungent—a message that is rooted in a doctrine of God—with an understanding of the ordained office of those who proclaim the Word.

CHAPTER 9

What William Perkins Teaches Us Today

Joel R. Beeke and Andrew Ballitch

As we commemorate the 500th anniversary of the Reformation at this conference, it is entirely appropriate that we consider England's William Perkins (1558–1602)—who served God's church as one of the last of the sixteenth century Reformers, as well as one of the fathers of seventeenth-century Puritanism.[1] Contemporary scholars have called Perkins "the principal architect of Elizabethan Puritanism," "the Puritan theologian of Tudor times," "the most important Puritan writer," "the prince of Puritan theologians," "the ideal Puritan clergyman of the quietist years," "the most famous of all Puritan divines," and the "father of Puritanism." They have classed Perkins with Calvin and Beza as third in "the trinity of the orthodox."[2] Perkins was more widely published in England than Calvin, and the first Protestant theologian to have a major impact in the British Isles, Europe at large, and North America. Many Puritan scholars marvel that Perkins's works have been largely unavailable in modern times until recently.[3]

---

1. J. I. Packer writes, "Puritanism was an evangelical holiness movement seeking to implement its vision of spiritual renewal, national and personal, in the church, the state, and the home; in education, evangelism, and economics; in individual discipleship and devotion, and in pastoral care and competence.... It was Perkins, quite specifically, who established Puritanism in this mould." J. I. Packer, *An Anglican to Remember—William Perkins: Puritan Popularizer*, St. Antholin's Lectureship Charity Lecture (London: St Antholin's Lectureship Charity, 1996), 1–2.

2. John Eusden, *Puritans, Lawyers, and Politics* (New Haven: Yale University Press, 1958), 11; Paul Seaver, *The Puritan Lectureships: The Politics of Religious Dissent, 1560–1662* (Palo Alto, Calif.: Stanford University Press, 1970), 114; Christopher Hill, *God's Englishman: Oliver Cromwell and the English Revolution* (New York: Harper and Row, 1970), 38; Packer, *An Anglican to Remember*, 1.

3. This paragraph is adapted from Joel R. Beeke, "William Perkins and His Greatest Case of Conscience," in Joel R. Beeke and Mark Jones, *A Puritan Theology: Doctrine*

In this chapter, we want to set before you a variety of ways in which Perkins still can teach us today by focusing on his life, systematic theology, pastoral-practical theology, and pulpit ministry. Let's pray that he, being dead, may yet speak to us (cf. Heb. 11:4).

PERKINS'S LIFE

1. Finding Comfort in the Sovereignty of God

Born in Warwickshire in 1558, little is known about his upbringing and family. His parents' names were Thomas and Hannah. He did not come from a great house or noble family, though the fact that he was able to enter Christ's College at Cambridge as a "pensioner," that is, as one able to pay the common expenses of his education, is a clue that he did not grow up in poverty. With such an ordinary background, Perkins was quite unremarkable when he entered Christ's College in 1577.[4]

During his early days as a student, in addition to dabbling in the study of astrology and other dark arts, Perkins frequently fell into public drunkenness. In fact, at one point, as he stumbled through the streets of Cambridge, he overheard a mother say to her misbehaving child, "Hold your tongue, or I will give you to drunken Perkins, yonder."[5] The Holy Spirit used this event to convict him of sin, which resulted in his conversion and the redirection of his attention and energy to the study of divinity. He graduated with his bachelor's degree in 1581 and his master's in 1584, at which point he was elected fellow at Christ's College and also appointed lecturer, or assistant curate,[6] at St. Andrews the Great, the church across the street from the college gates.

---

for Life (Grand Rapids: Reformation Heritage Books, 2012), 587. Cf. Louis Wright, "William Perkins: Elizabethan Apostle of 'Practical Divinitie,'" *Huntington Library Quarterly* 3 (1940): 171; George L. Mosse, *The Holy Pretence: A Study in Christianity and Reason of State from William Perkins to John Winthrop* (Oxford: Blackwell, 1957), 48.

4. Benjamin Brook, *The Lives of the Puritans: Containing a Biographical Account of Those Divines Who Distinguished Themselves in the Cause of Religious Liberty, from the Reformation under Queen Elizabeth, to the Act of Uniformity in 1662* (Pittsburgh: Soli Deo Gloria, 1994), 2:135.

5. Brook, *The Lives of the Puritans*, 2:129.

6. In other words, a junior member of the pastoral staff. His duties were many, including preaching; but he may have been dubbed lecturer because he read the prayers. It was an entry-level post.

From the platforms of pulpit, lectern, and writing desk, the Lord used Perkins to great effect. He was an apologist for the only recently reformed Church of England as it stabilized under Elizabeth I. As the father of Puritanism, he would exert significant influence in English non-conformity and later dissent. His impact was particularly potent in the areas of personal piety, preaching, and pastoral counseling. He gained international standing as a Reformed theologian with the publication of *A Golden Chaine* in 1590. While this work on the *ordo salutis* earned Perkins renown in his own day, it has made him unjustly infamous in ours. In it Perkins sets forth a conception of the triune God who is sovereign in the salvation of sinners, which he maintained throughout his life. It was this sovereign God in whom Perkins found comfort as he studied the Holy Scriptures during his conversion and subsequent ministry.

Still today, God's people learn to embrace His sovereignty with profound comfort and gratitude, realizing that were it not for this precious divine sovereignty they not only would never have been saved, but would, on the contrary, have rushed headlong into hell and everlasting destruction. Have you too learned to treasure the amazing wonder of the grace that sovereignly drew you from the horrible pit and miry clay of your own sin, set your feet on the gospel rock of Christ Jesus, and established your life in Him (cf. Ps. 40:2)? Can you testify that though you may once have despised the sovereignty of God as an infringement on your liberty as a free moral agent, now, having experienced His sovereign drawing power, it has become one of your favorite attributes of God?

2. Enduring Hardship and Ever Engaged in Ministry

In 1646, John Geree published a tract entitled *The Character of an Old English Puritan, or Non-Conformist*. Part of his definition of Puritanism is the motto "he who suffers [and endures] wins."[7] Perkins died in 1602, at the age of forty-four and was no stranger to suffering. He lost three of his seven children and never met his seventh, as his wife was pregnant when he passed away. He suffered with kidney stones throughout his entire adulthood, the last bout claiming his life after several excruciating weeks. As Perkins lay dying, a friend prayed for

---

7. John Geree, *The Character of an Old English Puritan, or Non-Conformist* (London: W. Wilson, 1646).

relief from suffering. Perkins embraced the brevity of life by crying out, "Hold, hold! Do not pray so; but pray the Lord to give me faith and patience, and then let him lay on me what he pleases."[8] The great man died in faith, supplicating the Lord for mercy and forgiveness. Yet despite a life marked by suffering and what we would call an untimely death, he proved incredibly productive as he embraced the possibilities of life by remaining engaged in ministry until the end.

Perkins believed that in order to die as a Christian should, one must prepare for death. Part of this preparation is a refusal to delay doing whatever good one has the power to do.[9] Perkins was not given to delay, but rather redeemed the time. He would write in all of his books, "Thou art a Minister of the Word: Mind thy business," revealing a man of intense focus on his calling.[10] During his eighteen-year tenure as preacher at St. Andrews, Perkins delivered six major expositional sermon series: Matthew 5–7, Matthew 4, Revelation 1–3, Hebrews 11, Jude, and Galatians 1–5, likely in this order. At the same time, he held his teaching post at Christ's College until 1595, the year he married. He wrote more than a dozen works on the Christian life and pastoral ministry. He wrote many doctrinal works as well, including a catechism, expositions of the Lord's Prayer and the Apostles' Creed, and two treatises on predestination in addition to *A Golden Chaine*. He also authored polemical works against witchcraft, astrology, and the Church of Rome.

Perkins was relentless in both his writing and preaching ministry, even in the face of suffering and early death. Beyond this, he faithfully balanced life and ministry. He did not have the luxury of devoting his time entirely to writing and delivering sermons. He also had students to care for and administrative responsibilities, having served as dean for several years. Marrying, he had to resign his fellowship at Cambridge, thus replacing those duties with the care of his wife and their numerous children. All the while he shouldered the time-consuming demands of pastoral ministry. The sovereign God who saved Perkins was the same sovereign God who empowered, sustained, and used him.

---

8. Brook, *The Lives of the Puritans*, 2:133.

9. William Perkins, *The Whole Works of That Famous and Worthy Minister of Christ in the Universitie of Cambridge, M. William Perkins* (London: John Legatt, 1631), 1:476.

10. Brook, *The Lives of the Puritans*, 2:131.

The study of historical figures such as Perkins who were sovereignly plucked from their debauchery as brands from the burning and then sovereignly used mightily by God for His glory and the good of many others, ought to move us to appreciate every detail of God's fatherly and gracious sovereignty in our own lives, moving us to pray that He would use us richly for His glory. Knowing that life is short, let us do all we can to serve God while we may. Knowing that in this life we shall have tribulation, let us glory in suffering and endure to the end, trusting in Christ and calling on God. Let Perkins's life teach you to pray every morning: "Lord, in this short life, make me useful and fruitful today; give me a single eye, Thy name to glorify—today!"

3. Balancing Unity and Controversy

Perkins had a clear view of what was of primary importance and what was secondary. When souls hung in the balance, Perkins was quick to refute error and at times did so vehemently.

An example of this is his magisterial apologetic piece, *A Reformed Catholike*. During Perkins's career, England's Protestantism was not entirely settled. The country had flip-flopped between Roman Catholic and Protestant monarchs over the course of the previous decades and the populace had not entirely given up Roman superstitions. There were also external threats, including political enemies in league with the Church of Rome and an influx of Jesuit missionaries working as undercover agents to undo the Reformation. Perkins saw the Church of Rome as teaching another religion, one as different from true Christianity as darkness is from light. The future of his beloved country remained uncertain in his estimation. So he took up his pen in an attempt to show the differences in substance between the two religions, in the hope of winning over those yet loyal to the Roman Church, and educating his countrymen. Perkins also wielded his pen against errors regarding God and salvation in the divisive Cambridge predestination controversy of the 1590s.

There is some debate over Perkins's relationship to Puritanism and therefore by definition his posture toward the Church of England. On the one hand, the content of his teaching and writing is clearly Puritan-minded throughout. On the other hand, he remained strongly devoted to the Church of England, living peaceably in it to the extent his conscience would allow as did many of the Puritans. In fact, most of them remained in the national church until ejected from it.

This debate centers to a significant degree on the interpretation of Perkins's two appearances before the authorities to be questioned on his alleged non-conformity. The first episode unfolded in 1587, when a sermon Perkins preached in the college chapel provoked a threefold complaint. He was reported to have taught that it was a corruption for a minister to give himself the elements of the Lord's Supper, that kneeling to receive the sacrament was superstitious and antichristian, and that facing "liturgical east" (i.e., in the direction of the altar in the chancel) at particular points in the worship service was objectionable. Perkins defended himself before the vice-chancellor and the heads of the colleges. He explained his reservations about such practices, but denied the harsh language attributed to him. No penalty was imposed and no other complaints are recorded.

In 1591, Perkins found himself summoned before the Star Chamber as a witness against the Presbyterians, Thomas Cartwright and Edmund Snape. Several years prior, all three of the men attended a meeting at St. John's College to discuss the national church's Book of Discipline. Perkins confirmed this and was then released.[11] This much is clear, Perkins never openly allied himself with the Elizabethan Presbyterians and had no toleration for separatism. His agenda was reform of the church from within.[12]

Perkins was valiant for truth when it came to doctrine and holiness, but seems to have lived peaceably within the Church of England. There is little evidence to suggest him chafing under the external requirements of the Book of Common Prayer.

In balancing unity and controversy, Perkins teaches us two important lessons today: first, we ought never to abandon the visible church lightly or easily. Second, wherever we choose to draw the line on various doctrines and issues, there should be a clear line between essential and non-essential matters, between those things worth fighting for and those that ought to be tolerated and lived

---

11. W. B. Patterson, *William Perkins and the Making of Protestant England* (Oxford: Oxford University Press, 2014), 46–48.

12. Joel R. Beeke and J. Stephen Yuille, *William Perkins*, Bitesize Biographies (Welwyn Garden City, England: EP Books, 2015), 58.

with. Perkins is a notable example of striving to find such a line in Scripture and acting accordingly.

PERKINS'S SYSTEMATIC THEOLOGY

4. Bowing Under and Rejoicing in the Authority of the Word

There is no doubt that Perkins believed that all Scripture is the inerrant Word of God, and, therefore, he built his entire life and ministry upon it. The Bible does not become the Word of God through the Spirit's work, or merely contain the Word of God. It is by nature the Word of God as a result of the Spirit's inspiration.[13] In his exposition of the Apostles' Creed, Perkins affirms that

> Divine, are the books of the old and new Testament, penned either by Prophets or Apostles. And these are not onely the pure *word of God*, but also the *scripture of God*: because not onely the matter of them; but the whole disposition thereof, with the style and phrase was set downe by the immediate inspiration of the holy Ghost.[14]

So what is "immediate inspiration"? Perkins defines it this way in his preaching manual: "the word of God written in a language fit for the Church by men immediately called to be *Clerkes*, or *Secretaries* of the holy Ghost."[15] While this verbal plenary conception of inspiration implies inerrancy, Perkins makes his stance explicit.[16] In his own words, Scripture "remaineth entire in it selfe, voide of deceit and errour."[17]

---

13. Paul M. Smalley, introduction to *The Works of William Perkins, Volume 2* (Grand Rapids: Reformation Heritage Books, 2015), x–xiv. Contra the neo-orthodox interpretation of John Augustine ("Authority and Interpretation in Perkins' Commentary on Galatians," in *A Commentary on Galatians*, by William Perkins, ed. Gerald T. Sheppard [New York: Pilgrim Press, 1989], xl).

14. Perkins, *Works*, 1:122. Emphasis in original.

15. Perkins, *Works*, 2:647. Emphasis in original. Perkins cites 2 Peter 1:21 as support. This contradicts the Barthian interpretation of Perkins. John H. Augustine, "Authority and Interpretation in Perkins' Commentary on Galatians," in *A Commentary on Galatians*, ed. Gerald T. Sheppard, by William Perkins, Pilgrim Classic Commentaries (New York: Pilgrim Press, 1989).

16. Contra Jack Rogers (*Scripture in the Westminster Confession* [Grand Rapids: Eerdmans, 1967], 416).

17. Perkins, *Works*, 2:646. Psalm 12:6 is Perkins's biblical support. This contradicts the anti-inerrancy thesis of Jack Rogers and Donald K. McKim, *The Authority and Interpretation of the Bible: An Historical Approach* (San Francisco: Harper & Row, 1979).

But the purity of Scripture is not the only thing that its nature as the Word of God guarantees. As God's written Word, the Bible is ultimately authoritative for Christians and effectual for accomplishing God's purposes. Perkins summarizes his conviction that the sixty-six books of canonical Scripture are both the source and the norm of theological discourse, by writing:

> The authoritie of these books is *divine*, that is, absolute and soveraigne: and they are of sufficient credit in and by themselves, needing not the testimony of any creature; not subject to the censure either of men or Angels; binding the consciences of all men at all times, and being the onely foundation of our faith, and the rule and canon of all truth.[18]

Thus, Scripture is the final authority in all matters of faith and practice. It reveals what God's human creatures are to believe, how they are to behave, and those things in which they are to rejoice. It speaks to every area of human life: the personal and private, the family and society at large. Scripture regulates the worship of God and is to be appealed to as the final arbitrator of disputes in the church.

Further, God's Word is effectual. As the Spirit sovereignly wills, preaching the Word results in conversion and applying the Word consoles the conscience. For Perkins, his comfort and joy were found in believing that all Scripture is breathed out by God and therefore is inerrant, effectual, and above all, authoritative for all of faith and life. This core conviction was foundational to his life and ministry.

Perkins teaches us today to bow under the supreme authority of Holy Scripture. The Word of God must be supreme for our faith and life, our beliefs and theology, our ethics and daily behavior, our worship and the way we approach God, and our fellowship and emotional life. Its authority and sufficiency covers everything. We must be persuaded that the Bible has the authoritative power to bring life from the dead, to transform our lives, to resist Satan, and to deal with suffering and death. This authoritative book scrutinizes our lives, challenges us, encourages us, and helps us to believe the truth.

Through Scripture's authoritative and sufficient content we find love, peace, contentment, and deliverance from despair. And yes, we find joy and happiness—in its teaching, its reliability, its authority,

---

18. Perkins, *Works*, 1:122. Emphasis in original.

its clarity, its sufficiency, its grace, its cleansing, its power, its guidance, its correction, its warnings, its promises, its suitability, its unity, its hope, its songs, its balance, its worldview, its freshness, and its thanksgiving. We find joy in its realism, its idealism, its optimism, and its predictions concerning the future.

There is no "silver bullet" secret to living the happy Christian life. Perkins would simply say to us: know your Bible—honor its authority with your faith and submission. Sit at the feet of its supreme author, the Holy Spirit, and let Him teach you and lead you to the Wonderful Counsellor, Jesus Christ, and then go out and do as the Bible directs and commands; be doers of the Word and not hearers only. Let the Bible control your entire life—and by the Spirit's grace, you will experience true happiness as the by-product of such believing and obedient thinking, speaking, and doing.

5. Experiencing the Piety of Predestination

Though predestination was not the center or governing structure of Perkins's theology (Christ as set forth in the Apostles' Creed was), he strongly emphasized predestination as the decretal basis of all salvation and sanctification. However, this did not stunt his emphasis on godliness, but enlightened it with a God-centered piety. Predestination was not mere orthodox theology for him or for the Puritans. It was essential to the gospel and to godliness.[19]

Primarily concerned with the conversion of souls to God and their subsequent growth in holiness, Perkins believed that a biblical experience of God's sovereign grace in predestination was vital for spiritual comfort and assurance. He believed that salvation worked out experientially in the souls of believers through God's covenanting mercies was inseparable from sovereign predestination in Christ. Far from being harsh and cold, sovereign predestination was the foundation upon which experiential faith could be built.[20] It offered solid hope to the true believer.

---

19. Dewey D. Wallace, Jr., *Puritans and Predestination: Grace in English Protestant Theology, 1525–1695* (Chapel Hill: University of North Carolina Press, 1982), 43–44.

20. Experimental or experiential preaching addresses how a Christian experiences the truth of scriptural doctrine in his life. The term *experimental* comes from *experimentum*, meaning trial, and is derived from the verb *experior*, to know by experience, which in turn leads to "experiential," meaning knowledge gained by experiment. Calvin used the Latin equivalents of experimental and experiential

Perkins's predestinarian theology did not make him cold and heartless when dealing with sinners and saints in need of a Savior. Rather, his warm, biblical theology set the tone for the stream of Puritan "practical divinity" literature that would pour forth from the presses in the seventeenth century. It inspired generations of preachers to call men to turn from sin to a loving Savior, and to follow Him through trials to glory.

We should learn from Perkins that predestination is not the enemy of sinners but their friend. Without divine election, there would be no hope for anyone, for we are all sinners. Because of election, repentant sinners are always welcome with God. There is not a single verse in all the Bible that tells us that we will not be welcomed by God if we cast ourselves with all our sins at His feet and put all our trust in His Son. The last invitation of the Bible says, "Whosoever will, let him take the water of life freely" (Rev. 22:17). We must not let the doctrine election rob us of comfort; rather we must let it do its God-appointed work and put solid ground under all our faith and hope as Christians.

As Perkins stressed, we must also let this doctrine of election humble our pride and magnify God's grace and glory, for it shows us that we can do nothing to save ourselves—God alone saves sinners. Election comforts and sustains us with God's unchangeable love for us when Satan attacks us with doubts and accusations. It grants us a vibrant vision of God's special love to us in Christ Jesus which fills us with joy, fueling our reverence and love for Him and moving us to diligent holiness of life.

6. Growing in the Centrality of Christ

The closest Perkins ever came to writing a systematic theology was his 1595 *An Exposition of the Symbole or Creed of the Apostles.* Of

---

interchangeably, since both words indicate the need for measuring experienced knowledge against the touchstone of Scripture. Experimental preaching seeks to explain in terms of biblical truth how matters ought to go, how they do go, and what the goal of the Christian life is. It aims to apply divine truth to the whole range of the believer's personal experience as well as to his relationships with family, the church, and the world around him. Cf. Robert T. Kendall, *Calvin and English Calvinism to 1649* (New York: Oxford University Press, 1979), 8–9; Joel R. Beeke, "The Lasting Power of Reformed Experiential Preaching," in *Feed My Sheep: A Passionate Plea for Preaching,* ed. Don Kistler (Morgan, Pa.: Soli Deo Gloria, 2002), 94–128.

course, while the Creed is structured along Trinitarian lines, almost two-thirds of it focuses on Christ, and it is here that Perkins devotes the largest attention. After articulating a classically orthodox conception of the person and natures of Christ, Perkins dedicates over one-third of the entirety of his work to walking through the passion narratives of the four Gospels. Christ's priestly work of atonement is precisely what gave Him the preeminent place in Perkins's theology.

For Perkins, election centers upon and is grounded in Christ. Salvation is never made to depend on a bare decree, but always upon the decreed and decreeing Christ. The election and work of Christ is both chosen by God in His decree and by the Son's willingness to always do the will of His Father. Christ is the foundation, means, and end of election. He writes:

> Election is God's decree whereby of his own free will he hath ordained certain men to salvation, to the praise of the glory of his grace.... There appertain three things to the execution of this decree: first the foundation, secondly the means, thirdly the degrees. The foundation is Christ Jesus, called of his Father from all eternity to perform the office of the Mediator, that in him all those which should be saved might be chosen.

> Q. How can Christ be subordinate unto God's election seeing he together with the Father decreed all things?

> A. Christ as he is Mediator is not subordinate to the very decree itself of election, but to the execution thereof only.[21]

Election includes the means of its execution in the work of Christ and of His Spirit. Without Christ, man is totally hopeless. Christ is the foundation of election, as the center column of Perkins's chart in *A Golden Chaine* shows. He is predestined to be Mediator. He is promised to the elect. He is offered by grace to the elect. And, finally, He is personally applied to their souls in all His benefits, natures, offices, and states.[22]

In Perkins's estimation, all Scripture points to Christ. In *How to Live Well*, he asserts, "The scope of the whole Bible is Christ with his benefits, and he is revealed, propounded, and offered unto us in

21. *The Work of William Perkins*, ed. Ian Breward, Courtenay Library of Reformation Classics 3 (Abingdon: Sutton Courtenay Press, 1970), 197–98.
22. Cf. Perkins, *Works*, 2:608.

the maine promise of the word: the tenour whereof is, that God will give remission of sinnes and life everlasting to such as will believe in Christ."[23] In *The Arte of Prophesying*, Perkins summarizes the whole witness of canonical Scripture in syllogistic form:

> (a) The true Messias shall be both God and man of the seede of David; he shall be borne of a Virgin; he shall bring the Gospel forth of his Fathers bosome; he shall satisfie the Law; he shall offer up himselfe a sacrifice for the sins of the faithfull; he shall conquer death by dying and rising againe; he shall ascend into heaven; and in his due time he shall return unto judgement. But (b) Jesus of Nazareth the Son of Mary is such a one: He (c) therefore is the true Messias.[24]

Here the major premise summarizes the writings of the Old Testament and the minor, those of the New. The conclusion of the witness of Scripture is this: Jesus is the Christ, the Savior of sinners.

With Christ as the center-piece of theology and the focus of Scripture, it is not surprising that for Perkins, Christ ought to permeate practical theology as well. The primary subject of preaching should be Christ, and "repent and believe" a regular application. The foundational ground of assurance must be the promises of God in Christ. The example of Christ ought to inform the Christian life. The rule of Christ should be adhered to in the church. The gospel of Christ must be the distinguishing factor between true and false religion.

Let Perkins be a faithful guide to those of you who desire to give Christ the primacy that He deserves in your theology, life, and ministry. Delve deeply into writers like Perkins who will help you come to Paul's experiential comfort: "For me to live is Christ" (Phil. 1:21), and "Christ is all in all" (Col. 3:11).

PERKINS'S PASTORAL AND PRACTICAL THEOLOGY

7. Needing the Pastor as Counselor
In the sixteenth and seventeenth centuries, pastoral counseling largely took the form of casuistry, or case divinity, where Scripture is applied to specific and concrete "cases," that is, questions of

---

23. Perkins, *Works*, 1:484.
24. Perkins, *Works*, 2:647.

conscience or duty. Roman Catholics long dominated in this field, but Perkins was an early Protestant proponent. In fact, he provided the "first extensive treatment of the subject by any Protestant in England" and "showed boldness and originality in writing about matters of conscience in his time."[25] His influence extended well into the seventeenth century through students at Cambridge, such as William Ames, John Downame, and Joseph Hall.[26]

Two theological motivations pushed Perkins and others to apply Scripture to the specifics of daily life. First, the Reformed doctrine of the "third use" of the Law compels those within the tradition to mine the Old Testament for direction in the Christian life. The Law not only serves as a mirror to reveal sin, its first use, and as a restraint of evil for those outside the kingdom, its second use; it also reveals how Christians are to live. As a "rule of life" the Scriptures teach "what duty God requires of man" (Westminster Shorter Catechism, Q. 3). A second theological motivation was the sufficiency of Scripture. Immediately following the famed declaration in 2 Timothy 3:16 about the inspiration and fourfold profitability of Scripture, verse 17 states, "that the man of God may be perfect, thoroughly furnished unto all good works" (2 Tim. 3:17). In Scripture we find everything needed to live a life of obedience to God. But "sufficient" does not mean *exhaustive*. Cases of conscience involve matters not specifically addressed in Scripture; and such cases must be addressed by diligently comparing Scripture with Scripture, endeavoring to apply the general teaching of the Word to the specific case in hand.

If the theological motivators were not enough, men like Perkins also experienced the acute demands of pastoral ministry. In the Puritan mind, the pastor was never less than a preacher, but he was certainly more. Part of the pastor's role as shepherd was visitation and counseling, guiding those under his care to lead lives pleasing to God, with consciences clear before Him. To help equip pastors for this work, Perkins wrote *The Whole Treatise of the Cases of Conscience*. The editor, Thomas Pickering, notes that Perkins's work accomplished its purpose because "his grounds and principles are drawn either directly, or by just consequence out of the written

---

25. Patterson, *William Perkins and the Making of a Protestant England*, 92.
26. Patterson, *William Perkins and the Making of a Protestant England*, 111.

word."[27] What are some of the questions Perkins answers? Here are a few: What is the difference between a troubled conscience and melancholy or depression? At what point can a Christian in good conscience flee persecution? When can a man defend himself with the force of physical violence? What kinds of recreation are appropriate? Such were the perennial, practical questions that Perkins sought to answer from the pages of Scripture, many of which need answering again and again as pastoral contexts change.

Let us learn from Perkins that the church should still seek advice from her pastors on cases of conscience, and pastors ought to formulate their answers, as did Perkins, from Scripture. Let pastors learn their need for intimate knowledge of Scripture and for good listening skills and love for their people, so that they may patiently bear with them and provide good counsel.

8. Knowing the Greatest Case of Conscience

Perkins's writing on assurance of faith set the agenda for the seventeenth century and for chapter 18 of the Westminster Confession of Faith. He wrote several books in the late 1580s and 1590s that explain how one may know he is saved: *A Golden Chaine: Or, The Description of Theologie: Containing the Order of the Causes of Salvation and Damnation;*[28] *A Treatise Tending unto a Declaration, Whether a Man be in the Estate of Damnation or in the Estate of Grace;*[29] *A Case of Conscience, the Greatest that ever was: how a man may know whether he be the childe of God or no;*[30] *A Discourse of Conscience: Where is set down the nature, properties, and differences thereof: as also the way to get and keepe a good Conscience;*[31] and *A Graine of Musterd-seede: Or, the Least Measure of Grace that is or can be effectuall to salvation.*[32]

Through his prolific writings, Perkins taught people how to search their consciences for even the least evidence of election based on Christ's saving work. Perkins viewed such efforts as part of the pastor's fundamental task to keep "balance in the sanctuary"

---

27. Perkins, *Works*, 2: No page number. The quote comes from Pickering's dedicatory epistle to *The Whole Treatise of The Cases of Conscience*.

28. Perkins, *Works*, 1:9–116.

29. Perkins, *Works*, 1:353–420.

30. Perkins, *Works*, 1:421–28.

31. Perkins, *Works*, 1:515–54.

32. Perkins, *Works*, 1:627–34.

between divine sovereignty and human responsibility.[33] Sinners had to be shown how God's immovable will moved the will of man and how to look for evidences of election and inclusion in God's covenant. They also had to be taught how to make their election sure by living as the elect of God.

Perkins proposed three grounds of assurance: the promises of the gospel, which are contained in God's covenant and are confirmed or ratified by the shedding of Christ's blood as the blood of the covenant; the testimony of the Holy Spirit witnessing with our spirit that we are the children of God; and the fruits of sanctification. These three interconnected grounds, all of which depend on the illuminating and applying ministry of the Holy Spirit, are so important that Perkins called them "the hinge upon which the gate of heaven turns."[34] The believer ought always to strive to grow in assurance by seeking as large a degree of assurance as possible from all three of these grounds or means.

The promises of God are always the primary ground of assurance. When embraced by faith, the promises of God produce the fruits of sanctification and often are combined with the witness or testimony of the Spirit. The believer may have difficulty at times realizing one or more of these grounds in his own experience. That is particularly true of the testimony of the Spirit. Yet that ought not to distress the believer, Perkins says, because even when the Spirit's testimony is not felt deeply enough to persuade the believer of his election, the effects of the Spirit's work will be demonstrated in sanctification.

In his writings, Perkins lists various marks or works of sanctification that the believer, in dependency on the Spirit, can use to grow his assurance. Here is one such list:

> I. To feele our wants, & in the bitternesse of heart to bewaile the offense of GOD in euery sinne. II. To striue against the flesh, that is, to resist, and to hate the vngodly motions thereof, and with griefe to thinke them burthenous [burdensome] & troublesome. III. To desire earnestly and vehemently the grace of GOD, and merit of Christ to obtaine eternall life. IV. When it is obtained, to account it a most precious iewell [jewel]. Phil. 3.8. V. To loue the minister of Gods word, in that he is a minister, & a Christian, in

---

33. Irvonwy Morgan, *Puritan Spirituality* (London: Epworth Press, 1973), ch. 2.
34. Perkins, *Galatians*, 278.

that he is a Christian: and for that cause, if neede require, to be ready to spend our blood with them. Matth. 10.42. 1 Joh. 3.16. V. To cal vpon GOD earnestly, and with teares. VII. To desire and loue Christs coming and the day of iudgement, that an end may be made of the daies of sinne. VIII. To flie all occasions of sinne, and seriously to endeauvor to come to newnesse of life. IX. To perseuere in these things to the last gaspe of life.[35]

Perkins taught that if a believer has, even to a small degree, experienced some of these marks of grace, he can be assured that he is being sanctified by the Spirit of God. All of these marks are alien or "unnatural" to those who are dead in trespasses and sins. In turn, since the entire golden chain of salvation—election, vocation (effectual calling), faith, justification, sanctification, and eternal glorification, etc.—are "inseparable companions," the believer "may infallibly conclude in his owne heart, that he hath, and shall have interest in all the other in his due time."[36]

Perkins was keenly aware of the need to set all marks of grace in a Trinitarian framework so that they did not result in a man-centered religion. In commenting on 1 John 4:7, Perkins wrote that believers know God "by a speciall knowledge, whereby they are assured that God the father of Christ is their father: Christ their Redeemer: the holy Ghost their sanctifier."[37] All assurance is Christological. It is based on Christ's merits (commenting on 1 John 2:12), received by faith in Him (on 1 John 5:4), and patterned after Him (on 1 John 3:3).[38] It depends on Christ's anointing with the Spirit, in which all believers share. Perkins viewed the ointment John refers to in 1 John 2:20, 27 as the grace of God's Holy Spirit that we receive from Christ, which is the fulfilment of the anointings with holy oil in the Old Testament.[39] In sum, the believer may be assured of his adoption by God the Father by discerning the marks of saving grace in his heart and life as they flow out of Christ and are produced in him by the Holy Spirit.

---

35. Perkins, *Works*, 1:113.

36. Thomas F. Merrill, ed., *William Perkins, 1558–1602, English Puritanist—His Pioneer Works on Casuistry: "A Discourse of Conscience" and "the Whole Treatise of Cases of Conscience"* (Nieuwkoop: B. DeGraaf, 1966), 111–12.

37. Perkins, *Works*, 1:427.

38. Perkins, *Works*, 1:423, 427, 425.

39. Perkins, *Works*, 1:424, 425.

From Perkins, we need to learn that it still is critical today that you strive to make your calling and election sure. Strive to get as much assurance as you can, with the Spirit's enlightening grace, from the promises of God, the testimony of the Holy Spirit, and the marks of saving, sanctifying grace.

9. Encountering Cultural Blind Spots

Perkins was a wise and godly man, yet he was a man of his times and therefore susceptible to being uncritical of his cultural perspective. This is apparent in several places, one being Perkins's approval of the death penalty for witchcraft. While it is true that Perkins condemned the excesses of witch trials in general and their superstitions in particular, he still clearly saw execution as the proper punishment for a witch. The offense warranted death, not only because of the harm it caused to others, but because the witch had bound him or herself to the enemy of God and His church. To be an enemy of the national church was to be an enemy of the state as well; and so gross sins should be punished as crimes.[40]

Related to capital punishment for religious crimes is the blind spot of a coterminous church and society. The magisterial Reformers, the tradition which includes Perkins, were seemingly unable to move past the medieval ideal of Christendom, or Christian geo-political entities. Perkins had no conception of religious liberty. The nearest thing for him would be perhaps an uneasy toleration of other religions such as Judaism. To be a citizen of the English commonwealth, vested with all the rights and privileges of citizenship, one had to be a communicant member of the Church of England. Non-conformity or separation was anathema.

While Perkins certainly had cultural blind spots, so do many Christians in the twenty-first century. Part of the value of studying a historical figure like Perkins is the opportunity it affords to reflect on our own conformity to the world around us, and our own uncritical appropriation of the culture we live in. For instance, Perkins believed that Scripture regulates worship, that God has not left mankind free to speculate or innovate about the form or content of public worship. For a very long time afterwards, Reformed Christians believed that

---

40. Perkins, *Works*, 3:639. *A Discourse of the Damned Art of Witchcraft* is Perkins's polemic against witchcraft and sorcery, framed by exegesis of Exodus 22:18.

we must worship God in no other way than He has commanded in His Word (Heidelberg Catechism, Q. 96). To do otherwise is sin against the Second Commandment. How many churches today have traded this conviction for a pragmatic approach? Rather than asking "What does the Bible say?" the questions often are: "What will draw people and keep them? What makes the most people happy?" Or worse yet, "What will give us the greatest scope to show our creativity and use our artistic talents?" Unsurprisingly, the answers to these questions are in stark contrast to one another.

Another example is the area of entertainment and recreation. Perkins actually raises questions about the amount and kinds of recreation permitted by Scripture. He demonstrates biblical intentionality even in the realm of pastimes. How strikingly different this is from what is asked today, if a question is raised at all, "Is it intrinsically wrong?" Perkins's blind spots should challenge us to check for our own blind spots today.

PERKINS'S PULPIT MINISTRY

10. Engaging in the Plainness of Powerful Exposition

Though Perkins is best known today for his theological treatises, his preaching made him popular during his lifetime, while his printed expositional works extended the influence of his pulpit ministry into the seventeenth century and beyond. In Perkins's mind, preaching the Word was the primary means of grace. The Holy Spirit works faith and regeneration through the proclamation of the gospel. Preaching the Word of God remedied the problems of unbelief, ignorance, superstition, and immorality; problems that plagued sixteenth-century England. The Word of God is the only substance or content of preaching;[41] the preacher's task was to proclaim, explain, and apply God's Word for salvation and sanctification. Given the nature and authority of the Word, preaching, not surprisingly, is God's chosen means for building His church. It is the epicenter of every Christian's faith, worship, and piety. In the preface to his preaching manual, *The Arte of Prophesying*, Perkins states that preaching serves a twofold purpose, "one, in that it serveth to collect [gather] the Church, and to

---

41. Perkins, *Works*, 2:646.

accomplish the number of the Elect; the other, for that it driveth away the Woolves from the fields of the Lord," for it is the means "whereby mens froward mindes are mitigated and moved from an ungodly and barbarous life, unto Christian faith and repentance." Preaching is efficacious because it aims at the mind through rationality, the conscience through addressing specific sins, and the heart through passionate and zealous pleading.[42]

Perkins modeled plain-style Puritan preaching. The method was threefold: interpretation of a given text, drawing out its doctrines, then elaborating or explaining them, and applying them to the hearers, also referred to as the "doctrine-use formula." What made the preaching plain was not any lack of insight, power, passion, or zeal, but rather may be summed up in Perkins's two requirements for the preparation and delivery of sermons: hiding human wisdom and demonstrating the Spirit. In preaching, the preacher ought to avail himself of every resource at his disposal, but should not bring it all with him into the pulpit. The technicalities of scholarly exegesis or dogmatics should be left out. Only errors that presently threaten the church to which one is preaching should be corrected. Only the most important or most useful doctrines found in the text should be propounded in a single sermon. Only human testimonies that are really helpful to convince the conscience should be cited.[43] In short, "the goal was to teach, not to dazzle."[44] Demonstration of the Spirit manifested itself in the graciousness of the preacher, his purity of heart and motivation, and holiness in his life.[45] Such humble and Spirit-filled preaching stood in marked contrast to "purple prose" of the richly ornamented, intricately rhetorical displays of learning celebrated widely by the non-Puritan-minded clergy of Perkins's day.

Preaching is still the primary means of grace today. It has been from the early church, to the Reformation, and will continue to be the divinely ordained "staff" to gather God's sheep and drive away wolves. Here Perkins's plain style method of preaching is gold for us. If we aim to impress, our hearers will not be impressed with God.

---

42. Joel R. Beeke and Mark Jones, *A Puritan Theology: Doctrine for Life* (Grand Rapids: Reformation Heritage Books, 2012), 682–85.

43. Perkins, *Works*, 2:664–71.

44. Beeke and Jones, *A Puritan Theology*, 689.

45. Perkins, *Works*, 2:670.

If our goal is to build up our reputations, God will be robbed of His glory. Essential to holiness of heart is the earnest desire that people become disciples of Jesus, not fans of the preacher. If Scripture is the Word of God, it needs no help from us to do its appointed work in our hearers. It need only be faithfully expounded and diligently applied.

11. Employing a Faithful Hermeneutic

Perkins based his entire writing and preaching ministry on a particular approach to biblical interpretation. When he came to a passage of Scripture, his aim was to find the natural sense. In his comments on Galatians 4:24 he said,

> that there is but one full and intire sense in every place of Scripture, and that is also the literall sense, sometimes expressed in proper, and sometimes in borrowed or figurative speeches. To make many senses of Scripture is to overturne all sense, and to make nothing certaine. As for the three spiritual senses (so called) they are not senses, but applications or uses of Scripture.[46]

The "many senses" here referenced are the three spiritual senses of the medieval *quadriga* or "fourfold sense" of Scripture: literal, allegorical, tropological, and anagogical. But while Perkins dismisses the medieval interpretive scheme, he also recognizes that the text, at times, demands a figurative reading. Woodenly literal interpretations are not always the natural sense, and in certain places there are multiple referents in the single natural sense. For example, when Paul uses Abraham's family as an allegory in Galatians 4, Perkins claims there "are not two senses, but two parts of one full and intire sense. For not only the bare history, but also that which is thereby signified, is the full sense of the holy Ghost."[47] In short, interpretation arrives at the natural sense of the words of Scripture, the words breathed out by God and addressed to the church throughout the ages. Thus prophecy and general application are folded into the natural sense.

Perkins maintained a three-step process in achieving his goal of determining the natural sense or meaning of Scripture. His three tools were the "analogy of faith" or better, the analogy of Scripture as a whole, due regard for the text in its context, and the need for

---

46. Perkins, *Works*, 2:298.
47. Perkins, *Works*, 2:298.

collation, or placing this text alongside others. Here are some definitions. First, "the *Analogy* of faith is a certaine *abridgement* or *summe* of the Scriptures, collected out of the most manifest and familiar places."[48] The analogy of faith is a collection of the clear loci of Scripture, a kind of systematic theology by which the interpreter weighs and interprets each part of Scripture. Second, regard for context means to consider the circumstances of the text under investigation. It includes answers to the questions, "Who? To whom? Upon what occasion? At what time? In what place? For what end? What goeth before? What followeth?"[49] These questions drive the interpreter to study the grammar and usage of the writer, and the literary and historical contexts in which he writes. Third, collation is comparison of one particular text with other passages found throughout the canon, which of course finds its warrant in divine inspiration.

The order we have just followed—analogy of faith, context, collation—is significant. The analogy of faith limits the interpretive options. For instance, on a first pass, one might conclude that James teaches works-righteousness; however, it is clear from the overall witness of Scripture that justification is by faith alone. Thus, the initial conclusion is not the true meaning of James. Study of context is essential to exegesis. Here grammatical, rhetorical, historical, and literary analysis is brought to bear on the text. The meaning of the words is determined by their surroundings. Collation then brings in other passages of Scripture to verify, amplify, or qualify a given interpretation.

Perkins is thus teaching us to use Scripture to interpret Scripture, which must be our goal. In the midst of today's hermeneutical chaos, Perkins throws a rope to drowning men! From those who disallow all Christological interpretation of the Old Testament to those who only ask, "What does this verse mean to you?" and from those who restrict all meaning to the human author's intent to those who disregard that intention as inaccessible, countless voices extrinsic to the Word of God compete for our ear. Perkins's words, faithful to the Reformed tradition, ring with refreshing sanity today: "the principall Interpreter of Scripture, is the holy Ghost," who, after all, is the

---

48. Perkins, *Works*, 2:651–52. Emphasis in the original.
49. Perkins, *Works*, 2:652.

author, and "the supreme and absolute meanes of interpretation, is the Scripture it selfe."[50]

12. Exercising the Wisdom of Continual Application

An integral part of the Puritan plain-style preaching method was application of the text to the hearers. In fact, the act of preaching was considered incomplete without it. Perkins served as a model in this regard. Perkins's preaching, and often his writing, was a continual exercise of applying the doctrines of Scripture to his hearers in particular "uses," according to their various states and needs. This method is observable even in many of his theological treatises and polemical works. In the context of sermon preparation, Perkins articulates his thoughts on the subject of application.

The Arte of Prophesying identifies the third main phase of preaching, following the drawing out of doctrines from a faithfully interpreted text by applying them in specific ways or "uses." Application is to be pointed and specific to one's hearers. Perkins approaches this task with three overlapping spheres of consideration. First, consider the text. Is it law or gospel or both? Law and gospel operate differently. Law reveals sin and stirs it up. Gospel offers grace in Christ. Law passages point out sin, whereas gospel passages teach what, by grace, is to be believed or done, as a remedy for sin.

Second, consider the audience. Perkins enumerates seven spiritual conditions or categories of hearers: (1) ignorant and unteachable unbelievers, (2) ignorant but teachable unbelievers, (3) knowledgeable but unhumbled unbelievers, (4) already humbled unbelievers, (5) believers, (6) backsliders, and (7) churches with a mix of believers and unbelievers or people who belong to more than one category above.[51] These possible conditions of one's hearers correspond to seven ways of applying a passage. Over a period of time, the preacher must be sure he is applying God's truth to all seven of these spiritual conditions.

Third, consider 2 Timothy 3:16. Here Perkins sees four varieties of application, to which end all Scripture proves profitable. Teaching and reproof are mental categories of application. One informs and

---

50. Perkins, *Works*, 2:651. Perkins quotes 2 Peter 1:20 and Nehemiah 8:8 respectively in support of these concepts.
51. Perkins, *Works*, 2:664–68.

reforms the mind and the other recovers it from error. Instruction in righteousness and correction are the practical categories of application. The former, instruction in righteousness, enables the individual to live well in the spheres of family, state, or church. The latter, correction, transforms ungodliness and unrighteousness into obedience. [52]

These overlapping grids of consideration—the passage as law or gospel, the hearers, and varieties of application—make Perkins's applications precise and relevant also for our day, especially for ministers. To follow in his footsteps, the preacher is compelled to serious study of the text, intimate knowledge of his congregants, and belief in the fact that all Scripture is indeed Spirit-inspired and profitable. There are those today who think application is the exclusive province of the Holy Spirit and not, therefore, appropriate for the preacher, yet specific application is a worthy endeavor, for it is by this means that the Spirit convicts, exhorts, builds up, and encourages. When application is neglected, the hearers are left to go on as they were before, unchanged and unconcerned. When application is merely general or left undeveloped, people may easily conclude that this particular text of Scripture does not apply to them, or they apply it to themselves in ways that are mistaken or harmful. But when it is well founded, clearly and pointedly stated, God's people, with the help of the Spirit, quickly bridge the gap between the specific situation highlighted from the pulpit and their own, and by the Spirit's grace, take the application to heart and seek to live it out in practice.

13. Valuing the Training of Preachers

The Puritans dreamed of seeing in every English pulpit a doctrinally sound preacher who could apply the Scriptures wisely, affectionately, and powerfully.[53] In the 1570s, the old guard clergy started to pass from the scene at the same time Oxford and Cambridge began graduating significant numbers of pastoral candidates.[54] One problem, however, was the lack of any substantive teaching of homiletics in the universities' curriculum. It was assumed that an educated

---

52. Perkins, *Works*, 2:668–69.
53. Diarmaid MacCulloch, *The Later Reformation in England, 1547–1603* (New York: Palgrave, 2001), 96.
54. Susan Doran and Christopher Durston, *Princes, Pastors, and People: The Church and Religion in England, 1500-1700* (London: Routledge, 2003), 168.

man could speak well on topics sacred or profane. But the Puritans disagreed, so they began to seek ways to supplement the official curriculum with training in preaching. In the 1560s and 1570s, this supplementation took the form of "prophesyings." At such a gathering, someone would deliver a sermon, which would then be critiqued by the other ministers according to the categories of form, delivery, content, and application. This form of on-the-job ministerial education was suppressed by Elizabeth in 1576.[55] For those disinclined to defy their Queen, the training ground for preachers morphed into clergy conferences and sponsored lectureships.[56] This same drive for the training of preachers motivated Perkins to write the first English preaching manual, *The Arte of Prophesying*.

We have already seen many elements of Perkins's work on preaching, but at the risk of redundancy, let's explore the layout of the book as a whole. The two parts of "prophecy" as Perkins defines it, are preaching the Word and public prayer, namely, speaking as the voice of God to the people and as the voice of the people to God. Perkins, of course, majors on the first. He begins by providing a defense of Scripture as God's Word and a brief description of the Bible's contents. Then follows the right method of interpretation of Scripture, the drawing out of its doctrines, and their application to the hearers. Perkins warns against using memory aids and extensive sermon manuscripts. He reminds his readers that power in preaching comes from demonstration of the Spirit, not displays of human wisdom. Again, the doctrine-use formula of Puritan plain style preaching comes to the fore. Perkins's work is eminently practical, aimed at training preachers to prepare and deliver sermons.[57]

But the faithful preacher is not only a man trained for the ministry. He is a man called to the ministry. In his *The Calling of the Ministry*, Perkins speaks of the minister as one sent from God to his church as

---

55. Patrick Collinson, *The Elizabethan Puritan Movement* (London: Cape, 1967), 168–239; Patrick Collinson, *Archbishop Grindal, 1519–1583: The Struggle for a Reformed Church* (Berkeley: University of California Press, 1979), 219–82; Peter Iver Kaufman, "Prophesying Again," *Church History* 68, no. 2 (June 1999): 337–58.

56. Patrick Collinson, "Lectures by Combination: Structures and Characteristics of Church Life in 17th-Century England," in Collinson, *Godly People: Essays on English Protestantism and Puritanism*, History Series (London: Hambledon Press, 1983), 467–98.

57. Perkins, *Works*, 2:646–73.

an interpreter of reconciliation. God Himself is the author of reconciliation, the Son the worker, and the Spirit the ratifier. The gospel is the instrument of the triune God, yet it is the minister who speaks the word of reconciliation to the people of God. True ministers are rare, as their work is also a calling to suffer as they fulfill their office by proclaiming humanity's lack of righteousness and offering salvation in Christ. But the minister also experiences blessing from God when mercy is shown and souls are delivered from hell.[58] On the high calling itself, Perkins says ministers must be broken over their sin and humbled in pondering their great function. They must find consolation only in Christ and be commissioned by God for the work of the ministry.[59] Perkins clearly teaches an inward call from God, and an outward call from His church, and both must be present. The individual's conscience judges his standing before God and willingness; the church judges the candidate's ability and readiness. With both of these in place, the minister should rest in his calling as if it came "in the voice of God."[60]

Of the many matters worth highlighting from Perkins's work on ministerial calling and training for today, we confine ourselves to three. First, an inner call without an external call is no call at all. The individual determines his desire and willingness to serve God as an ordained minister of the gospel. The individual does not judge by himself his own fitness in the areas of gifts and abilities, and readiness. This is the church's responsibility. This ought to give pause to those pursuing ministry as a vocation without the oversight and endorsement of a sponsoring local church.

Second, the church is essential in the training of pastors. Even though most seminary training today includes courses on preaching, formal theological education is unable to do all of the equipping necessary for pastoral ministry. Some preparation is only possible through significant experience in a local church. Then too, there is the role and responsibility of the courts of the churches to oversee the work of the seminaries, and to try candidates by examination in order to affirm their experience, certify their gifts, attest to their learning,

58. Perkins, *Works*, 3:430–38.
59. Perkins, *Works*, 3:442–61.
60. Perkins, *Works*, 3:462.

and determine their fitness and readiness for ministry. This is also part of the authentically Reformed view of the outward call.

Third, solid seminaries with biblically sound faculty and a student body where iron sharpens iron are critical for our day. Seldom will the Reformed church produce great Reformed preachers apart from sound Reformed seminaries. John Bunyan in the seventeenth century, Charles Spurgeon in the nineteenth century, and Martyn Lloyd-Jones in the twentieth century are the exceptions, not the rule. Solid, sound seminaries are the backbone of the entire Christian enterprise. Though they cannot make great ministers, as the Holy Spirit alone can do that, the Spirit normally uses sound professors of theology as means in His hand to prepare men of God to be stalwart proclaimers of truth in His church.

CONCLUSION

14. Remembering the Value of the Forgotten

Perkins, for all his popularity and renown among his contemporaries, was largely forgotten to history. We have noted his stature while he lived and for several generations afterwards as an internationally recognized theologian, and his impact in England through his preaching and teaching at Cambridge. Perkins's publications were significant as well, not just in England, but in continental Europe and North America. In Dutch alone, 185 seventeenth-century printings of his individual and collected works came off the press. Perkins played a role in the Dutch *Nadere Reformatie* with this written presence and through his most influential student, William Ames. His writings were also published in Switzerland and Germany. They were translated into Spanish, French, Italian, Irish, Welsh, Czech, and Hungarian.[61] A historian of New England has noted that "a typical Plymouth Colony library comprised a large and a small Bible, Ainsworth's translation of the Psalms, and the works of William Perkins, a favorite theologian."[62] Perry Miller once wrote, "Anyone

---

61. Joel R. Beeke and Randall J. Pederson, *Meet the Puritans: With a Guide to Modern Reprints* (Grand Rapids: Reformation Heritage Books, 2006), 475.

62. Samuel Morison, *The Intellectual Life of Colonial New England*, 2nd ed. (New York: New York University Press, 1956), 137.

who reads the writings of early New England learns that Perkins was indeed a towering figure in their eyes."[63]

Yet despite all of this approbation and influence, Perkins's works were largely neglected in the nineteenth and twentieth centuries. Even when other Puritan works were at last appearing in new printings in the later decades of the last century, Perkins's works were left to languish in obscurity for a very long time.

Hopefully it is clear at this point, that William Perkins is a significant historical figure, whose writings are profitable to the church today. The retrieval of Perkins's writings provides perspective that only historical distance can bring. It creates comradery with a brother in Christ from the Reformed tradition. It honors the sovereign God who saved him and used him mightily. For these reasons and many more, Perkins's complete works are being published again by Reformation Heritage Books, for the first time since the seventeenth century. At present all four of Perkins's exegetical volumes have been printed, his doctrinal and polemical works are being readied for the press (vols. 5–7), and his practical works (vols. 8–10) have been typed from the original, and soon will be edited for publication.[64] The goal is to have all ten volumes that comprise his complete works in print by the end of this decade or early in the next.

The reprinting of Perkins's works itself teaches us the important lesson that we never know how God will use our diligent exercise of the gifts He has entrusted to us for use in His kingdom. Therefore, we ought to labor while it is day, and always heed Solomon's wise advice: "Cast thy bread upon the waters: for thou shalt find it after many days" (Eccl. 11:1). Pray with us that a great harvest will be reaped from the reprinting of William Perkins's complete works in the twenty-first century all around this needy globe through the maturation of the saints, the salvation of the lost, the building up of Christ's church, and the greater glory of God Triune.

---

63. Perry Miller, *Errand into the Wilderness* (Cambridge, MA: Harvard University Press, 1956), 57–59.

64. Joel R. Beeke and Derek W. H. Thomas, gen. eds., *The Works of William Perkins,* vols. 1–4 (Grand Rapids: Reformation Heritage Books, 2014–2017); vols. 5–10, forthcoming.

CHAPTER 10

Learning from Women
of the Reformation

Rebecca VanDoodewaard

The work that sixteenth-century women did massively impacted the Reformation, but in a very different way than the men's work, since it was largely domestic or political instead of pastoral and ministerial. It was feminine work that left its mark because it was faithfully and thoughtfully done. Studying the lives of these women helps us learn principles of godly womanhood that the church needs today.

Katherina Luther

The first lesson we can learn from Reformation women is that a hard past does not negate present fruitfulness. The sixteenth century was not a comfortable time in which to live. Plague was a continual problem, war flared up frequently, food could be scarce or expensive. These led to low life expectancy and very high infant mortality.[1] The Reformation added religious and social upheaval to all this. People suffered a lot, in many ways. But one thing we clearly see from believing women in this time is that deep trials do not cripple fruitfulness; in fact, they can facilitate it.

Katherina Luther is known for her work as a wife, enabling her husband to do his seminal work of reforming. In between reviewing Luther's writing, hosting his students, and raising children, Katherina brewed beer, caught fish, butchered pigs, and read her Bible. Without her, Luther would not have been as healthy, productive, or happy. Some of Luther's pet names for her were heart-love, morning star of Wittenberg, Sir Katharina, Mrs. Doctoress, your

---

1. Nicholas Orme, "Childhood in Medieval England" on *Representing Childhood* (http://www.representingchildhood.pitt.edu/medieval_child.htm), accessed June 12, 2017.

Holiness, preacher, dear Katie. Her work facilitated and furthered the Reformation. Looking at Katherina's work, you would not guess her background.

In 1499, Katharina was born to a noble family in eastern Germany.[2] When she was little, her mother died, and when her father remarried, 6 year-old Katharina was dropped off at a cloister school. Three or four years later, her father sent her to a Cistercian convent for good.[3] We don't know all of his reasons, but one of them was that he was financially tight, so giving away a child saved money, including a dowry.

Donating children to the church was common at the time, but imagine what it did to a young girl. Her mother died and for some reason, she was chosen from among her siblings to leave the family and go live with a pseudo family.

We do not know how she coped with it growing up, but what we do see in her as an adult is a deep love for children, and especially for orphans. Together, Katharina and Martin had Johannes (1526); Elizabeth (1527); Magdalena (1529); Martin (1531); Paul (1533); and Margarete (1534). And they adopted orphans and poor relatives: George, Andreas, Cyriacus, Fabian, Elsa, and Lena Kaufmann; Hans Polner; Martin Luther Jr.; Anna Strauss; Hanna von der Saale; Florian von Bora, and possibly two others.[4] That makes a total of at least sixteen children that Katie cared for.[5]

This did not happen in an emotional void; you cannot take in a dozen children who are not yours and love them like a mother without deep inner motivation. Part of it probably came from Katharina's own understanding of her adoption into God's family; part of it had to come from her own suffering, and a desire to keep other children from the same grief. Katharina knew what it was like to be bereaved and abandoned at a vulnerable age. The hardship of her childhood prepared her to show compassion for hurting children as an adult. This first hardship bore fruit.

2. Kirsi Stjerna, *Women and the Reformation* (Oxford: Blackwell, 2009), 53.
3. Ernst Kroker, *The Mother of the Reformation*, trans. Mark E. DeGarmeaux (St. Louis: Concordia, 2013), 11.
4. "We hear Luther talk about these eleven foster children only occasionally. And there may have been more." Kroker, 122–152.
5. Stjerna, *Women and the Reformation*, 58.

In the convent, the young Katharina was inserted into strict monastic life. The hardship here, the second trial, was not the order or the quiet; it was the falsehood that Katharina was immersed in. Convents—and monasteries, too—are pseudo families with pseudo "mothers" and "sisters" and "fathers" offering a pseudo gospel. We are used to seeing monks and nuns as friendly, pious people in popular culture or even our communities, but we need to remember that monasticism is an anti-gospel institution that by definition abuses people who are part of it. At that point in the convent, Katharina did not realize that she was experiencing the hardship of spiritual abuse. She was simply part of the religious community there. The convent had a considerable collection of relics, which the nuns used in their religious rites: there were regular prayers, worship of Mary, and the isolation, silence, personal poverty, and strict hierarchy that seemed normal to any late Medieval European because of the Church's control over the population.[6]

But again, the Lord designed it for her good. What Katharina did not see, and could not see at the time, is that the convent was actually giving her a skill set that she would later use to help the man who started the Reformation. The nuns grew a lot of their own food, and though Katharina did not do a lot of physical work herself, she saw gardening and food production happening around her.[7] The convent owned a lot of cows, pigs, horses, and sheep; Katharina saw basic animal husbandry.[8] She saw that a small community could be pretty self-sustaining because of a few hard-working women.

The convent served as a pilgrimage destination; the nuns often housed these guests, and Katharina saw the importance of hospitality and community. Care for the sick was also part of monastic life; Katharina showed herself to be an excellent nurse later in life.[9]

And one huge advantage that nuns had over other women in this period was education; nuns were taught how to read. Katharina could read her native German as well as some Latin, which she also

6. Kroker, *Mother of the Reformation*, 14.

7. Stjerna, *Women and the Reformation*, 53.

8. Kroker, *Mother of the Reformation*, 15–17.

9. Kroker, *Mother of the Reformation*, 181.

spoke.[10] She was exposed to theological works, too. This prepared her very specifically for being the wife of an author and intellectual.

The convent was not only giving her practical skills; she also had a habit of prayer pressed into her. Later in life, she expressed appreciation for this habit that the convent taught her. So God prepared Katharina to be involved in reform before she realized that it was a possibility.

And in 1523, Katharina realized that reform was not only a possibility, but a necessity. The printing press allowed the production of Protestant literature, particularly pamphlets, and they were smuggled into convents across Germany. Katharina's convent was no exception; Luther's writings reached it around 1519.[11] She and a few other believing nuns eventually decided that they must escape. After asking their families for help and being refused, Katharina fled with eight other nuns to Wittenberg on Luther's advice.[12] The story about hiding inside fish barrels is not true; the women were just on the wagon, but the 60 miles would have been risky, dangerous, and uncomfortable enough.[13]

That is because escaped nuns were a huge problem in 1523. For one thing, they made the Roman Catholic Church angry: they had broken serious vows and were essentially fugitives. Even people who helped them were subject to execution if caught. The nuns had also made enemies of their families by embarrassing and betraying them in converting. Ex-nuns were awkward in society, too; these single women needed to integrate into a quickly changing city. They had not interacted with men for most of their lives, they had little or no experience with children, and few opportunities for employment. They were leaving a very secure, stable environment and future for totally unpredictable ones. These women were highly vulnerable socially, legally, and emotionally.

---

10. We know this from Luther's letters to her, which include Latin parts. See, for example, Martin Luther to Katharina Luther, October 4, 1529 in *The Letters of Martin Luther*, ed. and trans. Margaret A. Currie (London: MacMillan, 1908), 197. There are also records of her speaking Latin occasionally. Bainton, *Women of the Reformation in Germany and Italy* (Minneapolis: Augsburg Press, 1971), 295.

11. Stjerna, *Women and the Reformation*, 54.

12. Kroker, *Mother of the Reformation*, 32.

13. Kroker, *Mother of the Reformation*, 35.

Luther understood this, and quickly helped them all find places to live and work. So Katharina's third trial was servanthood, following the bereavement and spiritual abuse. She became a domestic servant for a Wittenberg family—from a pseudo family at the convent to a real family that was not hers as she adjusted to civilian life.

Although Katherina did bring some skills from the convent, she had never seen how a family, let alone a Christian one, functioned. And this was what she learned as a servant in two different homes. This third trial bore fruit.

Her two mistresses seem to have been excellent homemakers, so Katharina saw how to manage money and servants, children and visitors. She saw that families are not as predictable as convents, and how a wife and mother dealt with that. She saw Christian marriages functioning. Despite the good environments in these homes, or perhaps because of them, Katharina seems to have wanted her own home.

And in her first year as a servant, just months after leaving the convent, Katharina met a university student, Jerome Baumgärtner, and they fell in love—it was known in the town that they were a couple. Jerome had to leave town later that year, and Katharina heard nothing more from him. In 1524, Luther wrote to him, "If you intend marrying Katharine von Bora, make haste before she is given to someone else…she has not yet gotten over her love for you."[14] You can imagine what Katharina was going through here; living as a servant in someone else's home with a broken heart, the Protestant leadership in town trying to figure out what had happened to the relationship. And what had happened was Jerome's family. They were wealthy, politically involved, and very aware that marriage to a runaway nun would hurt their status. Essentially, Jerome was forced to choose between his family and Katharina, and he chose his family, marrying a wealthy, younger woman. He was not the only suitor Katharina had in these years, but he was the only one whom Katharina loved. This abandonment must have sunk deep into her, since it even affected her physically at the time.[15]

Of course, we know what happened: she married Dr. Luther himself in 1525, at the height of the Peasants' War. And he did not

---

14. He added, "I wish that you two were married." Martin Luther to Jerome Baumgärtner, October 12, 1524 in *Letters*, 129.

15. Stjerna, *Women and the Reformation*, 55.

marry her because he loved her; he married her to please his father, and to spite the pope and the devil.[16] Luther was a great man, but he was not an easy man: moody, sometimes depressed, intense, sometimes crass, walking around with a death sentence hanging over him, complaining about his bowels. Katharina cared for him and often brought him to his senses.

Did part of Katharina's love for Martin come from Martin's faithfulness to her? I think it did. Having a father then a suitor abandon you would make you very thankful for a faithful man. And I think that Katharina's devotion to her husband, her patience with her husband, was in part a deep appreciation for his steadfast love for her.

Because of course, he did fall in love with her. Luther's letters show "how soon and powerfully Katharina...swept him off his feet."[17] And for the rest of her marriage, all of Katharina's past experiences informed and empowered her service as a wife and mother.

If you look at how God set this up, looking back from Katharina's fruitfulness in marriage, providence is so clear. The training was so specific to the calling, moving from abandoned child to nun to servant to Reformer's wife, unknowingly gathering tools for ministry along the way. God knew just what Katharina would need to do to contribute to reform, and He provided before she realized what her role in that would be.

This sort of background, with everything from rejection to physical danger to bad teaching, could have crippled Katharina, emotionally and relationally. It didn't. She not only understood God's providence: she also had a theology of suffering and a strong sense that the work in front of her was important. She knew that Luther, and thus the church, needed her. This enabled her to put her past in a biblical perspective and also put her past to use.

This does not mean that she never struggled with the hardships she had been through. We don't know what she thought about from day to day as she dug up onions, washed sheets, and served meals, but she must have grieved over her lost childhood as she raised her own children. The broken engagement probably left questions for a time. But these things did not stunt her. Instead, God enabled her to

16. Bainton, *Germany and Italy*, 288.
17. Stjerna, *Women and the Reformation*, 56.

use the lessons from these hard, hard things, and be a blessing to His church.

Most people have not suffered like this. Some have suffered more, in different ways. So perhaps this example is more of an encouragement than a lesson: don't allow your past hardships to choke out service to Christ and His church today, and tomorrow.

Katharina Zell

The second thing we can learn from these women is what biblical womanhood looks like. Biblical definitions of womanhood and femininity are often different from ours. Excelling as a woman does not mean excelling in a man's role, or just applauding the men as they excel; it means pursuing excellence at your particular calling as a woman within biblical boundaries, regardless of traditional roles. Tradition does not have legitimate weight in defining masculine or feminine: tradition can get it wrong. The Bible never does. So we have to conform our standard of womanhood to the Bible's standard, believing God's testimony of femininity above our culture's distortion, and our distorted reactions to that.

We do not tend to think of the sixteenth century as a time when people had to sort out female identity issues. But Roman Catholicism had very strong ideas about women and what they should be doing. For example, lactating nuns and celibate wives were both considered holy. That's a problem! And because Roman Catholic tradition fell apart under a scriptural examination, the Protestant church had to deal with the fallout. Runaway nuns and priests' wives revealed real issues of gender and identity confronting early Protestantism. The church turned to Scripture for guidance.

What did it see there? It saw Miriam, the prophetess leading the Israelite women. It saw Jael, the stay-at-home mom assassinating an enemy general. It saw Abigail, the woman in a difficult marriage using her wealth to provide for David. It saw Dorcas, the older woman devoting herself to care for the poor. It saw Pricilla, the well-taught wife helping Paul with his teaching ministry. Clearly, biblical womanhood was not limited to convent walls or Roman Catholic nurseries. Nor was it limited to reading your Bible and raising Protestant babies. Biblical womanhood was—and is—using your gifts to serve the church in the ways in which you can facilitate its growth and health according to biblical patterns. Just like in Proverbs 31, biblical femininity is often expressed in active service. One example of this is Katharina Zell.

Born in 1497 in Strasbourg, Katharina was well educated as a child. She developed deep religious zeal while young, but struggled with assurance of salvation, feeling that her works were never enough to buy her way to heaven. In her late teens, Matthew Zell arrived in town, preaching Christ to the city.[18] Katharina realized that Christ's death had paid the penalty for her sins, that salvation is a free gift. Her search for spiritual security died with an understanding of Christ's completed work.

Pastor and parishioner married on December 3, 1525.[19] It was one of the first public Protestant marriages: a bold step for both husband and wife as it broke canon law and defied Rome. But it was a step that the Lord blessed.

Katharina's education and growing understanding of the Bible enabled her to defend truth in public as well as private. Sometimes it seems like she outdid her husband in this; Bucer shruggingly said that Katharina was "a trifle imperious."[20] But he also admitted that she was "God-fearing and courageous as a hero."

Katharina's first published work was a defense of clerical marriage—priests or pastors getting wives. Her work not only refuted false accusations about her own marriage, but also helped people rethink the issue. She went back to the Bible, showing that clerical celibacy had no scriptural grounds.[21] The work also defended Katharina's right, as a lay person and as a woman, to read Scripture and publically present arguments from it.[22] This writing made her known throughout Europe.

Katharina was also hospitable and used her domestic skills to care for refugees.[23] One year, scores of men arrived in Strasbourg,

---

18. Alise Anne McKee, *Katharina Schutz Zell*, 2 vols. (Leiden: Brill, 1999), 1:34–35.

19. McKee, *Katharina Schutz Zell*, 1:40.

20. Bucer in Bainton, *Germany and Italy*, 63.

21. Katharina Zell, *Church Mother: The Writings of a Protestant Reformer in Sixteenth-Century Germany*, trans. Elsie McKee (Chicago: University of Chicago Press, 2006), 72–73.

22. Stjerna, *Women and the Reformation*, 118.

23. Bainton, *Germany and Italy*, 63.

fleeing persecution. Katharina sheltered and fed them[24] and wrote to their wives, encouraging them to stand firm in their faith.[25]

Through her life, Katharina kept up correspondence with many intellectuals, including Erasmus and Calvin, discussing issues and principles. We know from these letters that she was well read, because she quoted a range of theologians, from Augustine to Savonarola.[26]

Between 1526 and 1533, Katharina gave birth to two babies, both of whom died in infancy: "Matthew seemed to cope better, but Katharina especially struggled."[27] Though the double loss was a deep valley for her, it did not seem to slow her service to others or care for the church.[28]

She continued her work, visiting people with leprosy, syphilis, and the plague.[29] Occasionally, she had to fight city magistrates to gain access, but she did it and won.[30]

In 1548, Zell died. After his death, Strasbourg changed its theological direction, and about ten years later, Katharina became involved in her most public and painful controversy. When her husband was alive, they had a student, Rabus, live in their home as an intern. He became Zell's successor and the city's most popular preacher. But despite his training, he attacked Reformed views and customs, urging high Lutheranism. Katharina was not going to tolerate a former student teaching bad theology: she wrote to Rabus.

Rabus answered her; the letters moved from theological-political issues to public, personal attacks on Katharina, whom he called "disturber of the peace of the church." She replied in a letter to the whole city: "Do you call this disturbing the peace that instead of spending my time in frivolous amusements I have visited the plague-infested and carried out the dead? I have visited those in prison and under sentence of death. Often for three days and nights I have neither eaten nor slept. I have never mounted the pulpit, but I have done more than any minister in visiting.... Is this disturbing the peace of the

24. Stjerna, *Women and the Reformation*, 120.
25. This letter was later published. McKee, *Katharina Schütz Zell*, 2:2; Zell, *Church Mother*, 50, 53, 43.
26. Stjerna, *Women and the Reformation*, 113.
27. McKee, *Katharina Schütz Zell*, 1:70–77; 2:306.
28. McKee, *Katharina Schütz Zell*, 1:107.
29. Bainton, *Germany and Italy*, 68, 65.
30. Stjerna, *Women and the Reformation*, 116.

church?... You young fellows tread on the graves of the first fathers of this church in Strasbourg and punish all who disagree with you."[31] It was a time that deeply grieved her.

By 1558, Katharina's study of the Scriptures increased, producing a commentary on Psalms 51, 130, and the Lord's Prayer, more meditative than her other writings, showing an author spiritually developed by the means of grace and sorrow. It was her last published work.

The date of her death is unknown. She was living March 3, 1562; a letter she wrote that day survives, saying that she was, "often half dead with her long sickness." Certainly by the end of that year, she was in glory.

Historians today call her a "lay Reformer." But she only did what every Christian should: used her gifts for gospel change in her own sphere, whatever ways possible. Bucer remarked, "Her zeal is incredible for Christ's lowliest and afflicted. She knows and searches the mysteries of Christ."[32] Submission did not equal passivity, but creative, active, and sacrificial service that had the praise of her husband, the recognition of the community, and the blessing of the Lord. Biblically channeled zeal resulted in a strong woman, free to exercise gifts.

Notice that the roles of author and public figure were not her goals: they simply came as she strove to serve her family and church. She was not responding to a call for more women in public theological dialogue and publishing. Public roles outside of the home were not things that Reformation women fought for: they came to fill them because they were excelling in the home and had the thoughtfulness, theological background, and energy to take on additional work when there was a need.

And public roles were not filled at the cost of private roles—the primary callings of caring for family. Husband and children were not sacrificed for career or "personal fulfillment." And there was contentment when God limited these women to private, domestic roles. But there was also great fruitfulness and freedom here. Reformation era believers could answer the issues of bad Catholic teaching on gender roles not because they were reacting to it, as we

31. Katharina Zell to Rabus in Bainton, *Germany and Italy*, 72, 73.
32. Bucer in Stjerna, *Women and the Reformation*, 129.

often react to feminism, but because they lived out the principles that they found in Scripture.[33]

Protestant orthodoxy at the time was generally very comfortable with the wide range of activities of these women. Reformation women and male theologians would have been appalled by a woman preaching or leading worship, but they were happy to have women learning, writing, and leading armies, because of the Bible's principle of believers using their gifts within inspired boundaries.[34]

The big question regarding gender roles in the church is not, "How much are women allowed to do?" but, "How can women best use their gifts to serve Jesus?" Jesus gives us very clear guidelines in His Word. And Reformation women give us solid examples in this area as we try to learn what womanhood can actually be, based not on our feelings or desires or tradition, but on unchanging biblical principles and priorities in a world that is very confused on this subject.

Anna Bullinger

The third lesson is what a home is. For many of the early Reformation women, childhood homes were distant places; because many girls were donated to convents, home was an early childhood memory with bitter associations. Others of these women came from wealthy backgrounds, growing up in a culture where home was a place to display money and power. The Reformation changed that. In the Reformation, home became the headquarters for a family's fruitfulness.

Our culture treats our homes as private places where we retreat, places of personal consumption and relaxation. Of course, homes ought to be places where we can rest and unwind when we need to. But as Christians in the sixteenth century studied the Scriptures, they saw examples like the Proverbs 31 woman, Lydia, and others who used their homes as tools, bases for Christian service. These women ran their households for maximum fruitfulness.

This is actually an expression of womanhood that Scripture commands. In 1 Timothy 5:14, Paul tells us that younger women, among other things, are be home managers. The Greek term gives the idea

---

33. Stjerna, *Women and the Reformation*, 131.

34. The notable exception to this rule is John Knox, who published his *First Blast of the Trumpet Against the Monstruous Regiment of Women* against the advice of his friends, including John Calvin.

of a ruler (οικοδεσποτεο), someone who excels in running a home because she has taken able charge of domestic affairs. We see this sort of thing in Europe as Protestantism takes hold, women helping their husbands and the church by running efficient, fruitful homes.

Anna Bullinger modeled this. Born around 1504, she was eight when her father died in battle.[35] Her mother donated Anna to a convent at Zurich and eventually she took holy orders.[36]

But while she lived as a nun, Zwingli's preaching changed the town, and eventually the convent. Heinrich Bullinger was sent to preach to the nuns; he met Anna, they fell in love, and around the time that the convent closed, they married on August 17, 1529.[37]

Bullinger ended up with a call to serve as the pastor of the Zurich cathedral, and he accepted. This was a great honor and it came with great responsibility, not only for the preacher but also for his wife. A busy husband was only one aspect of her calling, and Anna was certainly as busy as her husband. Babies arrived almost yearly until there were eleven children in the home.[38] Bullinger's father and mother lived in the home until they died. The couple took in Zwingli's widowed wife and children, caring for them as their own family. Bullinger also had the habit of having interns or other gifted students live in his house.[39]

And so Anna's family became very large, often with more than twenty people living in her house. She must have been good with money, because she fed and clothed everyone in the family on a relatively small salary. But it was hard. We have hints of her difficulty in a letter that Bullinger wrote to his oldest son who was a university student in Strasbourg: "Your mother makes big eyes when you already speak of needing another pair of shoes for the winter. It

---

35. Rebecca A. Giselbrecht, "Myths and Reality about Heinrich Bullinger's Wife Anna," *Zwingliana* 38 (2011): 55.

36. James Good, *Famous Women of the Reformed Church* (Birmingham: Solid Ground Christian Books, 2007, facsimile of 1901 edition), 32.

37. Heinrich Bullinger, *Heinrich Bullinger Diarium (Annales vitae) der Jahre 1504–1574* (Zurich: Theologische Buchhandlung Zürich, 1985), 18. Dr. David Noe kindly translated Bullinger's entry about the wedding.

38. Six sons, five daughters. Three of the boys die young; Anna raises the rest. Richard Rolt, *Lives of the Principle Reformers, Both Englishmen and Foreigners, Comprehending the General History of the Reformation...* (London: Bakewell and Parker, 1759), 149.

39. Good, *Famous Women*, 37–38.

is hardly fifteen weeks since you left us, when you took three pairs with you."[40]

The large family was not the only thing that Anna had on her plate. Her house was a home to Protestant refugees from all over Europe. Anna had believers coming from Italy starting in 1542. When persecution broke out in England in 1550 under Bloody Mary, Bullinger and the Zurich church took in the refugees.[41] Swiss refugees arrived in the spring of 1556: one hundred and sixteen of them showed up needing food and shelter. Anna set the example of hospitality for the city.

But Anna's visitors were not limited to those fleeing persecution. Her husband's talents and position brought theologians who wanted to talk: Calvin and Farel from Geneva; Bucer and Capito from Strasbourg; Phillippe de Mornay from France: the Bullinger home welcomed all of them.

Anna also cared for the needy in Zurich. She was always running out to bring food to poor people, visiting the sick in the congregation, and giving clothes to orphans. People started calling her "the Zurich-mother."[42]

In 1564, though, Bullinger contracted the plague; Anna nursed him so that he recovered, but she caught it herself and died shortly after.

Anna's work must have seemed like drudgery at times: endless meals, laundry, and morning sickness. But when we see it as a whole and the fruit that it bore, it is remarkable. Anna sheltered and fed hundreds every year, raised many children, cared for her mother and in-laws as they died, allowed young men to prepare for future ministry, and enabled her husband to further the gospel cause in Zurich and beyond. Bullinger's bestselling book, *Christian Matrimony*, reflects the happy marriage pattern that Anna and her husband had; they spread this pattern throughout Europe.[43] Anna's example as helpmeet became the Protestant standard for many decades. She lived out the pattern we see in Scripture of doing good to everyone (especially to the household of faith); caring for the poor, orphan,

---

40. Bullinger in Good, *Famous Women*, 38.

41. Good, *Famous Women*, 39–40.

42. Good, *Famous Women*, 43.

43. Heinrich Bullinger, *The Christen State of Matrimonye*, trans. Miles Coverdale (Amsterdam: Theatrum Orbis Terrarum, 1974, facsimile of the 1541 edition).

and widow; welcoming the stranger; bringing up children; honoring father and mother; and loving a husband.

This is typical of Protestant women in this era. They saw their homes as bases for ministry. Their work was never done—they never checked off everything on their list and headed for a coffee shop, though they did take time off occasionally, often at a husband's insistence. But what we see again and again in the Reformation is God taking ordinary obedience, simple, unglamorous hard work like this, and using it to transform a culture.

It is clear that Anna's work was a blessing to the people whom she served directly. But in this era, what Anna and other Protestant women did was radical. Just marrying a pastor was a public denunciation of monasticism. And then quietly raising children and opening your home to other Protestants added insult to injury. This biblical lifestyle directly challenged the Roman Catholic Church's teaching on clergy, marriage, and more. Not only were these women living quiet, fruitful lives, working with their hands; God also used their obedience to complete a shift in European culture.

Think about how convents and monasteries functioned before the Reformation: they served as hospitals, basic education facilities, hostels, and places of personal devotion. Believing housewives proved that they could pray, read, garden, care for the sick, host travelers, and foster an intellectual climate just as well as monks and nuns had for centuries. Protestant housewives did a lot to make monasticism socially obsolete. As their lives conformed to a biblical pattern, they showed that society could function just fine without the Roman Catholic institutions that had been propping it up. Though their work was not always visible, Protestant wives attacked Catholic presuppositions by their domestic work.

Notice that these women did not form a committee and strategize on how to compete with monasticism. They just obeyed: they worked hard and were self-disciplined, and God used that feminine obedience to do His own work.

So we really need to be thinking of how to use our homes as bases for ministry today. That would include hospitality, teaching, prayer, reading, learning, and more. How might God use that in a culture where homes are falling apart?

Katherine Willoughby

The fourth lesson these women have left us is what catholicity looks like. For confessional believers, the word, "catholicity" is often a synonym for "ecumenism." But the two are different: ecumenism is promoting unity between existing denominations, often by watering down doctrine till everyone can swallow it, while catholicity is a positive recognition that Christ's church is universal with different local expressions. Catholicity is a love for all who confess Christ and live as Christians, regardless of their denominational or cultural background. Ecumenism tries to create a homogeneous church; catholicity seeks to love the church universal while accepting legitimate distinctions of time, place, and even creed. In the first generation of Reformation believers, catholicity was part of survival, not only for the Protestant church as it faced Rome and schism, but also for the spiritual health of individual believers.

A Reformation woman who exemplifies this is Katherine Willoughby. She was born in 1519 in England to a wealthy noble couple. By the time she was fourteen, she was married to Henry VIII's friend, Charles Brandon, the Duke of Suffolk. He was a nominal Protestant, and Katherine was Roman Catholic.[44] As the Duchess of Suffolk, Katherine was brought into the inner circle of the royal court; she and her husband hosted the King, she received personal gifts from him, and was very influential at court, socially and later politically.[45] The couple had two sons.

During the early 1540s, Katherine became lady-in-waiting to the Protestant Queen, and so had increased access to Protestant literature and theologians. Sometime in this period, she seems to have been converted.

In 1545, Brandon died, leaving Katherine a widow with two sons. She was in her mid-twenties and one of the richest women in England.[46] By the following year, she was clearly in the evangelical camp, helping distribute banned theological works and advocating

---

44. Steven Gunn, *Charles Brandon: Henry VIII's Closest Friend* (Stroud, U. K.: Amberley, 2015), 146.

45. Melissa Franklin Harkrider, *"Women, Reform, and Community in Early Modern England: Katherine Willoughby, Duchess of Suffolk, and Lincolnshire's Godly Aristocracy, 1519–1580* (Woodbridge, U. K.: Boydell Press, 2008), 42, 48.

46. Gunn, *Charles Brandon*, 221.

for the use of Tyndale's vernacular New Testament.[47] She became increasingly Reformed in her convictions.

Two years after the duke died, Henry VIII died too, leaving England to his truly Protestant son, Edward VI. So the deaths of the duke and the king really changed Katherine's life. Because of these deaths, Katherine had the time, the cash, the freedom, and the connections to facilitate the English Reformation. And that's what she did: her encouragement and deep pockets helped "shape a new protestant culture."[48]

In 1550, she had started helping Protestant refugees from Europe and befriended John Foxe.[49] The year that she lost both her children, 1551, she hired Hugh Latimer as her chaplain.[50] Katherine used Latimer not just for her own growth, but also to shape her servants' and neighbors' theology—she had him preach often to different groups,[51] and because of her patronage, his sermons survive.[52] Katherine had them published, which is why we have them today. She funded other Protestant publications, too; sermons and devotional material, spreading Reformed thought through England.[53]

Working with a Protestant bishop, Katherine gave a lot of pastoral positions in the county to believing ministers, really promoting evangelical thought in the area.[54] She abolished holy days, saints' images, and pilgrimages in her lands.[55] She found Protestants to teach in the parish schools, and also set up grammar schools taught by evangelicals in order to make sure Reformed ideas were passed on to the next generation.[56]

---

47. Harkrider, *Women, Reform, and Community*, 50.

48. Susan Wabuda, "Bertie, Katherine, duchess of Suffolk (1519–1580)" in *Oxford Dictionary of National Biography*, Oxford University Press, 2004; online edition, Jan 2008 (http://www.oxforddnb.com/view/article/2273), accessed 4 May 2017.

49. Foxe later wrote and became famous for his *Book of Martyrs*. Roland Bainton, *Women of the Reformation in France and England* (Minneapolis: Fortress, 2007), 257.

50. He served from 1551–1552. Latimer's *Fyrste Sermon* was dedicated to the duchess and bore her coat of arms. Bainton, *France and England*, 256–57.

51. Harkrider, *Women, Reform, and Community*, 1.

52. Bainton, *France and England*, 257.

53. Harkrider, *Women, Reform, and Community*, 83–84.

54. Harkrider, *Women, Reform, and Community*, 64.

55. Bainton, *France and England*, 260.

56. Harkrider, *Women, Reform, and Community*, 86, 92.

Though it was Protestant, England was still under an Act of Parliament issued under Henry VIII forbidding the lower classes and women to read the Bible.[57] Katherine worked with other aristocrats to have this repealed, and it was, early in Edward's rule.

She financially supported Protestant professors at Cambridge, particularly Martin Bucer, who taught her boys. When Bucer was dying, Katherine was the one who cared for him.[58]

But the biggest lesson she leaves us is in her support of the continental refugees. Because Edward VI was Protestant, England was a safe place for believers, and thousands of Protestants fled from the continent to English cities, especially London, where Katherine was living. They were coming from France, Spain, Italy, Germany, Poland, and the Netherlands, where Roman Catholics were trying to stamp out reformation.

At this point, all legal churches in England belonged to the Church of England. It was a crime to pastor or support anything else. But when the number of refugees in London reached into the thousands in 1550, Katherine used her political connections and resources to obtain a charter that allowed them to establish a recognized church: the only congregations in England to legally exist outside of the Church of England.[59] "The charter granted them freedom to use their own rites and ceremonies,"[60] even though they were different from English ones. This was just one year after the Act of Uniformity was passed, so this charter, giving these refugee churches an exception to that, was extraordinary, and shows Katherine's influence and determination.[61]

Katherine never left the Church of England herself. She moved from conservative Roman Catholicism to evangelical, Reformed

---

57. This was the *Act for the Advancement of True Religion*, passed by the English Parliament on May 12, 1543. It was repealed by the first Parliament that met under Edward VI.

58. Bainton, *France and England*, 261.

59. Called, "Charter of the Church of the Strangers," the document was a very rare exemption under Edward VI from the *Act of Uniformity*. Jasper Ridley, *Bloody Mary's Martyrs: The Story of England's Terror* (New York, Carroll & Graf Publishers, 2001), 36–37.

60. Dirk W. Rodgers, "À Lasco [Laski], John (1499–1560)," in *Oxford Dictionary of National Biography*, Oxford University Press online edition, 2004 (http://www .oxforddnb.com/view/article/16081, accessed 4 May 2017).

61. Harkrider, *Women, Reform, and Community*, 65.

theology all within the state church. Her commitment to its growth and its health did not change. But personal loyalty to the Church of England did not keep her from a latitude in her acceptance of other believers' ecclesiology. When these refugees arrived, Katherine worked to make room for them in English religious society. She worked to facilitate the spiritual good of other Christians who did not believe exactly as she did.

Notice some things about this evangelical catholicity. First, it was not a toleration of error. Katherine had little time for people who twisted, ignored, or attacked Scripture, and everyone in England knew it; she was a public enemy of Roman Catholic bishops. She publicly opposed them, and worked to have them removed from their positions. She later put pressure on Church of England leaders who were weak in their commitment to biblical standards and called them out for compromising.[62] So this was not a lax approach to truth or to the church.

Second, this catholicity did not flow out of ignorance. Katherine knew what she believed and why. She was promoting Reformed thought through her patronage, specifically evangelical thought. She worked to correct unbiblical thought in herself, her family, her servants, and her tenants. She knew what the differences were between herself, her denomination, and the people whom she supported outside of it. She was not acting out of blissful unawareness that made her happy with anything.

Third, this catholicity was not liberal ecumenism. Katherine did not suggest that the refugees and the Church of England merge to form some international coalition of Protestant churches. There was a distinctness between the Church of England and the refugee congregations in London that was clear, and that Katherine and other believers were comfortable with. They realized that there would be differences on minor issues as well as differences in expressions of major issues because of cultural and creedal differences.

And Katherine did not pressure the refugees to join the English State Church; she put pressure on the English government to make

---

62. Katherine Bertie to William Cecil, Lord Burghley, March 4, 1559, State Papers 12/3 f.28 (State Papers Online, Gale, Cengage Learning, 2017). For a transcription see Paul F. M. Zahl, *Five Women of the English Reformation* (Grand Rapids: Eerdmans, 2001), 114–16.

allowances for them. Katherine realized that these refugees had a form of worship flowing out of different theological texts, different contexts, and to alter the worship would be asking them to change their polity and ignore their culture. Because the refugees were biblically orthodox in their beliefs, there was no reason for Katherine to oppose them, and she could actually make concessions for them, even though she did not believe exactly the same things. She was willing that they worshiped in their distinct, culturally shaped way as they strove to live out their confessional understanding of Scripture.

Though she was a believer, serving well, and growing quickly in theological understanding and love for God, she still struggled with sin, particularly an "explosive temper and sharp tongue."[63]

In 1553, Katherine married a second time to a man named Richard Bertie. He was a strong believer, but the marriage shocked everyone because he was one of her servants.

During this marriage, Katherine's faith was tested by persecution under Edward's sister Bloody Mary, which forced her to flee England and live as a refugee on the continent until Elizabeth I came to the throne. After years of wandering around in Germany and Poland, the family was back in England in 1559. Katharine spent the last years of her life supporting the reconstruction of English Protestantism. Once again, she funded Protestant publication and preaching, hired reformers like Miles Coverdale, patronized Protestant artists, gave away Bibles, and put pressure on Elizabeth's government to make the Church of England more biblical.[64] Because of her rank, she controlled a parish in London that was not part of the Established Church, and it became "a seedbed for puritan preachers" right there in the capital.[65] She supported all Protestants, including dissenters and other Christians outside the Church of England, interceding for ministers who preached without a government license.[66] Having been fruitful when free and faithful when persecuted, the duchess died after a long illness on September 19, 1580. Latimer's servant

---

63. Harkrider, *Women, Reform, and Community*, 54.

64. Harkrider, *Women, Reform, and Community*, 117–20.

65. Susan Wabuda, "Bertie, Katherine, duchess of Suffolk (1519–1580)," in *Oxford Dictionary of National Biography, Oxford University Press*, 2004, online edition, Jan 2008 (http://www.oxforddnb.com/view/article/2273, accessed 4 May 2017).

66. Bainton, *France and England*, 275–76.

remarked that for thirty-five years she had been "the mainstay of preachers, a comfort to martyrs, and God's instrument for the spread of the gospel."

So Katherine's catholicity, her universal love for all who name the name of Christ and live out of that profession, was a strong feature of her service. And it was actually a very common feature for believing women in this period. It is interesting that the more these women knew what they believed, and the more they were convinced of biblical truth, the more able they were to interact with believers from other backgrounds without feeling threatened on the one hand, and without personal compromise to biblical conviction on the other.

These women were flexible within biblical bounds in order to accommodate and serve other Christians. They were willing to make concessions where possible to other sheep while at the same time being absolutely intolerant of wolves in sheep's clothing as well as leaders within a confessional stream who did not really hold to it. Public attacks on false teachers and thoughtful care for other Christians are two sides of the catholicity coin. Often it was the women who were most catholic in the true sense who spoke out most strongly against Roman Catholicism. This should make sense because it is just an outflow of love for Jesus; love for the brethren and hatred of false teaching. Faithfulness to Christ means personal and ecclesiastical adherence to a biblical confession, knowing it, understanding it, committing to it, and being even *more* committed to the church universal. This sort of catholicity feeds a love for other Christians and is easy to love because it doesn't force its own culture or particular ecclesiology on other faithful Christians outside of our own denomination.

This is humility, isn't it? We realize that we don't have a stranglehold on truth: we can admit that and hold to a biblical confession strongly while respecting other believers who do the same. We are each striving to be faithful, as faithful as we can because it pleases the Lord. Real, biblical catholicity will make us devoted to the church universal even more than we are devoted to our own segment of it. That is what makes it useful.

Reformation women give us some good examples of what this looked like in real life. One historian says, "They believed in a practical Christianity that demonstrated itself not through ceremonies and sacerdotalism, but rather through everyday Christian living, including charity to other Protestants."[67]

Catherine de Bourbon

Last, the lives of these women show God's faithfulness. We can see this in the third woman in a short line of French Protestants. Mother, daughter, and granddaughter were part of the French royal family. All of them experienced intimidation, isolation, difficult marriages, and deep grief. Two of them suffered from chronic health problems. Humanly speaking, everything was against them. But since God was for them, they persevered.

Catherine de Bourbon was the daughter of Jeanne d'Albret, queen of Navarre. She was a later Reformation woman, born in 1559 to an alcoholic and adulterous father who died when she was a baby. Her wonderful mother taught her well. Catherine was also very close to her brother Henri, who was in line for the French throne. She grew up in the middle of horrific family and national conflict, but her mother made sure she was well educated by Theodore Beza. It seems that Catherine came to faith as a child.

When her mother took her to Paris on a visit to the Roman Catholic court in 1573, Catherine was under huge pressure to cave to the decadence and unbelief there, but she didn't. Jeanne wrote to a friend: "You cannot imagine how my daughter shines in this company. Everyone assails her about her religion and she stands up to them all."[68]

Jeanne died days later, leaving Catherine a last message through a governess. She urged her daughter "to stand firm and constant in God's service despite her extreme youth." She also insisted that "her daughter the princess be constantly instructed in [the fear of God and knowledge of the Gospel]...."[69] Catherine was only thirteen, and her mother's death was the beginning of life-long persecution.

---

67. Melinda Zook, *Protestantism, Politics, and Women in Britain, 1660–1714* (New York: Palgrave Macmillan, 2013), 129.

68. Jeanne d'Albret to Beauvoir, March 11, 1572 in Nancy Lyman Roelker, *Queen of Navarre: Jeanne d'Albret, 1528–1572* (Cambridge, MA: Harvard University Press, 1968), 376.

69. Jeanne d'Albret in Nancy Lyman Roelker, *Queen of Navarre*, 389.

Her mother's wishes were ignored: Charles IX and his mother Catherine de Medici took over Catherine's guardianship.[70] Henri and Catherine were kept in Paris, and lived through the St. Bartholomew's Day Massacre where thousands of Protestants, including some of Catherine's servants, were murdered. "Henri was forced to abjure the Protestant faith on behalf of both of them"[71] and Catherine developed depression.[72]

Henri eventually went back to rule Navarre and pushed for his sister's return. Catherine arrived back home at the age of sixteen, having been orphaned, seen her church massacred, and lived under significant personal persecution during her years in Paris. When she got back to Navarre, she renounced Roman Catholicism, making public profession of Protestant faith with her brother.[73]

By the age of seventeen, Catherine was acting as regent for Henri, who left Navarre to fight for the French throne;[74] Catherine managed troops, money, and international political connections. Through her life, Catherine suffered from migraines, like her mother. The headaches were sometimes debilitating, the worst one lasting fourteen months.[75] Somehow, Catherine managed to run Navarre despite this affliction.

In 1589, Henri became King of France. He gave up Protestantism because "Paris is worth a mass." Catherine was devastated by his unbelief. She wrote, "I am so distressed by it that I cannot express it adequately."[76] She was also under pressure to convert herself; Henri put Catherine under sustained intimidation to renounce Protestantism. She "remained a devout Calvinist despite severe pressures from her brother to follow his lead in abandoning their mother's faith."[77]

---

70. George Campbell Overend, *The Persecuted Princess: a Chapter of French History* (Edinburgh: Johnstone, Hunter, & Co., 1875), 42.

71. Jane Couchman, "Resisting Henri IV: Catherine de Bourbon and her Brother" in *Sibling Relations and Gender in the Early Modern World*, eds. Naomi J. Miller and Naomi Yavneh (Aldershot, U. K.: Ashgate, 2006), 65.

72. Overend, *Persecuted Princess*, 45.

73. Roelker, *Queen of Navarre*, 411.

74. Overend, *Persecuted Princess*, 53–54.

75. Catherine de Bourbon to Caumont-La Force, May, 1595, in Roelker, *Queen of Navarre*, 416.

76. Catherine de Bourbon to du Plessis-Mornay, July 1593, in Couchman, *Sibling Relations*, 71.

77. Roelker, *Queen of Navarre*, 124.

Still regent of Navarre, "Catherine remained devoted to her brother even after [his conversion]."[78] In 1590, we see a change in her own identity, though: before this point, she signed her letters, "Catherine de Navarre." That fall, she simply became "Catherine" for the rest of her life.[79]

Not only firm in her own faith, Catherine also interceded for other persecuted Protestants, opening her apartments in Paris as a Huguenot meeting place.[80] Because of her high position, she became the target of Roman Catholic attacks. Verbally abused from Catholic pulpits, threatened by mobs, and lied about in the press, Catherine felt the heat.[81] Henri, who was trying to keep the country from collapsing into civil war again, did not actually stop his sister's activities. But he did keep urging her conversion.

Catherine's letters to Henri were full of sisterly affection. But Henri used "his sister in a matrimonial chess game in order to cement [a political] alliance with former enemies."[82]

Catherine had fallen in love with a cousin, Charles, but in 1592 Henri discovered that they had signed a secret marriage contract. He arrested Charles[83] and put Catherine under house arrest.[84] Henri told her that she needed to marry Henri de Lorraine, who was a staunch Roman Catholic. Sickness and stress turned Catherine to writing poetry, like her grandmother did. The first one was a heart cry to God in the middle of deep trial:

> With your eye of pity, look on my labour,
> Give some relief from these mortal pains,
> Or if it pleases you, Lord, that I suffer them,
> Strengthen my heart against all these attacks.
> Let the tears, the cries, the sighs which my soul

---

78. Couchman, *Sibling Relations*, 64.

79. See Catherine de Bourbon to Monsieur de Sainct Genies, September 23, 1590 in *Lettres et Poesies de Catherine de Bourbon, Princesse de France, Infante de Navarre, Duchesse de Bar (1570–1603)* (Paris: Raymond Ritter, 1927), 76.

80. Roelker, *Queen of Navarre*, 414.

81. Overend, *Persecuted Princess*, 91–93.

82. Bainton, *France and* England, 75.

83. Roelker, *Queen of Navarre*, 412.

84. Couchman, *Sibling Relations*, 68.

> Brings forth in her grief, increase the flame
> Which your unfeigned zeal kindles within me.[85]

Pressure to marry continued.[86] Sister stood up to brother for years, until 1597, when she finally agreed to the marriage.[87]

What Catherine would not agree to was Roman Catholicism. She knew that the king had the authority to choose her husband, but "in matters of religion, she acknowledged no such right, and there was no limit to her resistance."[88] Henri voiced his frustration: "My sister is in the same bad mood…which is an unbearable affliction to me. That is why I am hurrying as much as I can to get her married."[89]

In 1598, Catherine made a significant impact on French religion as a delegate in the negotiations surrounding the Edict of Nantes.[90] Henri gave her the job of "persuading the cardinals and bishops that the Edict would serve their best interests."[91] It was a huge assignment, as one Protestant noted: "She will need to exercise her command of the arts of persuasion to the utmost…no woman has ever undertaken a more difficult task."[92] After many dinners and meetings, Catherine succeeded.[93] During the negotiations, Henri lessened the pressure on his sister in order to get Huguenot support for the Edict, which was pushed through.[94]

Months after the edict was signed, Catherine married the Roman Catholic Duke de Lorraine.[95] The Duke worked with Henri to isolate Catherine, dismissing her Protestant ladies-in-waiting after the wedding. Catherine, recovering from a serious fever, was devastated. She wrote: "a blow so cruel and hard to believe…. I cannot imagine that after obeying you… in taking a husband of the other religion… you would do such a cruel thing…. Have pity on a little sister!… I can

---

85. Translated from Catherine de Bourbon, "Sonnets du Madame" in *Lettres et Poesies*, 206–207.
86. See for example Catherine de Bourbon to Henri IV, September 22, 1595 in Couchman, *Sibling Relations*, 69.
87. Roelker, *Queen of Navarre*, 413–14.
88. Couchman, *Sibling Relations*, 70.
89. Henri IV to Caumont, June 18, 1598 in Couchman, *Sibling Relations*, 66.
90. Couchman, *Sibling Relations*, 68.
91. Noel Gerson, *The Edict of Nantes* (New York: Grosset and Dunlap, 1969), 119.
92. Duc de Montmorency to the Duchess de Montmorency, 1598, in Gerson, 119.
93. Sully in Gerson, *Edict of Nantes*, 125.
94. Couchman, *Sibling Relations*, 71; Roelker, *Queen of Navarre*, 414.
95. Couchman, *Sibling Relations*, 71–72.

bear everything else, but this reduces me to despair."[96] She got a few maids back, but her Huguenot ministers were replaced by priests who worked hard to convert her.[97]

In the summer of 1599, Catherine, then forty years old, suffered a miscarriage.[98] She was aware that the likelihood of having a child was slim because of her age and poor health, but desperately wanted a baby. She wrote to Theodore Beza, asking for prayer.

Henri worked with Catherine's in-laws to convert her, but with no effect. He wrote: "We have not been able to defeat my sister… with all our efforts and means…. I have spared neither advice nor persuasion, nor the authority I have over her."[99]

The marriage, as you can imagine, was complicated and hard.[100] These difficult relationships, isolation, poor health, and the grief of infertility combined to make life unwelcome. Catherine wrote, "I swear before God I wish for death a thousand times a day."[101]

Early in 1604, Catherine thought that she was expecting again, but she also had tuberculosis, and refused treatment in case it hurt the baby. The growth was actually an abdominal tumor that ended her life on February 13. She never realized what was really happening, and she died begging the doctors to save her child.[102] Henri did not attend her funeral and Catherine's body was buried beside her mother's.[103]

It's a sad story, isn't it? This kind of suffering is unusual, and grandmother, mother, and daughter all labored under it for their lifetimes.

But this is more than sad—it's incredible. You don't have three generations of women standing up to French kings and the power of Roman Catholicism just because. It's not coincidence or circumstance

---

96. Catherine de Bourbon to Henri IV, March, 1599, in Roelker, *Queen of Navarre*, 414–15.

97. Couchman, *Sibling Relations*, 72.

98. Catherine de Bourbon to Henri IV, August 18, 1599, in Roelker, *Queen of Navarre*, 415.

99. Henry IV to Monsieur de Bethune, March 21, 1602 in Couchman, *Sibling Relations*, 73.

100. Couchman, *Sibling Relations*, 73.

101. Catherine de Bourbon to Henri IV, August 7, 1600 in Bainton, *France and England*, 80.

102. Bainton, *France and England*, 81.

103. Roelker, *Queen of Navarre*, 416.

or even character. This sort of sacrificial faithfulness is supernatural. God was faithful to these women as individuals, as a family, and enabled them to stand up under the suffering. They did not only bear the suffering; they were incredibly fruitful through it all. These women are a poignant picture of God's faithfulness to His people.

All of these people together form a sort of Romans 12:1 exhibit. Worship is a lifestyle. These women show us what it can look like to be a living sacrifice. And they point us to the God who is the same today, and who still makes worshipers.

CHAPTER 11

What the Christology of the Reformation Teaches Us Today

Stephen G. Myers

Often, the guiding theological emphases of the Reformation are summarized using the "Five *Solas*"—*sola Scriptura, sola fide, solus Christus, sola gratia,* and *soli Deo gloria*. These five statements, in large part, encapsulate the theological content of the Reformation. One of these five solas is *solus Christus*—Christ alone. As Christians, we have faith in Christ alone; our hope and our salvation is in Christ alone; Christ alone is the Mediator between God and man. *Solus Christus* speaks of both the exclusivity and the exclusive glory of Jesus Christ in the redemption of God's people. But the prominence of *solus Christus* in the theology of the Reformation begs a question— when the Reformers and those who followed them proclaimed the exclusive glory of Christ, precisely who was the Christ they had in mind? How did they understand His person? How did they understand His work? What was the Christology of the Reformation? Who is the Christ behind *solus Christus*? When the Christology of the Reformation is examined, one finds an understanding of Christ that is able to support the weight of *solus Christus's* claims.

The Context of Reformation Christology

The richness of Reformation Christology is tightly connected to two specific factors. In the first instance, the theologians of the Reformation were articulating their doctrine in a milieu accustomed to the Roman Catholic presentation of traditional, creedal orthodoxy. This reality demanded that the Reformers address, in detail, every component of traditional Christian doctrinal language. In his *Institutes of the Christian Religion,* John Calvin framed the matter clearly. After speaking of Jesus as Prophet, Priest, and King, Calvin writes:

Yet it would be of little value to know these names without understanding their purpose and use. The papists use these names, too, but coldly and rather ineffectually, since they do not know what each of these titles contains.[1]

Every word that the Reformers would use in explaining who Christ is and what He has done, Roman Catholic theologians had been using for centuries, yet those words had come to have meanings quite different from the Reformers' understanding of their meaning. The Reformers, then, had to assume that even the traditional language of the Christian creeds needed detailed explanation in order to free that language from the Roman Catholic perceptions that had become attached to it. No area of Christological thought, and no terminology used to express that thought, could remain unexamined by the Reformers and this comprehensiveness bred a pronounced rigor in the Reformation's Christology.

Second, while the Reformers were articulating their doctrine against the backdrop of Roman Catholic teaching, at the same time, they also were refuting the errors of other men who were rejecting not simply the Roman Catholic presentation of creedal orthodoxy, but that very orthodoxy itself. Faced with such heterodox and even heretical doctrinal systems, the theologians of the Reformation and Post-Reformation eras seldom addressed Christology in isolation from other areas of doctrine. An example of this tendency is seen in John Owen's *Vindiciae Evangelicae: or, the Mystery of the Gospel Vindicated*, which contains some of Owen's finest work on Christology.[2] In that treatise, Owen systematically refutes the false teachings of the Socinians, a group that had emerged in the early days of the Reformation and who, among other things, rejected both the Trinity and the Deity of Christ. Given the Socinians' wholesale rejection of Christian truth, Owen is forced to begin at the beginning. Owen defends, first, a Christian understanding of Scripture, then a Christian understanding of the Being and perfections of God, and then a biblical view of mankind's condition both before and after the fall

---

1. John Calvin, *Institutes of the Christian Religion*, ed. John T. McNeill, trans. Ford Lewis Battles (Philadelphia: Westminster Press, 1960), 2.15.1.

2. John Owen, *Vindiciae Evangelicae: or, the Mystery of the Gospel Vindicated* in *The Works of John Owen*, ed. William H. Goold (1655; Edinburgh: Banner of Truth, 1966), 12.1–590.

before he even is able to begin to address the person and work of Jesus Christ.[3] When that treatment of Christology comes, then, it is shaped by what Owen already has written about who God is and who mankind is. For example, Owen had spent considerable time explaining that in order for God to be God, He had to be infinite and omnipresent, with no limitations placed upon His power and being.[4] As God Himself says in Jeremiah 23:24, He fills heaven and earth. Having shown infinity and omnipresence to be necessary to divinity, Owen comes to treat the person of Jesus Christ and he writes, in reference to the incarnate Son: "Though he humbled himself and was exalted, yet in nature he was one and the same, he changed not."[5]

Because he has discussed divine omnipresence before he has discussed the Incarnation of the divine Son, Owen is unable to avoid a profoundly mysterious issue. How does one understand the Incarnation of an omnipresent God? How does one hold together the seemingly contradictory facts that the Son of God is both in a specific geographical place as Jesus of Nazareth and, since He is God, He fills heaven and earth? Since Owen is presenting his Christology within a larger theological system, he is compelled to address all of the issues that necessarily arise.

The combination of these two factors—the need to refute entire systems of doctrine and the need to be very explicit about the terminology and concepts used in that refutation—created a richness and a depth to the Reformation's Christology. In the twenty-first century, when works of Christology are written, the author is free to choose what areas he wishes to explore and those areas can be dictated by specific contemporary Christological issues or simply by the personal interests of the author. For the Reformers, everything had to be addressed; it had to be set within a larger theological system, and all of the words used to express that comprehensive doctrine had to be clearly explained. There is little wonder, then, that the Holy Spirit used the theologians of this era to bring such clarity to the church's understanding of who Christ is and what He has done for His people. The resulting Reformation Christology can be stated simply, yet it plumbs mysteries whose glories the redeemed

---

3. Owen, *Vindiciae Evangelicae*, 85–169
4. Owen, *Vindiciae Evangelicae*, 86–98.
5. Owen, *Vindiciae Evangelicae*, 171.

will be singing longer than this earth shall endure—Jesus Christ is fully God, He is fully man, and He has won a full redemption for His people.

Jesus Christ is Fully God

The biblical support for the deity of Christ is both clear and plentiful. In John 1:1, the Scriptures declare that the Word, the Son, is God; in John 10:30, Jesus says, "I and my Father are one"; in Romans 9:5 and Titus 2:13, Paul refers to Jesus as God, a description earlier used by the disciple Thomas in John 20:28; in Philippians 2:6, Paul describes Jesus's identity with God; and throughout the New Testament, Jesus is worshiped as God. These facts are clear in the Scriptures. But there is a complicating factor. All of these things (John 1:1 excepted) are said about the man, Jesus of Nazareth. Therefore, when we consider what all of these things mean, we tend to start, conceptually, with a man—Jesus—and then make Him as much like God as we possibly can. But the starting point of our reflections on Jesus is that of a man. There is not necessarily anything wrong with that, of course—Jesus is a man!—but the complication is that often, we fail to do justice to the full deity of Christ simply because we cannot conceive of how a man can be or do the things that God is and does. As a result, we miss the enormity of what it means to say that Jesus is fully God. The theologians of the Reformation and Post-Reformation eras, however, were forced to deal with the implications of the full deity of Jesus Christ. An example of the Reformation era's attention to the deity of Christ is seen in the Reformers' treatment of precisely the issue later faced by John Owen in his previously discussed refutation of Socinian errors regarding the infinity and omnipresence of God. How does one understand the omnipresence of God alongside the familiar declaration that Jesus is fully God? During Jesus's earthly ministry, was the Son of God present everywhere; or was He only in specific places in the geography of Israel?

The glorious answer that the Reformed offered to that mysterious question often is called the *extra Calvinisticum*—the Calvinistic *extra*, or the Calvinistic "beyond." Whether accurately or not, this name clearly pins the doctrine to John Calvin, and in Calvin's own words, the doctrine is this:

For even if the Word in his immeasurable essence united with the nature of man into one person, we do not imagine that he was confined therein. Here is something marvelous: the Son of God descended from heaven in such a way that, without leaving heaven, he willed to be borne in the virgin's womb, to go about the earth, and to hang upon the cross; yet he continuously filled the earth even as he had done from the beginning![6]

Jesus Christ is the incarnate Son of God; and yet the Son of God is not confined within the physicality of Jesus. Or, to put it another way—during Jesus's earthly ministry, the eternal Son of God was on His knees, washing dirt from the feet of the disciples; and at the same instant, He was filling and upholding all of Creation. Jesus of Nazareth is not a container that encloses the Lord of Glory; rather, He is the person in whom the infinite Son is incarnate and even in that incarnate lowliness, the Son did not surrender His divinity. That is what Calvin is saying. Simultaneously, the Son of God was incarnate in Jesus of Nazareth and filling all of the earth with His divine presence and power.

Immediately, this sounds bizarre and perhaps even wrong. But it is the glorious mystery to which the Scriptures point. In John 1:18, the Scriptures tell us that even as the Son was in the flesh, making God visible to man, the Word was "in the bosom of the Father." In John 3:13, Jesus tells Nicodemus that He, Jesus, is both there with Nicodemus and in heaven. In Colossians 1:17, we read that all things "consist" by the Son, meaning that all of creation is held together by the Son. If this is true (and most certainly, it is), then even during His earthly ministry, the incarnate Son was holding together all of creation. If He were not—if, at the Incarnation, the presence and the potency of the Son was confined to the physical body of Jesus—then all creation would have dissolved. Even in the Incarnation, the Son of God remained transcendent; He veiled aspects of that transcendence during His earthly ministry, but He never surrendered it and He never became less than the infinite God.

A potential objection to this doctrine—certainly, an objection raised by the *extra*'s opponents during the Reformation—is that it presents a "partial Incarnation" in which the Son is partially, but not entirely, incarnate. According to this objection, the *extra* suggests that

---

6. Calvin, *Institutes* 2.13.4.

there is a part of the Son that remained un-incarnate. The response to this objection is rooted, once again, in a larger understanding of who God is. As God, the Son is a "simple," "immense" being. The "simplicity" of the Son means that He is not a composite being; He is not made up of constituent parts (Ex. 3:14; John 4:24; Luke 24:39). Since the Son cannot be divided into different "parts," wherever He is, He is all there. Humans, of course, are different. We are composite beings and so one part of us can be one place while another part is another place. For example, when you sit in a chair, your body is in the chair, but your feet are on the floor. There is a part of you—your feet—that are not in the chair. The Son of God, in His divine nature, is different. He is simple, and so wherever He is, He is fully and entirely there. The "immensity" of the divine Son means that there are no limitations on His being; there is nothing that circumscribes Him, no container that contains Him (1 Kings 8:27; Ps. 139:7–10; Acts 17:27–28). Given this immensity, the Son is omnipresent. Taken together, the simplicity and the immensity of the Son mean that He is everywhere completely present. In His divine nature, the Son is both entirely and completely in the body—the whole of Him is there—and the whole-ness of Him is filling heaven and earth. The divine nature of the Son is everywhere completely present. The *extra*, then, does not bespeak a partial Incarnation. Rather, it describes what cannot be compre-hended fully—the full Incarnation of the simple, immense Son. It is the ineffable reality to which Calvin and other Reformers were led as they considered the fullness of what it means to say that Jesus is fully God.

While Calvin undoubtedly taught this doctrine, the name *extra Calvinisticum* is a bit misleading in appearing to attribute the doc-trine's origination to him. The doctrine is much older than John Calvin. It is prominent in the Christology of the early church— particularly in men like Athanasius and Cyril of Alexandria; it is prominent in the Christology of the medieval church—in men such as Peter Lombard and Thomas Aquinas; and it is prominent in the Christology of the broader Reformation—in men such as Peter Mar-tyr Vermigli and Zacharias Ursinus.[7] Calvin's understanding of the

---

7. For a thorough account of the doctrine's history, see Andrew M. McGinnis, *The Son of God Beyond the Flesh: A Historical and Theological Study of the* extra Calvin-isticum (London: Bloomsbury, 2014).

transcendence of the incarnate Son is not novel to him. It has filled the church's understanding of who Jesus is since the very earliest of days. The name *extra Calvinisticum* does not reflect the pedigree of the doctrine, rather it reflects the context in which Calvin articulated it. Calvin had several rather sharp differences with the Lutheran branch of the Reformation on the doctrine of the Lord's Supper, and among these differences was that Lutheran doctrine held to the ubiquity of Christ's body. According to this doctrine, since Jesus Christ was fully God, and God is omnipresent, the body of Jesus is everywhere, most particularly in the elements of the Lord's Supper.[8] Calvin disagreed with this doctrine of the ubiquity of Christ's body, arguing that Jesus's body, as a fully, truly human body, was limited to a specific place just like any other human body. But at the same time as the Son was incarnate in that physically limited body, He was transcendently present in all of Creation. Jesus was, in the fullest sense, both fully man and fully God. As Calvin argued:

> the very same Christ, who, according to the flesh, dwelt as Son of Man on earth, was God in heaven. In this manner, he is said to have descended to that place according to his divinity, not because divinity left heaven to hide itself in the prison house of the body, but because even though it filled all things, still in Christ's very humanity it dwelt bodily [Col. 2:9], that is, by nature, and in a certain ineffable way.[9]

In other words, Christ can be, and is, present when His physical body is not. Christ is "ubiquitous," but His body is not. What that meant for the Lord's Supper is that Christ is spiritually present in the Supper even though His body remains in heaven. The Lutherans, obviously, disagreed with this understanding and, in an attempt to ridicule it and paint it as a bizarre novelty from Geneva, they called it the *extra Calvinisticum*. But it is not Calvin's doctrine; it is the long-held, Scriptural doctrine of the church. The Son of God is fully incarnate in Jesus Christ, yet the Incarnation does not exhaust the infinite being of the Son. In a way that we cannot conceive, the Son of God is, at the same moment, both in the flesh and beyond the flesh.

---

8. For the most responsible statement of this doctrine, see Martin Chemnitz, *The Two Natures in Christ*, trans. J. A. O. Preus (1578; Saint Louis: Concordia Publishing House, 1971), 423–67.

9. Calvin, *Institutes*, 4.17.30.

Do you see how wondrous the Jesus whom we worship is? As Jesus lay in His mother's arms in Bethlehem, and cried for the nourishment that He needed in order to survive, the very stars that filled the sky were there only because He held them there. As He walked the roads of Galilee, the earth would have vanished away in His absence. If you are a Christian, the One who hung in the darkness of Calvary, desolate under the judgment due to your sin, was the One who holds creation together. He is fully God. He did not hang on Calvary in weakness; He hung there because, in His divine strength, He was redeeming you out of His love for you. That is the love of the Son of God for His people. That is the glory of the Jesus who loves you. If you are not a Christian, know that this is the majesty of the Jesus who says, "Come unto me, all ye that labour and are heavy laden, and I will give you rest" (Matt. 11:28). Jesus is not a man of nostalgic interest or limp sentimentality. The Jesus with whom we deal—the Jesus who offers Himself in the gospel—is the living God.

Jesus Christ is Fully Man

This incredibly high view of Christ and of His divinity pervaded the Christology of the Reformation. But an insistence upon Christ's divinity never entailed a diminishing of His humanity. In fact, the Christology of the Reformers accentuated the full humanity of Christ in a way that sometimes was scandalous to their contemporaries. Interestingly, one of the two places in his *Institutes* where Calvin addresses the *extra Calvinisticum* comes in precisely such a setting. Calvin had laid out the full humanity of Christ and all of its implications in *Institutes* 2.13 and then he concludes that chapter by articulating the *extra*. Calvin's attention to the humanity of Christ had been so gritty and so human that he wanted to assure his readers that this same man also was unceasingly God. In the Christology of the Reformation, Jesus Christ is fully God and fully man. The Reformers and those who followed after them traced this humanity in a number of different ways, but there is one way in which Reformation Christology underscored the humanity of Jesus Christ that seems particularly useful for the twenty-first century church.

In reading through Christological discussions in the Reformation and immediately thereafter, with surprising regularity, one stumbles across references and allusions to monothelitism, a seventh century teaching which held that Jesus Christ, in the Incarnation, possessed only one will.[10] "Mono," of course, means "one" in Greek, and "thelema," in Greek, means "will"; so "monothelitism" is "one-will-ism." According to monothelite teaching, the incarnate Son had one will—specifically, a divine will. Opposed to this teaching was dyothelitism, the doctrine that Christ has two wills; a divine will and a human will. While this may seem to be a rather obscure argument, it raged in the church in the seventh century until finally, in 681, the Third Council of Constantinople condemned the monothelite position as heretical. One of the reasons this is significant is that, after 681, there was not really any simmering dispute within the church between monothelites and dyothelites. The issue largely was decided and had faded into the background of theological discussions.[11] But then, in the Reformation and Post-Reformation theologians, it reemerged with surprising prominence. Why was this doctrine of the two wills of Christ suddenly so widely used within the Christology of the Reformation? Among other things, it was seen by Reformation theologians as critical to understanding the full humanity of Christ.

Conceptually, dyothelitism is rooted in one's understanding of who Jesus is. In the words of the Westminster Shorter Catechism, Jesus Christ is "two distinct natures in one Person."[12] He is two natures—a full and perfect divine nature, and a full and perfect human nature—in one person—Jesus Christ. The concept of "nature"

10. For examples throughout the period, see Calvin, *Calvin's Commentaries* (Grand Rapids: Baker, 1999), 17:233; Peter Martyr Vermigli, *Dialogue on the Two Natures in Christ*, ed. and trans. John Patrick Donnelly (1561; Kirksville, Mo.: Sixteenth Century Essays and Studies, 1995), 29; Girolamo Zanchi, *Confession of Christian Religion*, ed. Luca Baschera and Christian Moser (1586; Leiden: Brill, 2007), 1:213; Samuel Rutherford, *The Covenant of Life Opened: Or, a Treatise of the Covenant of Grace* (Edinburgh: A. A. for Robert Broun, 1655), 309–10; Francis Turretin, *Institutes of Elenctic Theology*, ed. James T. Dennison, Jr., trans. George Musgrave Giger (1679–1685; Phillipsburg: P&R, 1992), 3:79; Benedict Pictet, *Christian Theology*, trans. Frederick Reyroux (1696; Philadelphia: Presbyterian Board of Publication, 1845), 245. For more on monothelitism, see Douglas Kelly, *Systematic Theology Volume Two: The Beauty of Christ: A Trinitarian Vision* (Fearn: Mentor, 2014), 246–48; Stephen Wellum, *God the Son Incarnate: The Doctrine of Christ* (Wheaton: Crossway, 2016), 338–48.

11. There were some debates about these matters in the thirteenth century, but they were relatively short-lived.

12. *Westminster Shorter Catechism*, 21.

can be vague, but a "nature" is essentially that which makes a thing what it is. Whatever makes a human a human is a human nature. Whatever makes God God is divine nature. A nature is that which makes a thing what it is.

As already has been seen, Jesus possesses a divine nature. Jesus is God, so everything that makes God God, Jesus is. Part of divine nature, part of what makes God God, is His will—His purposeful and intentional determining. If one removes the divine will from the divine nature, he is left with something less than God. The divine will is located in the divine nature.

Just as He possess a divine nature, Jesus also possesses a human nature. In Hebrews 4:15, the Scriptures declare that Jesus is perfectly and completely a man; the only difference between His humanity and ours is that He has no sin. Everything that makes man man, Jesus possesses. Part of human nature, part of what makes man man, is his will—his purposeful and intentional determining. If one removes a human will from human nature, he is left with something less than man. A human will is part of human nature.

What all of this means is that Jesus Christ—one person—has two wills, a divine will and a human will. Jesus's divine will is seen in places like Matthew 23:37; Luke 13:34; and John 5:21. This divine will is perfectly and precisely identical with the will of the Father and the Spirit. Jesus's human will is different. It is not sinful and it is not rebellious. It is a perfectly sinless will. Furthermore, it always is authoritatively led by Jesus's divine will. But it is a human will. As Calvin wrote, in Jesus, the divine will and the human will "differed from each other without any conflict or opposition."[13] The Scriptures do not fully explain either how that operated during Jesus's earthly ministry, or how it works in Jesus's glorified, exalted state. But the Scriptures do tell us that Jesus is fully God and fully man. He has a divine will and He has a human will. The depth that this brings to the humanity of Christ is incalculable. Not just in the things that one can see—the fleshly, tangible things of the body—but even in the interior, volitional impulses, Jesus is fully a man.

The Reformers rooted this doctrine in a familiar section of Matthew 26.[14] In that passage, it is the night of His betrayal; Jesus is

---

13. E.g. Calvin, *Commentaries*, 17:233.
14. See, e.g., Calvin, *Commentaries*, 17:233.

in the Garden of Gethsemane, and He prays to the Father to let the cup of God's wrath against sin pass from Him. In Matthew 26:38, Jesus tells His disciples, "My soul is exceeding sorrowful, even unto death." Jesus dreads what He knows lies ahead. Then, in verse 39, Jesus prays to the Father; and He says: "O my Father, if it be possible, let this cup pass from me; nevertheless, not as I will, but as thou wilt." Then, after a brief break, Jesus prays again, in Matthew 26:42: "O my Father, if this cup may not pass away from me, except I drink it, thy will be done."

The progression here is staggering. Jesus is submitting His will—His *human* will—to the will of the Father. He begins in dread, wanting nothing to do with the cross. Then, He pleads for a change of course, even while expressing a willingness to submit to the will of the Father. Then finally, Jesus prays for the Father's will to be done. Jesus's human will has been brought into submission to the will of the Father. He wants what the Father wants. It is not without heaviness, but He prays for what the Father wants. Jesus, the Son of God, is submitting His human will to the divine will. In the thick air of Gethsemane, one sees the two wills of Christ. The one, the divine will, that is identical with the Father's will; and the second, the human will, that initially shrinks from the ravages of Calvary but that then, obediently, is led by the divine will into submission. In Gethsemane, one hears the two wills of Christ. Jesus was not just a human anatomy that the Son of God activated. He was fully, truly, completely, from the inside out, a man, even in His will. That is what the Reformers and their theological descendants wanted so desperately to assert when they rebuked monothelitism and when they argued for the two wills of Christ. There is no level of consciousness or corner of the interior life in which Jesus Christ is not fully a man.

This might seem like somewhat abstract material, but it gets down to and it affects the way that Christians live their lives. Think about what it means. Jesus knows the struggle of bringing a human will into submission to the will of God. What one hears in the anguished cries of Gethsemane is Jesus bringing His human will into submission to the divine will. Jesus knows what will be involved in the cross. And His human will does not want it. It wants to pull back. Jesus's human will does not want the desolation of the cross. It does not want the disintegrating fury of the wrath of God against sin. It does not want to be the colliding point of God's perfect wrath and the sins of all of His people. But Jesus brings that will into submission. He brings it into such submission that He can pray, by the end, that the Father's will—the divine will—be done. Jesus did not live His days in some pristine environment in which doing God's will always was easy. Jesus knows what it is when doing the will of God is hard.

For Christians, there are depths of comfort here. If you are a Christian, you are called to a life of obedience. And that is hard. You struggle with all your might to make it appear to others that it is easy for you. But it is hard. And the real hardness of obedience is on the inside. You can grit your teeth and do things externally that will fit whatever standard you please. But to wrestle with the still-sinful will that resides inside and make it want the glory of God—that is the hardness of obedience.

Jesus, of course, was without sin. There was no sin even in His will. But He knows what it is when submitting your will to the will of God is hard, even terrifying and unpalatable. Jesus knows the aching hardness of submitting your will to the will of God; and He knows it from the weeping side of the tears. Jesus knows what it is to have precious things, beloved things—He knows what it is to have a life—and to lay it down before the will of the living God. When you know what it is that God would have you to do—in a difficult situation at work; in a relationship; in your interactions with a family member; in your dealing with a particular sin or a particular vice in your life—when you know what it is that God would have you to do, and you just do not want to do it, Jesus knows the anguish. Not the sin, but the anguish. He knows the pain of the letting go and the struggle of bowing down.

So run to Him. Pray for Jesus, by His Spirit, to strengthen you to submit to God's will as He submitted to God's will. It is not easy. Even for the perfect, sinless human will of Jesus, it was not easy. Pray that Jesus would give you strength to submit your will to the will of God. He knows what you mean when you ask it, and He is able; because just as Reformation Christology insisted, He is fully God and fully man.

Jesus Christ has Won a Full Redemption for His People

Along with stressing that Jesus Christ was both fully God and fully man, Reformation Christology was anxious to assert that He has won a full redemption for His people. This emphasis within Reformation Christology began with the nuanced way in which the Reformers interacted with the notion of "merit." On the one hand, the Roman Catholic Church had developed an understanding wherein "merit" was something that individual men and women could accumulate, receive from dead saints, or even purchase in order to escape the judgment of God. This notion of "merit" was fundamentally opposed to the gospel and the Reformers wanted nothing to do with it. But on the other hand, there were some groups withdrawing from Rome at the time of the Reformation who completely and radically rejected any idea of merit at all. In this line of thinking, "grace" is fundamentally opposite to the notion of "merit" and thus to assign any place to any merit was to begin a slide back into Roman legalism and works righteousness. Because of this antipathy to "merit," these more radical groups argued that there was not even anything meritorious in the shed blood of Jesus. That blood had not merited, won, or properly purchased anything at all. While the Reformers certainly did not want to articulate a Roman Catholic view of "merit," they likewise wanted to be clear that there was merit in the blood of Jesus. That sacrificial blood actually earned, and indeed deserved, redemption. There was procuring merit in the blood of Jesus because by that blood, God actually paid the debt due to His own justice to redeem His people.

John Calvin strongly resisted the complete rejection of merit. In *Institutes* 2.17, Calvin deals with how Christ truly merited grace and salvation for the people of God. Calvin begins with the stipulation that ultimately, grace and salvation flow from the good pleasure and decree of God. When one speaks of Christ "meriting" the redemption of His people, it is not as if Christ is procuring something that the Father was reticent to bestow. Rather, out of His mere good pleasure, God had decreed that through the work of Christ, the redemption that God desired for His people would be justly obtained. So the merit of Christ's work does not cause God's mercy; rather, the merit of Christ's work is the instrument through which God bestows His mercy. Christ came and merited redemption not so that God could love His people, but because He already did. With that critical stipulation made, Calvin gets to the point at issue—the procuring merit of Christ's work. Calvin states it bluntly: "By his obedience, however, Christ truly acquired and merited grace for us with his Father."[15] As counterintuitive as the language may sound, Christ earned grace. Indeed, Calvin is very specific about how this worked: "But when we say that grace was imparted to us by the merit of Christ, we mean this: by his blood we were cleansed, and his death was an expiation for our sins."[16]

Jesus's blood made us clean. His death removed our sin. The blood that Jesus Christ poured out on Calvary earned the forgiveness that His people receive. In keeping with this Reformation understanding, the matter can be stated quite strongly—because of the shed blood of Jesus, those who are His deserve to be cleansed. In this, Reformation Christology is articulating the dynamic of 1 John 1:9: "If we confess our sins, he is faithful and just to forgive us our sins and to cleanse us from all unrighteousness."

Notice what John says there. Why does God forgive the sin of His people? Does John say, "If we confess our sins, He is *merciful* to forgive us our sin"; "If we confess our sins, He is *gracious* to forgive us our sin"? No. John says, "If we confess our sins, he is *faithful* and *just* to forgive us our sins." It is the justice of God that brings cleansing and forgiveness to His people. When Jesus died under the curse of God against the sin of His people, He took God's wrath against that sin away. It is gone. The sins of God's people have been judged fully in Christ and therefore they deserve to be forgiven. Justice is satisfied. God forgives sin and He makes His people clean not because He does not care about their sin, and not because He overlooks it or winks at it. God forgives His people and makes His people clean because He has dealt with their sin in Christ. Jesus has merited their forgiveness and so God forgives their sin out of His justice. He gives that which has been merited. Christ's coming displays God's grace and mercy; but the forgiveness that Christ bestows, He merits.

That is sublime. But Calvin, rightly, nudges matters even further. Still in the same chapter of the *Institutes*, Calvin notes the words of Galatians 2:21: "If righteousness come by the law, then Christ

---

15. Calvin, *Institutes*, 2.17.3.
16. Calvin, *Institutes*, 2.17.4.

is dead in vain." From that verse, Calvin asserts that in Christ's death, believers have the righteousness that they would have had by keeping the law, if such obedience were possible. What "could" have come by obedience to the law, hypothetically, has come through Christ, instead. That connection being made, Calvin writes this: "For if righteousness consists in the observance of the law, who will deny that Christ merited favor for us when, by taking that burden upon Himself, he reconciled us to God as if we had kept the law?"[17]

In His obedience even unto death, Jesus merited for His people not only forgiveness, but positive righteousness. Jesus made His people, in God's eyes, like those who had kept the law! Jesus gives His people a law-keeping, God-pleasing righteousness. It is the same thing that Paul is describing in 2 Corinthians 5:21, when he writes: "For he hath made him to be sin for us, who knew no sin; that we might be made the righteousness of God in him."

Christ takes the sin of His people on Himself and, satisfying the divine wrath against that sin, He merits their forgiveness. Furthermore, the righteousness that Christ had won through a lifetime of perfect, unflinching obedience, He bestows upon His people, meriting for them righteousness. This "double exchange" is clear in Calvin and it would become even more clear in his theological descendants. There is, in Christ's work, an active obedience by which Jesus perfectly fulfills the law, wins righteousness by that obedience, and then gives, or imputes, that righteousness to His people so that they are counted "righteous." Not "guilty," and not even merely "forgiven," but "righteous." Jesus does not just take away His people's sin, He also gives them righteousness.

For Christians, the comfort of this truth knows no bottom. All of your sin—all of your filth and degradation and shame—Jesus has taken upon Himself and He has paid the debt that you owed to divine justice. Your sins are gone. They are gone. And in their place, Jesus has given to you—He has imputed to you—His very own righteousness. In the sight of the living God, you are righteous. Among men, the taint of sin lingers. Men and women look at you and they remember. "There is that man who did that horrible thing. There is that woman who was so hurtful. There is that man who was such a failure as a father; that woman who was so shameful." But it is not

---

17. Calvin, *Institutes*, 2.17.5.

so with God. He knows your deepest sin. And yet He looks on you and He sees the iridescent righteousness of Jesus. The Jesus in whom the Father declared Himself to be well pleased. There is no shame. There is no guilt. If you are a Christian, in you, God sees righteousness. You are clean. You are righteous. Because Jesus has merited it. With His life and with His death, Jesus has earned your place in the realms of endless day. Jesus Christ is fully God, fully man, and He has won a full redemption for His people.

Conclusion

In a day of often weak and superficial understandings of who Jesus is and what He has done, the Christology of the Reformation has stores of riches for us. It describes for us the only work that can merit, for sinners, acceptance and life before the holy God, and it presents to us the only Jesus who can accomplish that work. Jesus Christ is fully God, He is fully man, and He has won a full redemption for His people. Praise God for the truths He revealed to the Reformers; may those same truths invigorate us and stir our love for Jesus again.

CHAPTER 12

Missions: What Have We Learned from the Reformers?

Elias Medeiros

The subject of this article requires a justification. In order to answer this question, we need to first be convinced that the Reformers were engaged in the propagation of the gospel to all nations. This subject was the purpose of my first article, "The Reformers' Commitment to the Propagation of the Gospel to All Nations: A Historical Consideration," which is also part of this volume. In that article, I demonstrated, based on the primary and secondary sources available, that the Reformers, especially John Calvin, were intentionally and intensively committed to the propagation of the gospel to all nations. In that regard, I will highlight four lessons we can learn from the writings and work of the Reformers regarding the propagation of the gospel around the world.

Missional Terminology in Light of Scripture

The Reformers did not use terms such as "evangelism," "mission," "missions," "missionary," "missionary work," "mission field," and so forth. This does not mean they were not committed to evangelizing, discipling, training, and sending off "workers" and "laborers" to preach the gospel and win converts across the street and around the world. For the Reformers, biblical and theological precision were vitally important. The terms they used were God-glorifying, based on Scripture alone. Every term, description, and definition they used was subject to the Word of God (*sola Scriptura*).

The absence of the term "mission" or "missionary" in the Reformers' vocabulary does not imply indifference or lack of zeal, teaching, or practice on their part. The term "evangelism" was not used by the Reformers or the Puritans, but it does not mean they were indifferent to evangelizing or "professing" their faith publicly and privately.[1] Instead, they used other biblical terminology such as "fishing," "man-fishing," "throwing the nets," "professing," and so forth.

As a Reformed missiologist, I am convinced that this is one of the weakest areas in contemporary missiology: the lack of scriptural terminology as it relates to missions. The terms used and how we define them are crucial. Most of our missiological terms were defined by the disciplines of mission anthropology, mission strategy, and even mission history. We frequently use terms such as "mission," "missionary," "missionary work," "mission field," and "missional." These terms are not problematic per se. But when we attempt to define these terms we discover there is no universal agreement as to their meaning. Even mission scholars have come to the conclusion that it's nearly impossible to come up with an agreed-upon definition of the terms "mission" or "missionary."[2]

Many, if not most, missiologists approach Scripture using the principles of the social sciences (sociology, anthropology, history, and even mission strategy) as their hermeneutical grid. Instead of submitting the tenets of these disciplines to the scrutiny of biblical, exegetical, and theological evaluation, they interpret the Scriptures based on the terms and descriptions imported from these "sciences." For example, John 1:14 says, "And the Word became flesh and dwelt among us," which points to the theological and soteriological doctrine of the incarnation of Christ—Christ becoming man—true man and true God. Evangelical cultural anthropologists interpret and expand this verse to mean that John was talking about cultural identification. Their application goes like this: identify yourselves with the culture among which you will work. Evangelical anthropologists (when dealing with anthropology as a discipline) seldom interact with the theological treatises of the Reformed theologians as it pertains to biblical anthropology.

---

1. See Joel Beeke, *Puritan Evangelism: A Biblical Approach* (Grand Rapids: Reformation Heritage Books, 2012); Richard Baxter, "Directions About the Profession of our Religion to Others," in *The Practical Works of Richard Baxter*, vol. 1, *A Christian Directory* (Ligonier: Soli Deo Gloria, 1990).

2. See A. Scott Moreau, ed., "Mission and Missions," in *Evangelical Dictionary of World Missions* (Grand Rapids: Baker, 2000), 636–38; and Andreas J. Köstenberger and Peter T. O'Brien, *Salvation to the Ends of the Earth: A Biblical Theology of Mission*, *New Studies in Biblical Theology series* (Downers Grove, Ill.: InterVarsity, 2001), 21.

The remedy to this problem, of course, is to go back to Scripture. What terms do the Scriptures use when they refer to missions? The Reformers were careful not to elevate the writings and opinions of men over Scripture. In 1538, Luther wrote, "He who is well acquainted with the text of Scripture is a distinguished theologian. For a Bible passage or text is of more value than the comments of four authors."[3] Elsewhere, Luther wrote: "The writings of all the holy fathers should be read only for a time, in order that through them we may be led to the Holy Scriptures.... We are like men who study the signposts and never travel the road. The dear fathers wished by their writing to lead us to the Scriptures, but we so use them as to be led away from the Scriptures, though the Scriptures alone are our vineyard in which we ought all to work and toil."[4]

The Missionary Work of the Church and Suffering

A second lesson we learn from the Reformers is that the preaching of the gospel to all "across the street" and "around the world" for God's glory will not be accomplished without suffering. According to David Platt, "Martyrdom is the path, not the exception.... The Reformers remind us that it is right to give our bodies to defend the Bible and the gospel. Even if we don't die, we must give our lives to the same task.... A theology of danger and martyrdom is not a prominent theme in our churches today. Our views of safety and security are far too often American and not biblical."[5] I have already documented this in my other article. The Reformers, like the early church in the book of Acts, understood that suffering was an integral part of their "mission," which was the propagation of the gospel to all nations.

John Calvin received regular reports about ministers who were in prison because of the preaching of the gospel in Great Britain, Italy, France, Brazil, and so forth.[6] A glance at the table of contents

---

3. Martin Luther, *What Luther Says: An Anthology* (St. Louis: Concordia), 3:1355.

4. John Piper, *Martin Luther: Lessons from Life and Labor* (Minneapolis: Desiring God Foundation, 2012), 93–94.

5. David Platt, "Martyrdom and Mission: Why Reformers Died in their Day, How We Must Live in Ours." Sermon, Together for the Gospel, Louisville, Ky., April 12–14, 2016.

6. Jean Calvin and Jules Bonnet, ed., *Letters of John Calvin* (Edinburgh: T. Constable, 1858), 2:335, 373, 386.

of the volumes of John Calvin's published letters should convince any reader that the work done by the Reformers to spread the gospel among all nations was done under intense persecution. In his book, *Five English Reformers*, J. C. Ryle reports that "the broad facts of the martyrdom of our Reformers are a story well known and soon told."[7] He adds, "During the last four years of Queen Mary's reign no less than 288 persons were burnt at the stake for their adhesion to the Protestant faith...one was an archbishop, four were bishops, twenty-one were clergymen, fifty-five were women, and four were children."[8]

Most of us do not expect to be martyred as a result of sharing our faith, but we can't do this work without giving our life to the task. Consider the teaching of Jesus in Matthew 10:37–39: "He that loveth father or mother more than me is not worthy of me: and he that loveth son or daughter more than me is not worthy of me. And he that taketh not his cross, and followeth after me, is not worthy of me. He that findeth his life shall lose it: and he that loseth his life for my sake shall find it." In this regard, some mission historians have treated the Counter-Reformation very lightly. The Reformers were not just struggling against theological opposition. They were under persecution, fleeing from one place to another and living as refugees throughout Europe. They were under persecution and opposition in Great Britain, France, Germany, Italy, Portugal, Spain, Hungary, Poland, Bohemia, and Brazil, to mention only a few. The Reformers were fleeing and purposefully moving throughout Europe and even to the New World.

Sometimes we try to justify our failure to share the Good News by claiming many excuses; but consider the familiar words of Jesus in Matthew 16:24: "If any man will come after me, let him deny himself, and take up his cross, and follow me." Did Jesus offer a disclaimer about introverts or extroverts? Absolutely not! He said that we must deny ourselves for the sake of the cross. This is a radical call, but it is the biblical requirement of all disciples! Our Lord calls us to deny ourselves, to embrace the cross of suffering and sacrifice, and to join with other believers in following Him.

7. J. C. Ryle, *Five English Reformers* (Carlisle, Pa.: Banner of Truth, 1999), 6.
8. J. C. Ryle, *Five English Reformers*, 7–8.

Being and feeling comfortable should not be our goal. Instead, for the sake of God's glory, the edification of His people, the salvation of the lost among all peoples, and true joy in Him throughout our lives, the Spirit of God should make us increasingly uncomfortable. I am constantly praying for God to lead me to a lost person with whom I can share the gospel, or to a faithful Christian who I might be able to encourage. And in answer to these prayers, God has blessed me with many wonderful opportunities to talk to people about His saving love.

Living faithfully for Jesus in a world that despises Him will inevitably cause us to be persecuted and will likely require us to suffer at some point. Taking up a cross and following Jesus is not guaranteed to be an easy or pain-free process. Suffering is sure to be involved but receiving the eternal blessings which are ours in Christ is worth more than any momentary sacrifices we might be called upon to make. It is true that the Christian life is filled with blessings and joy, both now and forever, but we should also expect to face times of suffering during our earthly lives for the sake of the cause of Christ. In fact, every faithful follower of Christ should expect persecution and suffering.[9]

Some mission historians have dismissed the missionary work done by the Reformers in Brazil during the sixteenth and the seventeenth centuries. According to them, the work done by the Dutch Reformers (who sent more than one hundred religious workers to Brazil between 1624–1654) should be dismissed as not being real "missionary" activity since "these comparatively independent missionary endeavours...had no abiding result."[10] I was in a state of unbelief while reading Warneck's dismissal of these efforts and Ralph Winter's unfounded and undocumented declarations. Such indifference affects not only the truth of the missionary presence and work of the Genevan and Dutch Reformers in Brazil, but also belittles the testimony and work of those who were converted and martyred among my own people. For example, Pedro Poti, a Brazilian Indian,

---

9. Matthew 5:10–12; John 16:33.

10. Gustav Warneck, *Outline of a History of Protestant Missions from the Reformation to the Present Time* (New York: Revell, 1903), 47. Warneck was referring to the missionary efforts of the Dutch in Brazil between 1630–1654 and in North America in 1646.

was converted to the Reformed faith in my home state of Paraiba during the Dutch occupation in Northeast Brazil and was martyred by the Roman Catholic Portuguese authorities.[11] Pedro Poti's crime was that he had embraced the Reformed faith and did not renounce it after the Dutch were expelled, resulting in the Roman Catholic authorities attempting to force Poti to abandon his Protestant beliefs.[12]

The Sent Ones: The Ordained Ministers of the Gospel

A third lesson we can learn from the Reformers regarding missions is the conviction that if there is one person in the church who ought to be concerned about the preaching of the gospel and making disciples of all nations, to all the world over, and to every creature, it should be the ordained minister of the gospel. Consider this quote from John Calvin on Matthew 7:6: "As the ministers of the Gospel, and those who are called to the office of teaching, cannot distinguish between the children of God and swine, it is their duty to present the doctrine of salvation indiscriminately to all."[13] Commenting on the Great Commission in Matthew 28:19, Calvin writes, "The Lord commands the ministers of the gospel to go to a distance, in order to spread the doctrine of salvation in every part of the world.... Thus was fulfilled that prediction of Isaiah (49:6) and others of a similar nature, that Christ was given for a light of the Gentiles, that he might be the salvation of God to the end of the earth. Mark means the same thing by 'every creature,' for when peace has been proclaimed to those that are within the Church, the same message reaches those who are at a distance, and were strangers (Eph. 2:17, 19)."[14] And that the prophecy proclaimed in Isaiah 49:6 may be fulfilled, "Christ

---

11. Frans Schalkwijk, *Igreja e Estado no Brasil holandês: 1630–1654*. (São Paulo: Vida Nova, 1989), 308–309.

12. Antônio Paraupaba, Indian Chief in Rio Grande do Norte and contemporary of Pedro Poti, called Poti the "Pilar da Fé" (Pillar of Faith). See this testimony in Anthonio Paräupába, *Twee Verscheyden Remonstrantien ofte Vertogen Overgegeven aen de Heeren Staten Generael der Vereenighde Nederlanden* ('s Gravenhage: Hondius, 1657), 11–12. http://www.archive.org/details/tweeverscheyden00pargoog. See also Frans Schalkwijk, *The Reformed Church in Dutch Brazil (1630–1654)*, trans. by W. S. Smith and F. L. Schalkwijk (Utrecht: Uitgeverij Boekencentrum, 1998), 210–11.

13. John Calvin, *Commentary on a Harmony of the Evangelists, Matthew, Mark and Luke* (Edinburgh: Calvin Translation Society, 1845), 1:349.

14. John Calvin, *Commentary on a Harmony of the Evangelists, Matthew, Mark and Luke* (Edinburgh: Calvin Translation Society, 1846), 3:384.

was 'given for a light of the Gentiles, that he might be the salvation of God to the end of the earth.'"[15] Calvin was truly convicted that the ministers of the gospel are the ones to take the lead: "Though the ministers of the gospel be weak and suffer the want of all things: he will be their guardian, so that they will rise victorious over all the opposition of the world."[16]

George Gillespie, the youngest and one of the most brilliant members of the Westminster Assembly, followed Calvin's teaching in this regard. Gillespie stressed the calling and responsibility of every minister to preach the gospel "to all nations," to "all the world over," and "to every creature under heaven." He said that "the preaching of the gospel is the means and way ordained of God to save them that believe (Rom. 10:14; 1 Cor. 1:23)."[17] The pastor, the ordained minister, the preacher, is the person who should be deeply concerned about and committed to the preaching of the gospel, both "here" and "everywhere."

---

15. See Calvin's comments on Matthew 28:19, in John Calvin, *Commentaries on The Harmony of The Gospels*, vol 3. See also, John Calvin, *Sermons on Psalm 119* (Audubon, N.J.: Old Paths Publications, 1996). At the end of most of his twenty-two sermons on Psalm 119, Calvin concludes with this kind of longing, prayer, and application: "And furthermore not to forget to stir us up to call upon him, to the end that by his Holy Spirit he might put his helping hand even in our hearts, and not to suffer the doctrine which we hear by the mouth of his Preachers, to become unprofitable unto us, but that it may have the full power and strength: so that we may from day to day be confirmed therein: and more and more learn to forsake the world, and all whatsoever may withdraw us from the union and conjunction of our Lord and Master Jesus Christ, who is our head. *And that he will not only show unto us this favor and grace, but also unto all people and nations of the earth, etc.*" (Sermon 2 emphasis added). Here is another example: "That he will not only grant us this grace and favor, but also unto all people and nations of the earth, etc." (Sermon 3). Or, "Let us beseech him that he will not only give us this grace, but also all the people and nations of the world, etc." (Sermon 4), and so forth. See also his comments on Matthew 4:19; 7:6; John 4—just to name a few examples.

16. See Calvin's comments on Matthew 28:20, in John Calvin, *Commentaries on The Harmony of The Gospels*, vol 3.

17. George Gillespie, *A Treatise of Miscellany Questions; Wherein Many Useful Questions and Cases of Conscience Are Discussed and Resolved, for the Satisfaction of Those Who Desire Nothing More Than to Search for and Find Out Precious Truths in the Controversies of These Times* (Edinburgh: Robert Ogle, and Oliver & Boyd, 1844), 1–2. This book was first published by Patrick Gillespie, minister at Glasgow, in 1649.

The Church: God's Mission Agency

Fourth, we should learn that, for the Reformers, it was the church, under the leadership of the pastors, that was entrusted with the commission to make disciples of all nations. The Reformers' ecclesiology was central. They were Christ- and church-centered. Some mission historians have criticized John Calvin, claiming that he was against the orders of the Roman Catholic Church, which they saw as the missionary arms of the church. It has been argued among some missiologists that because John Calvin was anti-Roman Catholic he also opposed the creation of any organization to carry on the gospel among the nations. Calvin believed that the command to make disciples of all nations was given to the church and its ministers. This was Calvin's ecclesiology. He was committed to the biblical doctrine of the church.

If there is an organized organism to whom the responsibility of preaching the gospel to all nations has been given, it should be the church of the Lord Jesus Christ. Missions organizations can be a wonderful blessing to the people of God and a valuable help in the ongoing work of the church. However, many of the so-called "missionaries" today are not examined or recruited by local churches but are commissioned by independent missionary organizations. They come to the churches for financial support, but far too often there is little or no theological or ecclesiological accountability. I find this to be a very troublesome practice that needs to be reevaluated. The Reformers teach us a far better biblical way, if only we would follow their example.

Due to the seriousness of such work and the immediate need of hundreds, even thousands of workers and ministers of the gospel, Calvin perceived that "Geneva proved herself unable to provide the vast number of pastors requested by the burgeoning Calvinist churches within France." Calvin did not reduce the requirements for the pastors because of the demand. "Calvin's guidelines for the selection of pastors made heavy educational demands which seriously restricted the number of those eligible for such positions."[18]

Due to the seriousness attributed to the preaching and the need of well-trained ministers, the Reformers made it clear that those in

---

18. Alister E. McGrath, *A Life of John Calvin: A Study in the Shaping of Western Culture* (Malden: Blackwell Publishing, 1990), 184.

charge of the preaching of the gospel to all the nations should not simply be counted, but they should be weighed. Warneck was once concerned by the numerical growth of missionaries in the nineteenth and the beginning of the twentieth century. Warneck wrote, "The general cry is more missionaries. And let me add emphatically more men. But the petition that the Lord of the harvest should send forth laborers into His harvest, has also reference to their quality. Missionaries must be weighed, not merely counted. Spiritual equipment is, of course, the chief consideration. But the experience of more than a hundred years should prevent us from falling into the mistake of thinking that this alone suffices without a thorough training."[19]

Conclusion: A Reformed Definition of Terms
We should give thanks for the faithful and fruitful missionary work of the Reformers which has been so well documented in their literary work. These lessons are precious because they are biblical; and that is what we must all strive to be, as churches and as individual believers, if we truly want to please God as we proclaim His gospel throughout the whole world.

First, let us be thankful for the Reformers' commitment to *sola Scriptura*. For them, the thirty-nine books of the Old Testament and the twenty-seven books of the New Testament were the inspired, inerrant, infallible, invincible, sufficient, and efficient revealed Word of the living God. This means that every word and phrase coined outside of Scripture should not be automatically taken for granted.[20]

---

19. See *Ecumenical Missionary Conference. New York, 1900*, 2 vols. (New York: American Tract Society, 1900), 1:289. The New York Times of April 26, 1900, referred to that letter in these terms: "The principal feature of the meeting at Union Methodist Church was the reading of a letter from the Rev. Dr. Gustav Warneck, Professor of Missions at Halle University, Germany, who is regarded as one of the highest living authorities on missionary history and methods." https://www.nytimes.com/1900/04/26/archives/criticism-and-praise-letter-read-from-prof-warneck-and-address.html

20. I am also referring to words and terms such as "mission," "missions," "missionary," "missionary work," "mission field," and so forth. Köstenberger and O'Brien suggest that since "the Scripture itself does not define 'mission,'" they offer the following: "We consider that an inductive exegesis leading to a biblical theology should come first, after which an effort is made to relate the contributions of the different corpora, and even Testaments, to each other" (p. 21). See Andreas J. Köstenberger and Peter T. O'Brien, *Salvation to the Ends of the Earth: A Biblical Theology of Mission*, New Studies in Biblical Theology series (Downers Grove, Ill.: InterVarsity,

In other words, before we embrace any terminology we should make sure that such a word or phrase is part of the vocabulary of the Bible, and that such words and phrases are not simply imposed by the social sciences over the Scriptures.

Second, the terms "mission" and "missionary," as used today, were never employed by the Reformers. Calvin, for instance, used biblical terms such as "ministers of the Word," "preachers," "pastors," and "teachers," when referring to those sent to other parts of Europe and even to the New World.

During the Dutch occupation of Northeastern Brazil between 1630 and 1654, "more than fifty ministers labored in Dutch Brazil at one time or another."[21] Besides the term "minister," "various other terms were used with respect to this office: pastor, preacher, predikant, and domine. The designation 'predikant' had reference to the minister's central task, that of preaching."[22] The Reformers did not mention the word "missionary." There is no such office in the Scriptures. There are ministers, pastors, preachers, elders, evangelists; these are biblical terms for the biblical office of preacher. If someone would have asked Calvin or any Dutch Presbytery (classis) or Synod: "Are you sending 'missionaries' to Brazil?" they would have answered, as Calvin did, "we are sending ordained ministers to preach the gospel of the Lord Jesus Christ."

These servants of the Lord adhered to Reformed tradition and biblical terminology. As a matter of fact, "the [Dutch] ministers themselves [in the seventeenth century and prior to that] were quite conscious of their role in this regard [the task of preaching], often writing after their names the letters V.D.M., that is: 'Verbi Divini Minister,' 'Servant of the Divine Word.'"[23] The Dutch historian Frans Schalkwijk was also impressed with "the heterogeneity of the ministerial corps [ministering in Brazil], it being comprised of elements from several nations." He also discovered that "in addition to approximately forty ministers from the Netherlands, we encounter

2001). See also Andreas J. Köstenberger, "The Challenge of a Systematized Biblical Theology: Missiological Insights from the Gospel of John," in *Missiology* 23: 445–64.

21. Frans Schalkwijk, *Igreja e Estado no Brasil holandês: 1630–1654* (São Paulo: Vida Nova, 1989), 101. According to Schalkwijk, "in several cases much information [is still available] for an interesting monograph [doctoral dissertation]."

22. Schalkwijk, *Igreja e Estado no Brasil*, 101.

23. Schalkwijk, *Igreja e Estado no Brasil*, 101.

at least seven who, judging by their names or their correspondence, must have been from Germany…four…of English origin" and "no less than two French, and even two Spaniards."[24]

It was also noted by Schalkwijk that "the Christian Reformed Church in Brazil [between 1630–1654] devoted considerable attention to the work of missions [terminology employed by Schalkwijk]. Though some historians have maintained that the church neglected this task [in Brazil], they are in the minority."[25] Whom were they preaching and ministering to in Brazil? To the Indians, the Jews, their Dutch countrymen, the Portuguese, and African slaves.[26]

Third, we should avoid the use of nineteenth and twentieth century missiological vocabulary when we translate the Reformers. Based on the theology of "missions" exposed by the Reformers, I would recommend the following definition of terms, since such definitions allow us to approach the Reformers and assess their writings, interests, and works as it relates to the propagation of the gospel to all the nations through their biblical and theological perspectives:

"Mission"—the will and the work of God the Father, reconciling the lost to Himself, through the redemptive work of the Lord Jesus Christ, and by the convicting and applying work of the Holy Spirit, for the glory of God alone and the joy of all peoples.

"Missionary"—a worker, a witness, a servant of God through whom others may come to believe as the Lord assigns to each his task. In the context of the priesthood of all believers, every believer is a servant through whom others may come to believe across the street and around the world. In the context of offices of the church, this is the ordained minister of the Word, whose responsibility it is to preach the gospel to all creatures under the sovereign work of God. God is the one who calls, empowers, and sends His servants here and there, now and then.

---

24. Schalkwijk, *Igreja e Estado no Brasil*, 107.

25. Schalkwijk, *Igreja e Estado no Brasil*, 149. Warneck and Winter are part of such a minority. Unfortunately, their light declarations have been taken for granted and have influenced numerous mission historians, church historians, and others throughout the world.

26. Schalkwijk, *Igreja e Estado no Brasil*, 149–54.

"Missionary work"—is the preaching of the gospel to all creatures, to all nations, and to the whole world, according to
God's choosing, God's timing, and God's sending. Geography plays no role in defining, characterizing, or categorizing
a "missionary." What we preach "over there" is the same
gospel we preach "over here." The God who sends and
maintains His servants over there is the same who sends
and maintains His servants over here according to His
plans, timing, and will.

"Mission field"—the "mission field" is the world (Matt. 13:38):
Jerusalem, all Judea, Samaria, and "the uttermost part of
the earth" (Acts 1:8). What distinguishes a "mission field" is
not geographical or even cultural distances, but belief and
unbelief, saved and lost, converted and unconverted. A lost
soul among the unreached people groups is not more val-
ued before God than an unconverted neighbor on my street.

Contributors

ANDREW BALLITCH is associate pastor at Hunsinger Lane Baptist Church in Louisville, Kentucky.

JOEL R. BEEKE is President and Professor of Systematic Theology and Homiletics at Puritan Reformed Theological Seminary. He also serves as a pastor of the Heritage Reformed Congregation in Grand Rapids, Michigan.

IAN HAMILTON served as minister of Cambridge Presbyterian Church, England, for many years. Currently he teaches at Edinburgh Theological Seminary and at Greenville Presbyterian Theological Seminary.

MICHAEL HAYKIN is Professor of Church History and Biblical Spirituality at the Southern Baptist Theological Seminary, Louisville, Kentucky.

ELIAS MEDEIROS has worked in pioneer church planting in the Amazon region of Brazil, as well as in Recife, Brazil. He has pastored Presbyterian churches in Northeast Brazil, and taught at several theological institutions. Since 1993, he has served as the Harriet Barbour Professor of Mission at Reformed Theological Seminary in Jackson, Mississippi.

STEPHEN MYERS is Associate Professor of Historical Theology for the PhD program at Puritan Reformed Theological Seminary. Prior to his appointment at PRTS, Dr. Myers served as the pastor of Pressly Memorial Associate Reformed Presbyterian Church in Statesville, North Carolina.

CARL TRUEMAN held the Paul Woolley Chair of Church History, serving as professor of church history at Westminster Theological Seminary for many years. Recently, he accepted a call to serve as professor in the Department of Biblical and Religious Studies at Grove City College in Pennsylvania.

WILLIAM VANDOODEWAARD is Professor of Church History at Puritan Reformed Theological Seminary. Prior to coming to PRTS, he taught at

Patrick Henry College, near Washington, D.C., and at Huntington University in Indiana.

REBECCA VANDOODEWAARD is a wife, mother, and author of several books, including *Reformation Women: 16th Century Figures That Shaped Christianity's Rebirth*.